# Modern JAPANESE Grammar WORKBOOK

The *Modern Japanese Grammar Workbook* is an innovative book of exercises and language tasks for all learners of Japanese. The book is divided into two parts:

- Section A provides exercises based on essential grammatical structures
- Section B practises everyday functions (e.g. making introductions, apologizing, expressing needs).

All sentences are written both in romanization and in Japanese script and a comprehensive answer key at the back enables learners to check on their progress.

Key features of the book include:

- Exercises graded on a 3-point scale according to their level of difficulty
- Cross-referencing to the related *Modern Japanese Grammar*
- Topical exercises drawn from realistic scenarios to help learners develop their vocabulary and practical communication skills
- Opportunities to practice both written and spoken Japanese

The *Modern Japanese Grammar Workbook* is an ideal practice tool for learners of Japanese at all levels. No prior knowledge of grammatical terminology is assumed and it can be used both independently and alongside *Modern Japanese Grammar* (ISBN 978-0-415-57201-9), which is also published by Routledge.

**Naomi H. McGloin** is Professor of Japanese Language and Linguistics at the University of Wisconsin-Madison, USA.

**Mutsuko Endo Hudson** is Professor of Japanese Language and Linguistics at Michigan State University, USA.

**Fumiko Nazikian** is Senior Lecturer and Director of the Japanese Language Program at Columbia University, USA.

**Tomomi Kakegawa** is Associate Professor of Japanese at the University of Wisconsin-Eau Claire, USA.

## *Routledge Modern Grammars*
Series concept and development – Sarah Butler

### Other books in the series

*Modern Mandarin Chinese Grammar*
*Modern Mandarin Chinese Grammar Workbook*

*Modern French Grammar, Second Edition*
*Modern French Grammar Workbook, Second Edition*

*Modern German Grammar, Second Edition*
*Modern German Grammar Workbook, Second Edition*

*Modern Italian Grammar, Third Edition*
*Modern Italian Grammar Workbook, Second Edition*

*Modern Brazilian Portuguese Grammar*
*Modern Brazilian Portuguese Grammar Workbook*

*Modern Russian Grammar*
*Modern Russian Grammar Workbook*

*Modern Spanish Grammar, Third Edition*
*Modern Spanish Grammar Workbook, Third Edition*

# Modern
# JAPANESE
# Grammar
# WORKBOOK

**Naomi H. McGloin**
**Mutsuko Endo Hudson**
**Fumiko Nazikian**
**Tomomi Kakegawa**

 Routledge
Taylor & Francis Group

LONDON AND NEW YORK

First published 2014
by Routledge
2 Park Square, Milton Park, Abingdon, Oxon OX14 4RN

and by Routledge
711 Third Avenue, New York, NY 10017

*Routledge is an imprint of the Taylor & Francis Group, an informa business*

*British Library Cataloguing in Publication Data*
A catalogue record for this book is available from the British Library

*Library of Congress Cataloging in Publication Data*
A catalog record for this book has been requested

ISBN: 978-0-415-27093-9 (pbk)
ISBN: 978-0-203-64127-9 (ebk)

Typeset in ITC Stone Serif
by Graphicraft Limited, Hong Kong

Printed and bound in Great Britain by
TJ International Ltd, Padstow, Cornwall

# Contents

Contents

# Introduction

The *Modern Japanese Grammar Workbook* is a companion to *Modern Japanese Grammar: A Practical Guide*, and is designed to help you to strengthen your command of Japanese. It can be used alongside a Japanese textbook in a regular language program, or as review material for independent study. The Answer Key at the end of the book allows you to check your answers as you work through the exercises.

The exercises in the *Workbook* focus on structures in Part A 'Structures,' and communication in Part B 'Functions.' It will be a good idea to work from Part A if you can identify specific points on which you need practice, such as particles, transitive-intransitive verbs, the passive construction, evidential markers (e.g. **you** 'seem'), and honorifics (**keigo**). Part B is organized according to language use in particular situations. Here you can practice ways of doing things, such as describing a place, showing gratitude, apologizing, expressing surprise, and asking the way.

With abundant structural and, especially, usage exercises, this *Workbook* is unique, and the types and content of the exercises are firmly anchored on the authors' research on Japanese pragmatics and language pedagogy. Exercises are derived from realistic contexts and reflect actual use. Settings, topics, and speaker roles and relationships range greatly. The exercises deal mainly with spoken language (face-to-face, telephone) but also written language (e.g. e-mails, diaries, online reviews).

The *Workbook* is appropriate for near-beginners to intermediate and post-intermediate learners at the high school and college level and for teachers as a resource book. Instructions for the exercises are given in English, and all problems and answers are presented in both Japanese script (hiragana, katakana, and kanji) and romanization.

Exercises are graded on a 3-level scale according to whether they use:

*   basic vocabulary and grammatical knowledge
**   wider vocabulary and grammatical knowledge
*** advanced vocabulary and grammatical knowledge

We hope you find the exercises not only helpful but enjoyable!

Naomi Hanaoka McGloin
Mutsuko Endo Hudson
Fumiko Nazikian
Tomomi Kakegawa

# Notes on romanization

The romanization used in both the *Modern Japanese Grammar: A Practical Guide (PG)* and the *Modern Japanese Grammar Workbook* are slight variants of the Hepburn system. One major modification is how long vowels are romanized. In *PG*, long vowels are represented by double letters, as in **aa**, **ii**, **uu**, **ee**, **oo**. In the *Workbook*, long /a, i, u/ are written by double letters, but long /e/ and /o/ are transcribed as **ei** and **ou**, following Japanese **kana** spelling conventions.

| Hiragana | *PG* | *Workbook* |
|---|---|---|
| せんせい | sens<u>ee</u> | sens<u>ei</u> |
| かんそう | kans<u>oo</u> | kans<u>ou</u> |

This convention is adopted for the *Workbook* because, if one wants to look up words in dictionaries, one needs to follow the **kana** spelling convention.

The Japanese word meaning 'to say' is pronounced as **yuu**, but is written with hiragana for *i* and *u* (いう) in dictionaries; therefore, it is romanized as **iu** in the *Workbook*. Note also that all long vowels in loan words (e.g. クール, メール, ゴール) are written with double letters (e.g. **kuuru** 'cool,' **meeru** 'mail,' **gooru** 'goal').

# Acknowledgments

The authors would like to express their appreciation to Manuel Fernandez, Grover Hudson and Jim McGloin for proofreading our English and for their unflagging support, and to Shigeru Eguchi for preparing the illustrations used in the book. We also thank the University of Wisconsin-Eau Claire Office of Research and Sponsored Programs (ORSP) for a University Research and Creative Activity Grant, which enabled co-author Kakegawa to work on this *Workbook* during summer 2013.

# Part A

# Structures

# 1
# Introduction: major features of Japanese grammar

1 ★

Fill in the blanks with the words provided in the box to render the Japanese equivalent of the English sentences. You may use the same word more than once. Note that the English words that appear in parentheses will not appear in Japanese.

Example: ①私の母 __は__ __教師__ です .
①**Watashi no haha** __wa__ __kyoushi__ __desu__ .

②高校 **koukou** _____ _____ _____ _____。

③学校 **gakkou** _____ _____ _____ _____。

④毎日 **mainichi** _____ _____ _____。

①My mother is a teacher. ②(She) teaches English at high school.
③(Her) school is located in Yokohama. ④(She) is very busy every day.

> 教師・横浜・英語・あります・教えています・忙しい・とても・です・を・で・に・は
>
> **kyoushi · Yokohama · Eigo · arimasu · oshiete imasu · isogashii · totemo · desu · o · de · ni · wa**

⇨ 1.1, 1.2, 1.3

2 ★

Bracket the part of the sentence that modifies the underlined word.

Example: ① [私の] 専攻は現代文学です。

② たいてい簡単な漢字や短い話を読む時は辞書を使いません。③ 今、村上春樹が書いた本を読んでいます。④ まだ速く読むことはできませんが、とても面白いと思います。

Example: ① [Watashi no] <u>senkou</u> wa gendai bungaku desu.

② **Taitei kantan na <u>kanji</u> ya mijikai <u>hanashi</u> o yomu toki wa jisho o tsukaimasen. ③ Ima, Murakami Haruki ga kaita <u>hon</u> o yonde imasu. ④ Mada hayaku <u>yomu</u> koto wa dekimasen ga, totemo <u>omoshiroi</u> to omoimasu.**

⇨ 1.2

**3** ⋆ Choose the particle **ga** (for subject) or **wa** (for topic).

(A)
You are talking to a passerby (**tsuukounin**) on the street in Tokyo.

あなた： すみません。あそこに大きい建物【① が・は】ありますよね？
あれ【② が・は】何ですか。
通行人： ああ、あれ【③ が・は】ホテルです。
あなた： そうですか。銀行【④ が・は】どの建物ですか。
通行人： 銀行【⑤ が・は】あれです。

Anata: Sumimasen. Asoko ni ookii tatemono 【① ga・wa】 arimasu yo ne? Are 【② ga・wa】 nan desu ka.
Tsuukounin: Aa, are 【③ ga・wa】 hoteru desu.
Anata: Sou desu ka. Ginkou 【④ ga・wa】 dono tatemono desu ka.
Tsuukounin: Ginkou 【⑤ ga・wa】 are desu.

(B)
You are talking with your Japanese host sister Ako at home.

あこ： ねえ、昨日買ったイチゴ【① が・は】どこ？
あなた： え？あれ【② が・は】全部食べちゃったけど？
あこ： ええっ？今晩お客さん【③ が・は】来るから、買ったのに …
あなた： ごめん … あ、雨【④ が・は】降って来た！

Ako: Nee, kinou katta ichigo 【① ga・wa】 doko?
Anata: E? Are 【② ga・wa】 zenbu tabechatta kedo?
Ako: Ee? Konban o-kyaku-san 【③ ga・wa】 kuru kara, katta noni . . .
Anata: Gomen . . . A, ame 【④ ga・wa】 futte kita!

⇨ 1.4

**4** ⋆ Match the Japanese sentences with their English equivalents.

① 子供に歌を聞かせた。**Kodomo ni uta o kik-ase-ta.**
② 子供に歌を聞かせたかった。**Kodomo ni uta o kik-ase-ta-katta.**
③ 子供に歌を聞かれなかった。**Kodomo ni uta o kik-are-na-katta.**
④ 子供に歌を聞かせられたくない。**Kodomo ni uta o kik-ase-rare-taku-nai.**
⑤ 子供に歌を聞かせられない。**Kodomo ni uta o kik-ase-rare-nai.**

(a) I wanted to have my child hear the song.
(b) I cannot have my child hear the song.
(c) I do not want to be forced to hear the song by my child.
(d) I had my child hear the song.
(e) I did not have the song heard by my child. (OR I was not heard singing by my child.)

⇨ 1.5, 15, 20, 21, 27

**5** *

What is omitted in the following? The intended meaning is provided in English for each sentence.

> Example: _____ 今日早く朝ごはん _____ 食べた。→ 私は；を
> _____ **kyou hayaku asa-gohan** _____ **tabeta.** → **watashi wa; o**

(A)
You are at a convenience store. [単三電池 **tansan denchi** 'AA battery']

あなた： あのう、単三電池 ①_____ ありませんか。
店員： 申し訳ありません、②_____ 今 ③_____ ちょっと切らしておりまして。
あなた： そうですか。じゃ、④_____ また来ます。

**Anata:** Anou, tansan denchi ①_____ arimasen ka.
**Ten'in:** Moushiwake arimasen, ②_____ ima ③_____ chotto kirashite orimashite.
**Anata:** Sou desu ka. Ja, ④_____ mata kimasu.

(B)
Close friends Shigeru and Kei are talking about their classmate.

茂： あいつ ①_____、明日も授業 ②_____ サボるのかなぁ。
恵： いや、③_____ 明日は来るだろ、試験 ④_____ あるから。
茂： ⑤_____ 今夜どこ ⑥_____ 行こう ⑦_____。
恵： ⑧_____ どこでもいいよ。

**Shigeru:** Aitsu ①_____, ashita mo jugyou ②_____ saboru no kanaa.
**Kei:** Iya, ③_____ ashita wa kuru daro, shiken ④_____ aru kara.
**Shigeru:** ⑤_____ kon'ya doko ⑥_____ ikou ⑦_____.
**Kei:** ⑧_____ doko demo ii yo.

⇨ 1.6

# 2
# Pronunciation

**1** ★ How many syllables and moras does the following word consist of?

国会議事堂案内（こっかい ぎじどう あんない）**Kokkai gijidou annai** 'Diet Building Guide' → _____ syllables; _____ moras

⇨ 2.1, 2.2

**2** ★ (A)
What do you think are the original (unclipped) forms of the following abbreviations?

      Example: アポ **apo** ← アポイントメント **apointomento** 'appointment'

①アクセ **akuse** ②エンタ **enta** ③コラボ **korabo** ④カーナビ **kaanabi**
⑤コンパチ **konpachi** ⑥ アプリ **apuri**

(B)
How do you think the following compounds would be shortened?

      Example: 空＋オーケストラ **kara** + **ookesutora** 'empty + orchestra'
               → カラオケ **karaoke**

① 着信＋メロディ **chakushin** + **merodi** 'incoming + melody (ringtone)'
② コピー＋ペースト **kopii** + **peesuto** 'copy + paste'
③ マスコミュニケーション **masu komyunikeeshon** 'mass communication'
④ モバイル＋ゲーム **mobairu geemu** 'mobile (phone) game'
⑤ 就職＋活動 **shuushoku** + **katsudou** 'job hunting + activities'

⇨ 2.2

**3** ★ How are the following compounds pronounced as a result of sequential voicing (*rendaku*)?

      Example: にほん **Nihon** 'Japan' + はし **hashi** 'bridge'
               → にほんばし **Nihon-bashi** (name of a bridge/an area in Tokyo)

① あお **ao** 'blue' + そら **sora** 'sky' →
② きょうだい **kyoudai** 'sibling' + けんか **kenka** 'fight' →
③ ひ **hi** 'sun' + とけい **tokei** 'clock' → (sundial)
④ みか **mika** '3 days' + つき **tsuki** 'moon' → (crescent moon)

⇨ 2.3

**4** ★ Indicate the pitch of each mora as high (H) or low (L) paying attention to where the accent of the word is. An accent is indicated by an acute mark on the vowel (**á, í, ú,** etc.). Note that some words have no accent. **Ga,** which appears below, is a particle indicating the subject.

Example 1: **otokó** 'man' → LHH; **otokó + ga** → LHHL
Example 2: **sakana** 'fish' → LHH; **sakana + ga** → LHHH

① **kása** 'umbrella' → _____; **kása + ga** → _____
② **kao** 'face' → _____; **kao + ga** → _____
③ **himáwari** 'sunflower' → _____; **himáwari + ga** → _____
④ **imoutó** 'younger sister' → _____; **imoutó + ga** → _____

⇨ 2.4

# 3
# Writing system

**1 ★**  Rewrite the following words in *hiragana*. Long vowels are indicated by a macron on a vowel (â, î, û, etc.) here.

① **ashi**  ② **ume**  ③ **onna**  ④ **obâchan**  ⑤ **kagami**  ⑥ **kekkô**  ⑦ **shûmatsu**

⇨  3.1, Appendix 1

**2 ★**  Rewrite the following words in *katakana*. Long vowels are indicated by a macron on a vowel (â, î, û, etc.) here.

① **gitâ** 'guitar' ___ ___ ___; ② **futtobôru** 'football' ___ ___ ___ ___ ___ ___; ③ **konpyûtâ** 'computer' ___ ___ ___ ___ ___ ___ ___; ④ **nyan** 'meow' ___ ___ ___; ⑤ **sofuto** 'software' ___ ___ ___; ⑥ **kinkon** 'ding-dong' ___ ___ ___ ___

⇨  3.2, Appendix 2

**3 ★**  Two headlines from Asahi Shimbun (Asahi Newspaper) Digital (06/26/2013) are quoted below. In the romanized transliteration and English glosses, the words originally appearing in *kanji* are capitalized, those in *katakana* italicized, and those in *hiragana* in the normal script. Examine the use of the three types of writing system in the headlines, and answer the questions afterwards.

(A)
①九電　②株主総会　③周辺　④で　⑤脱原発派　⑥が　⑦集会　⑧と　⑨デモ

①**KYUUDEN**　②**KABUNUSHI SOUKAI**　③**SHUUHEN**　④**de** ⑤**DATSU-GENPATSU-HA**　⑥**ga**　⑦**SHUUKAI**　⑧**to**　⑨*demo*

①KYUUSHUU ELECTRIC POWER CO.　②STOCKHOLDER GENERAL MEETING ③SURROUNDING AREA　④at　⑤DE-NUCLEARIZATION GROUP ⑥(particle for subject)　⑦MEETING　⑧and　⑨*demonstration*

*De-nuclearization group [held] a meeting and demonstration in the area near the General Meeting for Stockholders of Kyuushuu Electric Power Co.*

(B)
①原発事故後　②の　③エネルギー政策　④めぐる　⑤主な　⑥動き

①**GENPATSU JIKO-GO**　②**no**　③*enerugii* **SEISAKU**　④**meguru**
⑤**OMO-na**　⑥**UGO-ki**

①AFTER NUCLEAR PLANT ACCIDENTS　②(particle for linking)
③*energy* POLICIES　④surround　⑤MAJOR-(inflection)　⑥moves-(inflection)

*Major moves surrounding the energy policies after the nuclear plant accidents*

What are the functions of *kanji*, *katakana*, and *hiragana*, respectively, in these headlines?

*Kanji* is used to represent _____
*Katakana* is used to represent _____
*Hiragana* is used to represent _____

⇨　3.1, 3.2, 3.3

# 4
# Words

**1** * Read the sentences below describing different word categories, and code them using 'J' for Japanese native words (*wago*), 'C' for words of Chinese origin (*kango*), 'F' for words of other foreign origin (*gairaigo*), and 'M' for mimetics (words depicting sounds, states, etc.).

a.  (  ) They represent basic words, especially those relating to nature and body parts; e.g. **yama** 'mountain' and **me** 'eye.'

b.  (  ) They represent words that came from various languages, other than those imported from Chinese before modern times.

c.  (  ) Many represent concepts and matters of an abstract, scholarly and formal nature.

d.  (  ) Most of them have simple sounds such as **ou** 'carry on one's back' and **kokoro** 'heart, spirit.'

e.  (  ) Within these words, the same segment is often repeated to represent a repeated action and prolonged state; e.g. **suyasuya** 'manner of sleeping peacefully,' **gorogoro** 'sound of thunder.'

f.  (  ) Many contain one or more complicated sounds such as long vowels (e.g. ê, ô), long consonants (e.g. tt, ss), syllable-final nasal (n), and palatals (e.g. ky, sh); e.g. **kekkon** 'marriage,' **ryokô** 'travel,' **gêjutsu** 'art.'

g.  (  ) Voiced consonants (e.g. *b*, *g*, *z*), *r*, and *p* rarely occur in initial position in this type of word.

⇨ 4.1, 4.2

**2** * Mark the following descriptions as true (○) or false (×).

a.  (  ) One would say **Nani** ('what') **ga** (subject) **imasu ka** ('is there?') to mean 'What is there?' when inquiring about an animal.

b.  (  ) In Japanese, 'No one is there' is expressed as **Dare ka imasen**.

c.  (  ) Referring to beer, for example, **nanbon** means 'how many bottles?,' and **nanbon ka** 'several bottles,' and **nanbon mo** 'many bottles.'

d.  (  ) Words like **dare mo**, **nani mo**, and **doko ni mo** can be used either in affirmative or negative sentences.

e.  (  ) Words like **nan demo**, **dare demo** and **doko demo** can only appear in negative sentences.

⇨ 4.3, 4.4, 5.2.3

# 5
# Sentences and sentence patterns

1 ★

Identify the underlined sentences in passages (A) and (B) as (a) nominal, (b) adjectival, (c) existential, or (d) verbal sentences. Note that if there is a topic in the sentence, it can also be classified as a 'topic-comment sentence.'

(A)
[大勢 **oozei** 'many'; 詳しく **kuwashiku** 'in detail']

①私は今年の九月から〇〇大学の大学院に入りました。②専攻は日本語です。③将来大学で日本語を教えたいと思っています。④日本語に興味を持ったのは大学二年生の時です。⑤私の大学には留学生が大勢いたのですが、⑥彼らと話しているうちに日本語をもっと詳しく知りたいと思うようになりました。

①**Watashi wa kotoshi no kugatsu kara 〇〇Daigaku no daigakuin ni hairimashita.** ②**Senkou wa Nihongo desu.** ③**Shourai daigaku de Nihongo o oshietai to omotte imasu.** ④**Nihongo ni kyoumi o motta no wa daigaku ninensei no toki desu.** ⑤**Watashi no daigaku ni wa ryuugakusei ga oozei ita no desu ga,** ⑥**karera to hanashite iru uchi ni Nihongo o motto kuwashiku shiritai to omou you ni narimashita.**

(B)
[面倒 **mendou** 'a pain in the neck'; 計算 **keisan** 'arithmetic'; 苦手 **nigate** 'not good at'; 苦労 **kurou** 'have a hard time']

①私は外国に旅行するのが好きだ。②いろいろ新しいものを見るのは本当に楽しい。だから暇があると　③旅行をする。でも、④外国に行って面倒だと感じる習慣の一つにチップの習慣がある。⑤私は計算が苦手なので、⑥いつも苦労する。

①**Watashi wa gaikoku ni ryokou suru no ga suki da.** ②**Iroiro atarashii mono o miru no wa hontou ni tanoshii.** Dakara hima ga aru to ③**ryokou o suru.** Demo, ④**gaikoku ni itte mendou da to kanjiru shuukan no hitotsu ni chippu no shuukan ga aru.** ⑤**Watashi wa keisan ga nigate na** node, ⑥**itsumo kurou suru.**

⇨ 5.2

# 6
# Register and style

1 ★ For each of the following sentences, write "S" if it is in spoken style and "W" if it is in written style.

(a) (  ) 京都を訪れたのは紅葉の美しいころだった。
   **Kyouto o otozureta no wa kouyou no utsukushii koro datta.**

(b) (  ) あのね、この間京都に行って来たよ。
   **Ano ne, kono aida Kyouto ni itte kita yo.**

(c) (  ) あのう、実は、先日京都に行って参りまして。
   **Anou, jitsu wa, senjitsu Kyouto ni itte mairimashite.**

(d) (  ) ご無沙汰しておりますが、その後いかがお過ごしでしょうか。
   **Gobusata shite orimasu ga, sonogo ikaga o-sugoshi deshou ka.**

(e) (  ) ひさしぶり。元気？
   **Hisashiburi. Genki?**

(f) (  ) 日本に住んでいたものの、日本語は全然上手になりませんでした。
   **Nihon ni sunde ita monono, Nihongo wa zenzen jouzu ni narimasendeshita.**

(g) (  ) 日本に住んでいたけど、日本語全然上手にならなくてさあ。
   **Nihon ni sunde ita kedo, Nihongo zenzen jouzu ni naranakute saa.**

(h) (  ) クッキー全部食べちゃったの？
   **Kukkii zenbu tabechatta no?**

⇨ 6.1, 6.2

2 ★★ The following is a conversation between a professor and a student. If two male students, who are friends, are having a similar conversation, how would the conversation go? How about if two female student friends are talking?

[時差ぼけ **jisa boke** 'jet lag'; 伺います **ukagaimasu** 'to go (humbly)']

先生：　　スミスさん、久し振りですね。
スミス：　あ、先生、ご無沙汰しています。
先生：　　いつ帰って来たんですか。
スミス：　きのう戻って来たばかりです。
先生：　　ふーん。じゃ、時差ぼけで大変でしょう。留学はどうでしたか。
スミス：　とても楽しかったです。いろいろ日本文化が体験できてよかったです。
先生：　　それはよかったですね。また今度話を聞かせてください。
スミス：　はい、近いうちに先生のオフィスに伺います。
先生：　　じゃ、また。
スミス：　失礼します。

Sensei: Sumisu-san, hisashiburi desu ne.
Sumisu: A, sensei, go-busata shite imasu.
Sensei: Itsu kaette kita n desu ka.
Sumisu: Kinou modotte kita bakari desu.
Sensei: Fuun. Ja, jisaboke de taihen deshou. Ryuugaku wa dou deshita ka.
Sumisu: Totemo tanoshikatta desu. Iroiro Nihon bunka ga taiken dekite yokatta desu.
Sensei: Sore wa yokatta desu ne. Mata kondo hanashi o kikasete kudasai.
Sumisu: Hai, chikai uchi ni sensei no ofisu ni ukagaimasu.
Sensei: Ja, mata.
Sumisu: Shitsurei shimasu.

⇨ 6.2, 6.3, 30.1, 30.2, 30.5

**3** ∗ Who would be likely to make the following utterances? If it is a woman, put F, for a man, put M. If it can be said either by a woman or a man, put N.

a. (　) よかったわよ。　　　　　Yokatta wa yo.
b. (　) 大丈夫だよ。　　　　　　Daijoubu da yo.
c. (　) 上手だね。　　　　　　　Jouzu da ne.
d. (　) 行くぜ。　　　　　　　　Iku ze.
e. (　) 行かないか。　　　　　　Ikanai ka.
f. (　) あの店で買ったのよ。　　Ano mise de katta no yo.
g. (　) 先に行くね。　　　　　　Saki ni iku ne.
h. (　) あの人にできるかしら。　Ano hito ni dekiru kashira.
i. (　) 腹へったなあ。　　　　　Hara hetta naa.
j. (　) もうお腹いっぱい。　　　Mou onaka ippai.

⇨ 6.3

# 7

# Nouns and noun phrases

1 ★★

Put the words in each set into the correct order to render the equivalents of the English phrases. Insert the particle **no** where needed.

(1) ウェイター・という・喫茶店・彼女がよく行く・「こまち」
**weitaa · to iu · kissaten · kanojo ga yoku iku · 'Komachi'**
*the waiter of the coffee shop 'Komachi,' where she (my girl friend) often goes*

(2) 子供・大きな・あの・犬
**kodomo · ookina · ano · inu**
*that child's big dog*

(3) 中学生・家・先生・むすめ
**chuugakusei · ie · sensei · musume**
*the house of the teacher of my daughter, (who is) a junior high school student*

(4) 「ゆず」・旅館・山・という・中・主人
**'Yuzu' · ryokan · yama · to iu · naka · shujin**
*the owner of the inn called 'Yuzu,' which is in the mountains*

(5) ゆうれいが出る・お寺に・うわさ・ある・という
**yuurei ga deru · o-tera ni · uwasa · aru · to iu**
*the rumor that a ghost appears in a certain temple*

⇨ 7.2

2 ★

Fill in the blanks with one of the following particles: **to, ya, no, o, ka, toka, nari**.

(1) 大学で数学（　　）日本語（　　）専攻した。
**Daigaku de suugaku (　　) Nihongo (　　) senkou shita.**

(2) 大学で数学（　　）日本語（　　）英文学など（　　）勉強した。
**Daigaku de suugaku (　　) Nihongo (　　) eibungaku nado (　　) benkyou shita.**

(3) きのうスピーチ（　　）練習（　　）した。
**Kinou supiichi (　　) renshuu (　　) shita.**

(4) A: いつ会いましょうか。
**Itsu aimashou ka.**
B: あした（　　）あさってはどうですか。
**Ashita (　　) asatte wa dou desu ka.**

(5) ビール（　　）ワイン（　　）何でも好きなものを注文してください。
**Biiru (　　) wain (　　) nan demo suki na mono o chuumon shite kudasai.**

(6) 赤ちゃんの誕生祝いには着るもの（　　）おもちゃなどが喜ばれる。
**Akachan no tanjou iwai ni wa kiru mono (　　) omocha nado ga yorokobareru.**

⇨ 7.3

# 8
# Pronouns

Fill in the blanks in the following conversation with appropriate pronouns from the box below, considering the context and the relationships between the speakers.

> あなた・あんた・おまえ・わた（く）し・あたし・おれ・あなたがた・
> あんたたち・おまえら・わたしたち・おれたち
>
> **anata · anta · o-mae · wata(ku)shi · atashi · ore · anata-gata · anta-tachi · omae-ra · watashi-tachi · ore-tachi**

(A)
At a job interview [面接官 **mensetsukan** 'interviewer,' 応募者 **oubosha** 'applicant,' 長所 **chousho** 'strong points']

面接官： ＿＿＿＿＿ の長所は何ですか 。
応募者： ＿＿＿＿＿ はだれとでもうまくやっていける方なので、そういう所が長所なのではないかと思います。

**Mensetsukan:** ＿＿＿＿＿ **no chousho wa nan desu ka.**
**Oubosha:** ＿＿＿＿＿ **wa dare to demo umaku yatte ikeru hou na node, sou iu tokoro ga chousho na no de wa nai ka to omoimasu.**

(B)
Reporting to the whole committee after group discussions at work

課長： どのグループから始めますか。
平野： では、＿＿＿＿＿ のグループから始めたいと思います。

**Kachou:** **Dono guruupu kara hajimemasu ka.**
**Hirano:** **De wa, ＿＿＿＿＿ no guruupu kara hajimetai to omoimasu.**

(C)
Shou and Tadashi, both males in their 20s, are very close friends.

[金欠 **kinketsu** 'have no money']

翔： ＿＿＿＿＿ 今、金欠なんだ。一万円貸してくれよ。
正： いやだよ。＿＿＿＿＿、返してくれたことないんだから。

**Shou:** ＿＿＿＿＿ **ima, kinketsu na n da. Ichiman'en kashite kure yo.**
**Tadashi:** **Iya da yo. ＿＿＿＿＿, kaeshite kureta koto nai n da kara.**

⇨ 8.1

**2** *

A couple of children and Kana, a woman in her 20s, are talking in a park, and see a man who appears to be in his 40s. What do each of the underlined words mean: 'I/me,' 'we/us,' 'you (singular),' 'you (plural),' 'she/her,' or 'he/him'?

子供達： ①<u>お姉ちゃん</u>、何やってるの？
佳奈： ②<u>お姉ちゃん</u>ね、今絵をかいてるの。
子供達： ふうん。③<u>ぼくたち</u>も絵かけるよ。
佳奈： そうお？じゃ、これ貸してあげるから、④<u>ぼくたち</u>もかいてよ。
　　　　 かけたら ⑤<u>お姉ちゃん</u>に見せてね。
子供達： いいよ。あ、あの ⑥<u>おじさん</u>、絵がすっごいうまいんだよ。

Kodomo-tachi: ①<u>O-neechan</u>, nani yatte ru no?
Kana: ②<u>O-neechan</u> ne, ima e o kaite ru no.
Kodomo-tachi: Fuun. ③<u>Boku-tachi</u> mo e kakeru yo.
Kana: Souo? Ja, kore kashite ageru kara, ④<u>boku-tachi</u> mo kaite yo. Kake-tara ⑤<u>o-neechan</u> ni misete ne.
Kodomo-tachi: Ii yo. A, ano ⑥<u>ojisan</u>, e ga suggoi umai n da yo.

**3** *

Choose an appropriate pronoun, considering the meaning of the sentence.

a. 智樹は【ぼく・自分・彼】のことをハンサムだと思っている。
   **Tomoki wa 【boku · jibun · kare】 no koto o hansamu da to omotte iru.**
   *Tomoki thinks he (= Tomoki) is handsome.*
b. 父と母は【お互い・自分・彼ら】を信頼し合っている。
   **Chichi to haha wa 【o-tagai · jibun · kare-ra】 o shinrai shi-atte iru.**
   *My father and mother trust each other.*
c. もう18歳になったんだから、【あなた・わたし・自分】のこと
   は【あなた・わたし・自分】で決めなさい。
   **Mou juuhassai ni natta n da kara, 【anata · watashi · jibun】 no koto wa 【anata · watashi · jibun】 de kimenasai.**
   *You're 18 now. Make your own decisions for yourself.*
d. 【あなたがた・自分たち・お互い】を責めるのはよしなさい。
   **【Anata-gata · jibun-tachi · o-tagai】 o semeru no wa yoshinasai.**
   *Stop blaming each other.*

⇨ 8.2

**4** :

Write down the English meanings of the underlined phrases below.

a. <u>恋する君</u>へ。
   <u>**Koisuru kimi**</u> e.
b. うちの息子は、<u>親の私</u>でさえ理解できないんだから、困ったものですよ。
   **Uchi no musuko wa, <u>oya no watashi</u> de sae rikai dekinai n da kara, komatta mono desu yo.**
c. <u>良い家族や健康に恵まれた彼女</u>は本当に幸せ者です。
   <u>**Yoi kazoku ya kenkou ni megumareta kanojo**</u> wa, hontou ni shiawase mono desu.
d. [冒険 **bouken** 'adventure']
   <u>いつまでも若々しいあなた</u>、ちょっと冒険をしてみませんか。
   **Itsu made mo wakawakashii anata, chotto bouken o shite mimasen ka.**

⇨ 8.3

# 9

# Demonstratives (*ko-so-a(-do)* words)

**1** *At a party Mr. Arita, the host, introduces Mr. Tanaka of Tokyo Bank to
Mr. Hayashi of Oosaka Motors. Complete the dialogues.

有田： 林さん、①＿＿＿＿＿＿＿＿＿＿。

田中： 田中一郎と申します。どうぞよろし
くお願いします。

林 ： 大阪モーターズの林大輔です。どう
ぞよろしく。

有田： じゃ、②＿＿＿＿＿＿＿＿＿＿。('This
way, please')

林　　有田　　田中
**Hayashi**　**Arita**　**Tanaka**

Arita: **Hayashi-san, ①＿＿＿＿＿＿＿.**
Tanaka: **Tanaka Ichirou to moushimasu.**
**Douzo yoroshiku o-negai shimasu.**
Hayashi: **Oosaka Mootaazu no Hayashi Daisuke desu. Douzo yoroshiku.**
Arita: **Ja, ②＿＿＿＿＿＿＿. ('This way, please')**

有田： 林さんは広島モーターズの山田さんをご存知ですか。
林 ： え？③＿＿＿＿＿＿＿＿＿。('which person?')
有田： ④＿＿＿＿＿＿＿＿＿人です。('that person over there with glasses on')
林 ： ああ、知っています。

Arita: **Hayashi-san wa Hiroshima Mootaazu no Yamada-san o go-zonji**
**desu ka.**
Hayashi: **E? ③＿＿＿＿＿＿＿. ('which person?')**
Arita: **④＿＿＿＿＿＿＿ hito desu. ('that person over there with glasses on')**
Hayashi: **Aa, shitte imasu.**

⇨ 9.1, 9.2, 30.4

**2** ∗ You are shopping in a department store. Looking at the illustrations, fill in the blanks with appropriate demonstrative words.

あなた anata      店員 ten'in

あなた： あのう、すみません。（ ① ）時計はいくらですか。
店員： （ ② ）は35,000円です。

**Anata:** Anou, sumimasen. ( ① ) tokei wa ikura desu ka.
**Ten'in:** ( ② ) wa 35,000 en desu.

あなた： そうですか。（ ③ ）カメラはいくらですか。
店員： （ ④ ）は140,000円です。

**Anata:** Sou desu ka. ( ③ ) kamera wa ikura desu ka.
**Ten'in:** ( ④ ) wa 140,000 en desu.

あなた： じゃあ、（ ⑤ ）小さいカメラはいくらですか。
店員： （ ⑥ ）カメラは20,000円です。
あなた： じゃあ、（ ⑦ ）をください。

**Anata:** Jaa, ( ⑤ ) chiisai kamera wa ikura desu ka.
**Ten'in:** ( ⑥ ) kamera wa 20,000 en desu.
**Anata:** Jaa, ( ⑦ ) o kudasai.

⇨ 9.1.1, 9.2

# 10
# Particles

1 ★

Fill in the blanks with appropriate particles from the box below. You may use the same particle more than once.

> が・を・に・の・で・へ・と・まで・から
> ga・o・ni・no・de・e・to・made・kara

(A)
On her way to the train station Maria Lopez runs into a neighbor Ms. Takahashi who likes to talk.

I.

| ロペス： | おはようございます。 |
| 高橋： | おはようございます。ロペスさんはいつも早いですねぇ。 |
| ロペス： | ええ、毎朝6時（①）起きます。 |
| 高橋： | そうですか。これから大学（②）行くんですか。 |
| ロペス： | ええ、駅（③）歩いて、そこから電車（④）行きます。 |
| 高橋： | そうですか。電車（⑤）乗ったら、気（⑥）つけて下さいね。時々変な人（⑦）いるから。 |

**Ropesu:** Ohayou gozaimasu.
**Takahashi:** Ohayou gozaimasu. Ropesu-san wa itsumo hayai desu nee.
**Ropesu:** Ee, maiasa rokuji（①）okimasu.
**Takahashi:** Sou desu ka. Kore kara daigaku（②）iku n desu ka.
**Ropesu:** Ee, eki（③）aruite, soko kara densha（④）ikimasu.
**Takahashi:** Sou desu ka. Densha（⑤）nottara, ki（⑥）tsukete kudasai ne. Tokidoki hen na hito（⑦）iru kara.

II.

| 高橋： | 大学（⑧）は何（⑨）勉強しているんですか。 |
| ロペス： | 専攻は工学です。子供（⑩）時から、数学（⑪）好きだったので。 |
| 高橋： | いいですね。うち（⑫）むすめは数学（⑬）ぜんぜんできなくて困ってるんですよ。 |
| ロペス： | あ、でも、ピアノ（⑭）とてもお上手だ（⑮）聞きましたけど。 |
| 高橋： | いえ、いえ、大したことないですよ。 |

**Takahashi:** Daigaku（⑧）wa nani（⑨）benkyou shite iru n desu ka.
**Ropesu:** Senkou wa kougaku desu. Kodomo（⑩）toki kara suugaku（⑪）suki datta node.

Takahashi: Ii desu ne. Uchi ( ⑫ ) musume wa suugaku ( ⑬ ) zenzen dekinakute komatte ru n desu yo.

Ropesu: A, demo, piano ( ⑭ ) totemo o-jouzu da ( ⑮ ) kikimashita kedo.

Takahashi: Ie, ie, taishita koto nai desu yo.

III.

[滞在 **taizai** 'stay'; 何とか **nan toka** 'something, so-and-so'; くじら **kujira** 'whale']

高橋: 日本滞在はいつ ( ⑯ ) ですか。
ロペス: 来年の夏 ( ⑰ ) 国 ( ⑱ ) 帰る予定です。
高橋: お国はどちら？
ロペス: メキシコ ( ⑲ ) プエルトバジャルタです。
高橋: え？そのプエルト何とかって、どこ ( ⑳ ) あるんですか。
ロペス: メキシコ ( ㉑ ) 西側です。きれいなビーチ ( ㉒ ) あっていい所ですよ。時々私の部屋 ( ㉓ ) くじら ( ㉔ ) 見えるんです。一度あそび ( ㉕ ) いらして下さい。
高橋: どうもありがとう。ほんといつか行きたいわねぇ。

Takahashi: Nihon taizai wa itsu ( ⑯ ) desu ka.

Ropesu: Rainen no natsu ( ⑰ ) kuni ( ⑱ ) kaeru yotei desu.

Takahashi: O-kuni wa dochira?

Ropesu: Mekishiko ( ⑲ ) Pueruto Bajaruta desu.

Takahashi: E? Sono Pueruto nan toka tte, doko ( ⑳ ) aru n desu ka.

Ropesu: Mekishiko ( ㉑ ) nishigawa desu. Kirei na biichi ( ㉒ ) atte ii tokoro desu yo. Tokidoki watashi no heya ( ㉓ ) kujira ( ㉔ ) mieru n desu. Ichido asobi ( ㉕ ) irashite kudasai.

Takahashi: Doumo arigatou. Honto itsuka ikitai wa nee.

IV.

[はなれて **hanarete** 'away (from X)']

高橋: ご家族 ( ㉖ ) はなれて暮らすのはさびしくないですか。
ロペス: はい、だいじょうぶです。高橋さん ( ㉗ ) ご主人はどんなお仕事ですか。
高橋: 主人は銀行 ( ㉘ ) 勤めているんですよ。
ロペス: そうですか。あのう、じゃ、そろそろ …
高橋: そうね。じゃ、またね。今度は駅 ( ㉙ ) 前 ( ㉚ ) 喫茶店 ( ㉛ ) 会いましょうか。
ロペス: はい、いつかご主人 ( ㉜ ) もお会いしたいです。じゃ、行ってきま〜す！

Takahashi: Go-kazoku ( ㉖ ) hanarete kurasu no wa sabishiku nai desu ka.

Ropesu: Hai, daijoubu desu. Takahashi-san ( ㉗ ) go-shujin wa donna o-shigoto desu ka.

Takahashi: Shujin wa ginkou ( ㉘ ) tsutomete iru n desu yo.

Ropesu: Sou desu ka. Anou, ja, sorosoro . . .

Takahashi: Sou ne. Ja, mata ne. Kondo wa eki ( ㉙ ) mae ( ㉚ ) kissaten ( ㉛ ) aimashou ka.

Ropesu: Hai, itsu ka go-shujin ( ㉜ ) mo o-ai shitai desu. Ja, itte kimaasu!

(B)
You are in a taxi giving the driver directions.

| 運転手： | どちら（①）？ |
| あなた： | ○○会社（②）お願いします。これ（③）住所です。 |
| 運転手： | ああ、ちょっと分かんないなぁ。すみません、行き方、分かりますか。 |
| あなた： | ええ、この道（④）まっすぐ行って、二つ目（⑤）角（⑥）右（⑦）曲がってください。あそこ（⑧）信号（⑨）見えますよね、あの角です。 |
| 運転手： | あ、はい。 |
| あなた： | あの黒いビルの前（⑩）止めてください。 |

| Untenshu: | Dochira（①）? |
| Anata: | ○○gaisha（②）o-negai shimasu. Kore（③）juusho desu. |
| Untenshu: | Aa, chotto wakannai naa. Sumimasen, iki kata, wakarimasu ka. |
| Anata: | Ee, kono michi（④）massugu itte, futatsume（⑤）kado（⑥）migi（⑦）magatte kudasai. Asoko（⑧）shingou（⑨）miemasu yo ne. Ano kado desu. |
| Untenshu: | A, hai. |
| Anata: | Ano kuroi biru no mae（⑩）tomete kudasai. |

(C)
Yoshiko and Hajime, a married couple, are talking about visiting the Moritas.

[道 **michi** 'how to get there'; 俳優 **haiyuu** 'actor']

| 由子： | ねえ、森田さんの家、道、分かる？ |
| 一： | うん、まあね。中野駅（①）電車（②）おりたら、すぐ（③）はず。あ、そう言えば、名刺の裏（④）地図（⑤）かいてもらったんだ。 |
| 由子： | あ、ほんと。何かおみやげ買わなくちゃ…。 |
| 一： | いや、それより子供さん方（⑥）ケーキでも焼いたら？ |
| 由子： | そうだね。ね、聞いた？あそこのとなり（⑦）おじょうさん、七月（⑧）俳優（⑨）福山何とか（⑩）結婚するんだってさ。 |
| 一： | へえー。 |

| Yoshiko: | Nee, Morita-san no uchi, michi, wakaru? |
| Hajime: | Un, maa ne. Nakano-eki（①）densha（②）oritara, sugu（③）hazu. A, sou ieba, meishi no ura（④）chizu（⑤）kaite moratta n da. |
| Yoshiko: | A, honto. Nanka o-miyage kawanakucha... |
| Hajime: | Iya, sore yori kodomo-san-gata（⑥）keeki demo yaitara? |
| Yoshiko: | Sou da ne. Ne, kiita? Asoko no tonari（⑦）o-jousan, shichigatsu（⑧）haiyuu（⑨）Fukuyama nan toka（⑩）kekkon suru n da tte sa. |
| Hajime: | Heee. |

⇨ 10.1, 10.2

**2** * Fill in the blanks with **dake** or **shika**.

(1) A: ゆうべはよく寝られましたか。
B: いいえ、五、六時間（　　）寝られませんでした。
A: **Yuube wa yoku neraremashita ka.**
B: **Iie, go-rokujikan （　　） neraremasendeshita.**

(2) A: この店はクレジットカードが使えますか。
B: いいえ、現金（　　）使えません．
A: **Kono mise wa kurejitto kaado ga tsukaemasu ka.**
B: **Iie, genkin （　　） tsukaemasen.**

(3) A: 赤ワインと白ワイン、両方買いますか。
B: いいえ、今日は白ワイン（　　）買います。
A: **Aka wain to shiro wain, ryouhou kaimasu ka.**
B: **Iie, kyou wa shiro wain （　　） kaimasu.**

(4) 先生：もう時間ですよ。
学生：すみません、あと5分（　　）待ってくださいませんか。
**Sensei:　Mou jikan desu yo.**
**Gakusei: Sumimasen, ato gofun （　　） matte kudasaimasen ka.**

⇨　10.3

**3** * The following is an e-mail message from Jim Curtis to his future host family in Japan. Fill in the blanks with appropriate particles chosen from the box. You may use the same particle more than once.

が・を・に・の・で ・へ・と・まで ・から
**ga・o・ni・no・de・e・to ・made・kara**

[翻訳家 **hon'yakuka** 'translator'; 社会科 **shakaika** 'social studies'; 面倒をかける **mendou o kakeru** 'to trouble someone']

近藤様ご一家へ
　　初めまして。9月からお宅にお世話になりますジム・カーティス（①）申します。これからはジム（②）呼んで下さい。
　　今日はかんたんな自己紹介をさせていただきます。僕は今、○○大学（③）3年生で、経済（④）専攻しています。趣味は読書と山（⑤）登ることです。それから、料理（⑥）好きで、よくパスタ（⑦）作ります。出身はニュージャージー州（⑧）プリンストン（⑨）いう町です。
　　家族は五人です。父は翻訳家で、家（⑩）仕事をしています。母はニューヨーク（⑪）ある会社（⑫）勤めていて、マーケティングの仕事をしています。兄（⑬）2人います。上（⑭）兄は高校（⑮）社会科の教師です。下（⑯）兄は今法律（⑰）勉強（⑱）していますが、あと1年（⑲）卒業します。
　　僕はまだ日本（⑳）行ったこと（㉑）ないので、今度行くの（㉒）楽しみ（㉓）しています。色々ご面倒をおかけする（㉔）思いますが、どうぞよろしくお願いします。

　　　　　　　　　　　　　　　　　　　　　　　　　　ジムより

Kondou-sama go-ikka e

Hajimemashite. Kugatsu kara o-taku ni o-sewa ni narimasu Jimu Kaatisu ( ① ) moushimasu. Kore kara wa Jimu ( ② ) yonde kudasai.

Kyou wa kantan na jiko shoukai o sasete itadakimasu. Boku wa ima ○○Daigaku ( ③ ) sannensei de, keizai ( ④ ) senkou shite imasu. Shumi wa dokusho to yama ( ⑤ ) noboru koto desu. Sore kara, ryouri ( ⑥ ) suki de, yoku pasuta ( ⑦ ) tsukurimasu. Shusshin wa Nyuujaajii-shuu ( ⑧ ) Purinsuton ( ⑨ ) iu machi desu.

Kazoku wa gonin desu. Chichi wa hon'yaku-ka de, ie ( ⑩ ) shigoto o shite imasu. Haha wa Nyuuyooku ( ⑪ ) aru kaisha ( ⑫ ) tsutomete ite, maaketingu no shigoto o shite imasu. Ani ( ⑬ ) futari imasu. Ue ( ⑭ ) ani wa koukou ( ⑮ ) shakaika no kyoushi desu. Shita ( ⑯ ) ani wa ima houritsu ( ⑰ ) benkyou ( ⑱ ) shite imasu ga, ato ichinen ( ⑲ ) sotsugyou shimasu.

Boku wa mada Nihon ( ⑳ ) itta koto ( ㉑ ) nai node, kondo iku no ( ㉒ ) tanoshimi ( ㉓ ) shite imasu. Iroiro go-mendou o o-kake suru ( ㉔ ) omoimasu ga, douzo yoroshiku o-negai shimasu.

Jimu yori

⇨ 10.1, 10.2

# 11
# Topic marker *wa*

1 ★

Rewrite the following sentences with the underlined words as the topic. The first one has been done for you as an example.

(1) 紫式部が<u>源氏物語を</u>書いた。 → <u>源氏物語は</u>紫式部が書いた。
  **Murasaki Shikibu ga <u>Genji Monogatari o</u> kaita.**
  → <u>**Genji Monogatari wa**</u> **Murasaki Shikibu ga kaita.**

(2) <u>子供が</u>外で遊んでいる。
  <u>**Kodomo ga**</u> **soto de asonde iru.**

(3) <u>田中さんに</u>会ったことがありません。
  <u>**Tanaka-san ni**</u> **atta koto ga arimasen.**

(4) 電話で<u>先生と</u>話しました。
  **Denwa de <u>sensei to</u> hanashimashita.**

(5) <u>日本で</u>温泉に入った。
  <u>**Nihon de**</u> **onsen ni haitta.**

(6) 代表が三人<u>イギリスから</u>来た。
  **Daihyou ga sannin <u>Igirisu kara</u> kita.**

⇨ 11.1

2 ★

Fill in the blanks with **wa** or **ga**.

(1) A: 日本に行きたいんですが、いつ（ ① ）いいでしょうか。
  B: やっぱり春か秋（ ② ）いいでしょうね。春（ ③ ）桜の花（ ④ ）きれい だし、秋（ ⑤ ）紅葉（ ⑥ ）素晴らしいです。
  A: **Nihon ni ikitai n desu ga, itsu（ ① ）ii deshou ka.**
  B: **Yappari haru ka aki（ ② ）ii deshou ne. Haru（ ③ ）sakura no hana（ ④ ）kirei da shi, aki（ ⑤ ）kouyou（ ⑥ ）subarashii desu.**

(2) A: だれかやってくれませんか。
  B: 私（　）やります。
  A: **Dareka yatte kuremasen ka.**
  B: **Watashi（　）yarimasu.**

(3) A: Bさん、これ、やってくれませんか。
  B: すみません、私（　）今ちょっと忙しいので。
  A: **B-san, kore, yatte kuremasen ka.**
  B: **Sumimasen, watashi（　）ima chotto isogashii node.**

(4) ［外を見て **Soto o mite**］あ、雪（　）降ってる！
  **A, yuki（　）futte ru!**

(5) 昔ある所におじいさん（ ① ）住んでいました。おじいさん（ ② ）お金（ ③ ）なくて、貧しい暮らしをしていました。

**Mukashi aru tokoro ni ojiisan ( ① ) sunde imashita. Ojiisan ( ② ) o-kane ( ③ ) nakute, mazushii kurashi o shite imashita.**

(6) 私（ ① ）兄弟（ ② ）二人います。姉（ ③ ）料理（ ④ ）得意で、姉（ ⑤ ）作った料理（ ⑥ ）とてもおいしいです。

**Watashi ( ① ) kyoudai ( ② ) futari imasu. Ane ( ③ ) ryouri ( ④ ) tokui de, ane ( ⑤ ) tsukutta ryouri ( ⑥ ) totemo oishii desu.**

(7) A: 病院を探しているんですが、病院（ ① ）どこにありますか。
　　B: あそこに銀行（ ② ）ありますね。病院（ ③ ）あの銀行のむこうですよ。

A: **Byouin o sagashite iru n desu ga, byouin ( ① ) doko ni arimasu ka.**
B: **Asoko ni ginkou ( ② ) arimasu ne. Byouin ( ③ ) ano ginkou no mukou desu yo.**

(8) A: 加藤さんって方に会いたいんだけど、知ってる？
　　B: うん、あそこに立っている黒いスーツを着ている人（　　）加藤さんだよ。

A: **Katou-san tte kata ni aitai n da kedo, shitteru?**
B: **Un, asoko ni tatte iru kuroi suutsu o kite iru hito (　　) Katou-san da yo.**

⇨ 11.2, 11.3, 11.5

**3** ☆☆☆

The following is the beginning of a folktale called "Urashima Tarou." Change the underlined particle **ga** to the topic marker **wa**, if appropriate in the context.

昔浦島という漁師が[1]いました。ある日海のそばを歩いていると、子供たちが[2]大きなかめをいじめています。浦島が[3]かわいそうだと思ったので、そのかめを助けてやりました。次の日浦島が[4]朝早くからつりに出かけました。浦島が[5]海でつりをしていると、「浦島さん、浦島さん」という声が[6]聞こえます。変だなと思いながら声のする方を見るとかめが[7]泳いでいました。かめが[8]「浦島さん、私が[9]きのうのかめです。きのうはどうもありがとうございました。今日はお礼に海の中にある竜宮（りゅうぐう=Dragon Palace）へお連れしたいと思います。どうぞ私のせなかにお乗りください。」と言いました。浦島が[10]喜んでかめのせなかに乗りました。

**Mukashi Urashima to iu ryoushi ga[1] imashita. Aru hi umi no soba o aruite iru to, kodomotachi ga[2] ookina kame o ijimete imasu. Urashima ga[3] kawaisou da to omotta node, sono kame o tasukete yarimashita. Tsugi no hi Urashima ga[4] asa hayaku kara tsuri ni dekakemashita. Urashima ga[5] umi de tsuri o shite iru to, 'Urashima-san, Urashima-san' to iu koe ga[6] kikoemasu. Hen da na to omoi nagara koe no suru hou o miru to kame ga[7] oyoide imashita. Kame ga[8] 'Urashima-san, watashi ga[9] kinou no kame desu. Kinou wa doumo arigatou gozaimashita. Kyou wa orei ni umi no naka ni aru ryuuguu (Dragon Palace) e o-tsure shitai to omoimasu. Douzo watashi no senaka ni o-nori kudasai' to iimashita. Urashima ga[10] yorokonde kame no senaka ni norimashita.**

⇨ 11.2, 11.5

# 12
# Verbs

1 * Complete the following conjugation chart. As for くる **kuru** 'to come,' write your answers in hiragana or romaji, and not kanji.

| Plain negative nonpast | Polite affirmative nonpast | Plain affirmative nonpast | Conditional | Volitional |
|---|---|---|---|---|
| 書かない **kakanai** | ① | 書く **kaku** 'write' | ② | 書こう **kakou** |
| ③ | 会います **aimasu** | 会う **au** 'meet' | ④ | ⑤ |
| ⑥ | ⑦ | 読む **yomu** 'read' | ⑧ | ⑨ |
| ⑩ | ⑪ | 待つ **matsu** 'wait' | 待てば **mateba** | ⑫ |
| とらない **toranai** | ⑬ | とる **toru** 'take' | ⑭ | とろう **torou** |
| ⑮ | 食べます **tabemasu** | 食べる **taberu** 'eat' | ⑯ | 食べよう **tabeyou** |
| ⑰ | ⑱ | くる **kuru** 'come' | ⑲ | ⑳ |
| ㉑ | ㉒ | 見る **miru** 'see' | 見れば **mireba** | ㉓ |
| ㉔ | ㉕ | する **suru** 'do' | ㉖ | しよう **shiyou** |

⇨ 12.1

**2** ★ Fill in the chart below with corresponding intransitive or transitive verbs.

| Intransitive verbs | Transitive verbs |
|---|---|
| とまる **tomaru** 'X stops' | ⑥ |
| ① | しめる **shimeru** 'close X' |
| かわる **kawaru** 'X changes' | ⑦ |
| ② | つける **tsukeru** 'turn X on' |
| あく **aku** 'X opens' | ⑧ |
| はいる **hairu** 'X enters' | ⑨ |
| ③ | だす **dasu** 'take X out' |
| おきる **okiru** 'X wakes up' | ⑩ |
| ④ | なおす **naosu** 'repair/cure X' |
| ⑤ | こわす **kowasu** 'break X' |

⇨ 12.2

**3** ★★ Indicate whether the underlined verbs are transitive (vt) or intransitive (vi).

(1) 台風で木が<u>倒れて</u>しまいました。
(2) 悪いけど、このいす、<u>直して</u>くれる？
(3) みなさん、明日の映画の時間が<u>変わりました</u>。
(4) いい写真だねぇ。みんなよく<u>写ってる</u>。
(5) 宿題は明日の3時までに<u>出して</u>ください。
(6) みっちゃん、早く行かないと、店が<u>閉まっちゃう</u>よ。
(7) 今夜はお祝いだから、シャンペンを<u>冷やして</u>おきましょう。
(8) ご病気が早く<u>治ります</u>ように。
(9) このコーヒーカップ、先週買ったばかりなのに、<u>割れ</u>ちゃった。
(10) そのドア、無理に<u>開ける</u>と、<u>こわれます</u>よ。

(1) Taifuu de ki ga <u>taorete</u> shimaimashita.
(2) Warui kedo, kono isu, <u>naoshite</u> kureru?
(3) Minasan, ashita no eiga no jikan ga <u>kawarimashita</u>.
(4) Ii shashin da nee. Minna yoku <u>utsutte</u> ru.
(5) Shukudai wa ashita no sanji made ni <u>dashite</u> kudasai.
(6) Mitchan, hayaku ikanai to, mise ga <u>shimatchau</u> yo.
(7) Kon'ya wa o-iwai da kara, shanpen o <u>hiyashite</u> okimashou.
(8) Go-byouki ga hayaku <u>naorimasu</u> you ni.
(9) Kono koohii kappu, senshuu katta bakari na noni, <u>warechatta</u>.
(10) Sono doa, muri ni <u>akeru</u> to, <u>kowaremasu</u> yo.

⇨ 12.2

**4** ★ Choose an intransitive or transitive verb, whichever is appropriate.

(1) A: あ、電気が【ついてる・つけてる】。
    B: うん、まだ【起きてる・起こしてる】んだね。
    A: **A, denki ga 【tsuite ru・tsukete ru】.**
    B: **Un, mada 【okite ru・okoshite ru】 n da ne.**

(2) A: 何してるの？
    B: せんたくものを【かわいてる・かわかしてる】の。
    A: **Nani shite ru no?**
    B: **Sentaku-mono o 【kawaite ru・kawakashite ru】 no.**

(3) A: この本の評判 (reputation) はどうですか 。
    B: とてもいいですよ。よく【売れて・売って】います。
    A: **Kono hon no hyouban (reputation) wa dou desu ka.**
    B: **Totemo ii desu yo. Yoku 【urete・utte】 imasu.**

(4) A: ジョンはころんで足の骨を【折れちゃった・折っちゃった】らしいですよ。
    B: あぶないですねぇ。大丈夫でしょうか。
    A: **Jon wa koronde ashi no hone o 【orechatta・otchatta】 rashii desu yo.**
    B: **Abunai desu nee. Daijoubu deshou ka.**

(5) 子: 仕事が【見つからない・見つけない】んだ … 。
    母: 【見つかろう・見つけよう】としたの？
    子: **Shigoto ga 【mitsukaranai・mitsukenai】 n da . . .**
    母: **【mitsukarou・mitsukeyou】 to shita no?**

(6) A: 暑いから、まど、【あいて・あけて】くれる？
    B: さっき【あこう・あけよう】としたんだけど、【あかなかった・あけなかった】の。
    A: **Atsui kara, mado, 【aite・akete】 kureru?**
    B: **Sakki 【akou・akeyou】 to shita n da kedo, 【akanakatta・akenakatta】 no.**

(7) A: ただいま！ああ、疲れた。おふろはもう【わいてる・わかしてる】？
    B: うん、さっき【わいて・わかして】おいたから。
    A: **Tadaima! Aa, tsukareta. O-furo wa mou 【waite ru・wakashite ru】?**
    B: **Un, sakki 【waite・wakashite】 oita kara.**

(8) A: すみません、ストーブを【きえて・けして】もらえますか。
    B: あ、ストーブはもう【きえて・けして】ありますよ。
    A: **Sumimasen, sutoobu o 【kiete・keshite】 moraemasu ka.**
    B: **A, sutoobu wa mou 【kiete・keshite】 arimasu yo.**

⇨ 12.2, 19.2.1, 19.2.4, 19.2.8

**5** ★ Many verbs can be turned into the potential form, but there are only a handful of commonly used spontaneous verbs, including those in the table below. Fill in the blanks with appropriate forms of potential or spontaneous verbs from the table.

| | Potential | Spontaneous |
|---|---|---|
| | 見られる **mirareru** 'can see/look' | 見える **mieru** 'can be seen, is visible' |
| | 聞ける **kikeru** 'can hear/listen' | 聞こえる **kikoeru** 'can be heard, is audible' |
| | 思える **omoeru** 'can think' | 思われる **omowareru** 'can be thought, seem' |
| | できる **dekiru** 'can do' | できる **dekiru** 'be made, become existent' |

(1) A: あ、ほら！あそこに富士山が＿＿＿＿ますよ。
   B: 本当だ。わぁ、きれい！
   A: **A, hora! Asoko ni Fuji-san ga ＿＿＿＿ masu yo.**
   B: **Hontou da. Waa, kirei!**

(2) A: もしもし、田中ですが、あのう、午後からの会議は …
   B: すみません、よく＿＿＿＿ないんですけど。もうちょっと大きい声でお願いします。
   A: **Moshi moshi, Tanaka desu ga, anou, gogo kara no kaigi wa . . .**
   B: **Sumimasen, yoku ＿＿＿＿nai n desu kedo. Mou chotto ookii koe de o-negai shimasu.**

(3) A: この辺はずいぶん変わりましたねぇ。
   B: ええ、大きいビルがどんどん＿＿＿＿て、もう昔の面影 (vestige) はありませんね。
   A: **Kono hen wa zuibun kawarimashita nee.**
   B: **Ee, ookii biru ga dondon ＿＿＿＿te, mou mukashi no omokage (vestige) wa arimasen ne.**

(4) A: ラジオでクラシック音楽が聞きたいんだけど。
   B: だったら、FMで＿＿＿るよ。
   A: **Rajio de kurashikku ongaku ga kikitai n da kedo.**
   B: **Dattara, FM de ＿＿＿＿ru yo.**

(5) A: ニューヨークはいいですね。おいしいおすしが食べられて。
   B: ええ、最新のミュージカルも＿＿＿＿ますし。
   A: **Nyuuyooku wa ii desu ne. Oishii o-sushi ga taberarete.**
   B: **Ee, saishin no myuujikaru mo ＿＿＿＿masu shi.**

(6) 現在残されている遺跡 (ruins) から、武蔵野のあたりには1万5千年も前から人が住み始めたと＿＿＿＿る。
   **Genzai nokosarete iru iseki (ruins) kara, Musashino no atari ni wa ichiman gosennen mo mae kara hito ga sumi-hajimeta to ＿＿＿＿ru.**

(7) A: 洞窟 (cave) の中って暗くて何も＿＿＿＿ないんですね。
   B: ええ、声が＿＿＿＿＿＿から、いいですけどね。
   A: **Doukutsu (cave) no naka tte kurakute nani mo ＿＿＿＿nai n desu ne.**
   B: **Ee, koe ga ＿＿＿＿＿＿ kara, ii desu kedo ne.**

⇨ 12.5, 12.6

29

**6** * Fill in the blanks with appropriate forms of giving and receiving verbs.

> やる・あげる・さしあげる・くれる・くださる・もらう・いただく
>
> **yaru · ageru · sashi-ageru · kureru · kudasaru · morau · itadaku**

(1) 今年は大学から奨学金を _____ているので、助かります。
**Kotoshi wa daigaku kara shougakukin o _____te iru node, tasukarimasu.**

(2) 夫： おっ、ハワイのおみやげか。だれが（僕達に）_____たの？
妻： お隣の奥さんよぉ。いいよねぇ、あそこの家は。
**Otto:** O, Hawai no o-miyage ka. Dare ga (boku-tachi ni) _____ta no?
**Tsuma:** O-tonari no okusan yoo. Ii yo nee, asoko no uchi wa.

(3) In a TV commercial [私ども **watakushi-domo** 'we (*humble*)'; 期間中
**kikan-chuu** 'during (the period of)']
（私どもは）セールの期間中、お客様にプレゼントを _____ています！
**(Watakushi-domo wa) seeru no kikan-chuu, o-kyaku-sama ni purezento**
**o _____te imasu!**

(4) 花に水を _____ のを忘れないで下さいね。
**Hana ni mizu o _____ no o wasurenai de kudasai ne.**

(5) マリって子、（私が）誕生日のプレゼントを _____たのに、ありがとうも言わ
ないのよ。
**Mari tte ko, (watashi ga) tanjoubi no purezento o _____ta noni,**
**arigatou mo iwanai no yo.**

(6) このハンカチ、きれいでしょ？社長さんの奥様が _____たの。
**Kono hankachi, kirei desho? Shachou-san no okusama ga _____ta no.**

(7) 母： あら、そのおかし、だれに _____たの？
子： 公園で知らないおじさんが _____たの。
母： 知らない人から物を _____ちゃだめよ。
**Haha:** Ara, sono o-kashi, dare ni _____ta no?
**Ko:** Kouen de shiranai ojisan ga _____ta no.
**Haha:** Shiranai hito kara mono o _____cha dame yo.

⇨ 12.7, Exercises in 42

**7** * Satoshi is looking for a part-time job. Looking at his 'can-do' list, describe what he can and cannot do using the potential form of verbs. '○' means that he can, and '×' that he cannot.

| | | |
|---|---|---|
| • 英語を話す | • **Eigo o hanasu** | ○ |
| • 車を運転する | • **Kuruma o unten suru** | ○ |
| • 一日5時間働く | • **Ichinichi gojikan hataraku** | × |
| • エクセルを使う | • **'Ekuseru' o tsukau** | ○ |
| • 朝早く会社にくる | • **Asa hayaku kaisha ni kuru** | × |
| • ビデオクリップを編集する | • **Bideo kurippu o henshuu suru** | ○ |

Example: さとしさんは英語が話せます。
**Satoshi-san wa Eigo ga hanasemasu.**

_____

_____

_____

_____

_____

⇨ 12.6

# 13
# Adjectives

1 *

The following passage is a journal entry written by an employee of a small company. Change the form of each adjective appropriately so that it fits logically in the sentence. Some adjectives need not be changed.

昨日は一日中とても ①＿＿＿＿＿＿ （忙しい）。朝から ②＿＿＿＿＿＿ （暑い）ので、5時に起きてしまった。③＿＿＿＿＿＿ （ねむい）から、④＿＿＿＿＿＿ （冷たい）アイスコーヒーを飲んで、目を覚ました。⑤＿＿＿＿＿ （新しい）ブランドのコーヒーで、⑥＿＿＿＿＿ （おいしい）。七時半に家を出て、仕事に行った。家から会社までは ⑦＿＿＿＿＿＿ （近い）。歩いて15分だ。会社に着いたら、まだ誰もいなくて、⑧＿＿＿＿＿ （静か）。10時ごろ電話がかかってきて ⑨＿＿＿＿＿ （大変）ことになった。前の日に納品 (to deliver) した商品に ⑩＿＿＿＿＿＿ （多い）の欠陥 (defects) が見つかったのだ。

**Kinou wa ichinichi-juu totemo ①＿＿＿＿＿ (isogashii). Asa kara ②＿＿＿＿ (atsui) node, goji ni okite shimatta. ③＿＿＿＿＿ (nemui) kara, ④＿＿＿＿ (tsumetai) aisu koohii o nonde, me o samashita. ⑤＿＿＿＿ (atarashii) burando no koohii de, ⑥＿＿＿＿ (oishii). Shichiji-han ni ie o dete, shigoto ni itta. Uchi kara kaisha made wa ⑦＿＿＿＿ (chikai). Aruite juugo-fun da. Kaisha ni tsuitara, mada daremo inakute, ⑧＿＿＿＿ (shizuka). Juuji goro denwa ga kakatte kite ⑨＿＿＿＿ (taihen) koto ni natta. Mae no hi ni nouhin ('deliver') shita shouhin ni ⑩＿＿＿＿ (ooi) no kekkan ('defects') ga mitsukatta no da.**

⇨ 13.1, 13.2, 13.4

2 *

Fill in the blanks with appropriate forms of the adjectives given below.

先生：　旅行はどうでしたか。
学生：　（　①つまらない　　）。
先生：　え、どうしてですか。
学生：　ホテルがとても（　②たかい　　）んです。それで、お金がほとんどなくなってしまって、あまり観光できなかったんです。
先生：　そうですか。（　③ざんねん　　）ね。
学生：　先生の休みはどうでしたか。
先生：　引っ越しをしたので、ちょっと（　④たいへん　　）。

**Sensei:　Ryokou wa dou deshita ka.**
**Gakusei:　(　① tsumaranai　　).**
**Sensei:　E, doushite desu ka.**
**Gakusei:　Hoteru ga totemo (　② takai　　) n desu. Sorede, o-kane ga hotondo nakunatte shimatte, amari kankou dekinakatta n desu.**
**Sensei:　Sou desu ka. (　③ zannen　　) ne.**

32

Gakusei: Sensei no yasumi wa dou deshita ka.

Sensei: Hikkoshi o shita node, chotto（　　④ taihen　　）.

⇨ 13.1, 13.2

**3** * Fill in the blanks with appropriate forms of the following adjectives.

> おもしろい・つまらない・たのしい・しずか・にぎやか・たいへん・
> いそがしい・ひま・ふるい・あたらしい・やすい・たかい・おいしい・
> まずい・ちいさい
>
> **omoshiroi・tsumaranai・tanoshii・shizuka・nigiyaka・taihen・
> isogashii・hima・furui・atarashii・yasui・takai・oishii・
> mazui・chiisai**

(1)

A: 明日、(a)＿＿＿＿＿＿？

B: うん、(b)＿＿＿＿＿＿けど、なんで？

A: 最近 (c)＿＿＿＿＿＿て、出かけてなかったから、どこか行きたいなと思って。

B: あ、じゃあ駅前に (d)＿＿＿＿＿＿レストランがオープンしたって聞いたから、
行ってみない？

A: うん、いいね。

B: けっこう (e)＿＿＿＿＿＿て、ボリュームがあって、(f)＿＿＿＿＿＿って言ってたよ。

A: Ashita, (a)＿＿＿＿＿＿？

B: Un, (b)＿＿＿＿＿＿kedo, nande?

A: Saikin (c)＿＿＿＿＿＿te, dekakete nakatta kara, dokoka ikitai na to
omotte.

B: A, jaa ekimae ni (d)＿＿＿＿＿＿resutoran ga oopun shitatte kiita kara,
itte minai?

A: Un, ii ne.

B: Kekkou (e)＿＿＿＿＿＿te, boryuumu ga atte, (f)＿＿＿＿＿＿tte itte ta yo.

(2)

C: Dさんの出身ってどこですか。

D: 僕ですか。僕は福井です。

C: へえ、そうなんですか。

D: (a)＿＿＿＿＿＿町でね、魚は (b)＿＿＿＿＿＿けど、あんまり (c)＿＿＿＿＿＿
ところだよ。

C: でも、よく帰省してますよね。

D: アハハ、まあ、(d)＿＿＿＿＿＿ところだけど、(e)＿＿＿＿＿＿、落ち着くか
ら。それに、やっぱり (f)＿＿＿＿＿＿魚が食べたくなるからね。

C: D-san no shusshin tte doko desu ka.

D: Boku desu ka. Boku wa Fukui desu.

C: Hee, sou na n desu ka.

D: (a)＿＿＿＿＿＿machi de ne, sakana wa (b)＿＿＿＿＿＿kedo, anmari
(c)＿＿＿＿＿＿tokoro da yo.

C: Demo, yoku kisei shite masu yo ne.

D: Ahaha, maa, (d)＿＿＿＿＿＿tokoro da kedo, (e)＿＿＿＿＿＿, ochitsuku
kara. Soreni, yappari (f)＿＿＿＿＿＿sakana ga tabetaku naru kara ne.

(3)

E: 今回のプロジェクトどうだった？
F: いろいろ問題があって、(a)＿＿＿＿＿＿＿よ。
E: そうだったの？けっこう (b)＿＿＿＿＿＿そうに見えたけど。
F: それは、(c)＿＿＿＿＿＿時もあったけど、陰で苦労してたんだよ。
E: そうなんだ。お疲れさま。

E: **Konkai no purojekuto dou datta?**
F: **Iroiro mondai ga atte,** (a)＿＿＿＿＿＿**yo.**
E: **Sou datta no? Kekkou** (b)＿＿＿＿＿＿**sou ni mieta kedo.**
F: **Sore wa,** (c)＿＿＿＿＿**toki mo atta kedo, kage de kurou shite ta n da yo.**
E: **Sou na n da. O-tsukare-sama.**

⇨ 13.1, 13.2, 13.3, 28.1

# 14
# Adverbs

**1** ★ The following is a recommendation for a healthy lifestyle. Change the words provided in the blanks into appropriate adverbial forms.

健康のために、夜は（ ①早め ）寝て、朝も（ ②早い ）起きること。そして、ゆっくりと（ ③いい ）かんで食べること。仕事の合間に（ ④適度 ）体を動かすこと。

**Kenkou no tame ni, yoru wa（ ① hayame ）nete, asa mo（ ② hayai ）okiru koto. Soshite, yukkuri to（ ③ ii ）kande taberu koto. Shigoto no aima ni（ ④ tekido ）karada o ugokasu koto.**

⇨ 14.2

**2** ★ Choose the appropriate adverbs.

A: 最近、調子どう？
B: 【① なかなか・あまり】いいよ。タバコも【② めったに・まれに】すわないし。
A: そうなの？私なんか【③ まれに・ぜんぜん】眠れないから、体調悪くて。
B: それは良くないね。【④ おそらく・ぜひ】運動不足だね。
A: うん、そうかも。
B: だったら、【⑤ けっして・ぜひ】うちのクラブに入るといいよ。
A: え〜、でも運動苦手だから、【⑥ また・まだ】そのうちにね。
B: わかった。じゃ、【⑦ まんがいち・たいして】気が向いたら、電話して。

A: **Saikin, choushi dou?**
B: 【① Nakanaka・amari】**ii yo. Tabako mo**【② mettani・mareni】**suwanai shi.**
A: **Sou na no? Watashi nanka**【③ mareni・zenzen】**nemurenai kara, taichou warukute.**
B: **Sore wa yokunai ne.**【④ Osoraku・Zehi】**undou busoku da ne.**
A: **Un, sou kamo.**
B: **Dattara,**【⑤ kesshite・zehi】**uchi no kurabu ni hairu to ii yo.**
A: **Ee, demo undou nigate dakara,**【⑥ mata・mada】**sono uchi ni ne.**
B: **Wakatta. Ja,**【⑦ man ga ichi・taishite】**ki ga muitara, denwa shite.**

⇨ 14.3

**3** ★★★ The following is a horoscope for **yagi-za** (Capricorn). Fill in the blanks with appropriate adverbs from the box below. Use each word just once.

> a. まったく・b. ひそかに・c. のんびり・d. とつぜん・
> e. 少しずつ・f. おおいに・g. じっさいに・h. じっくり
>
> a. **mattaku**・b. **hisoka ni**・c. **nonbiri**・d. **totsuzen**・
> e. **sukoshizutsu**・f. **ooi ni**・g. **jissai ni**・h. **jikkuri**

今日はどこか遠くの国に旅行をしてみたくなりそうな日です。そこは、① ＿＿＿＿ あこがれていた外国かもしれません。今の生活に ② ＿＿＿＿ 不満がなくても、③ ＿＿＿＿ 日常から離れてみたくなるのは自然な気持ち。今から ④ ＿＿＿＿ 計画的に貯金をすれば、⑤ ＿＿＿＿ 旅立てるかもしれませんよ。また、行ってみたい場所のガイドブックを ⑥ ＿＿＿＿ 読んだり、ネットで画像を見つけたりして、想像の中で ⑦ ＿＿＿＿ 旅をするのもおすすめ。遠くの世界に思いを馳せ、⑧ ＿＿＿＿ 楽しんでください。

**Kyou wa dokoka tooku no kuni ni ryokou o shite mitakunari sou na hi desu. Soko wa, ① ＿＿＿＿ akogarete ita gaikoku kamo shiremasen. Ima no seikatsu ni ② ＿＿＿＿ fuman ga nakute mo, ③ ＿＿＿＿ nichijou kara hanarete mitaku naru no wa shizen na kimochi. Ima kara ④ ＿＿＿＿ keikakuteki ni chokin o sureba, ⑤ ＿＿＿＿ tabidateru kamo shiremasen yo. Mata, itte mitai basho no gaidobukku o ⑥ ＿＿＿＿ yondari, netto de gazou o mitsuketari shite, souzou no naka de ⑦ ＿＿＿＿ tabi o suru no mo o-susume. Tooku no sekai ni omoi o hase, ⑧ ＿＿＿＿ tanoshinde kudasai.**

⇨ 14.1, 14.2

# 15
# Negation

1 ★ Complete the sentences with negative forms. Use the appropriate tense and style.

> Example: きのうは暑かったですが、きょうは _____。
> → きのうは暑かったですが、きょうは 暑くありません。
> **Kinou wa atsukatta desu ga, kyou wa _____.**
> → **Kinou wa atsukatta desu ga, kyou wa <u>atsuku arimasen</u>.**

(1) 父は日本人ですが、母は _____。
   **Chichi wa nihonjin desu ga, haha wa _____.**

(2) 建物の中は静かですが、外は _____。
   **Tatemono no naka wa shizuka desu ga, soto wa _____.**

(3) 大都市の物価は高いけれど、いなかに行くと _____ よ。
   **Daitoshi no bukka wa takai keredo, inaka ni iku to _____ yo.**

(4) 私はたいてい運動をしますが、きのうは _____。
   **Watashi wa taitei undou o shimasu ga, kinou wa _____.**

(5) きのうはセールがあったけど、今日は _____ と思うよ。
   **Kinou wa seeru ga atta kedo, kyou wa _____ to omou yo.**

(6) 彼には先週会ったので、今週は _____ と思います。
   **Kare ni wa senshuu atta node, konshuu wa _____ to omoimasu.**

(7) きのうたくさん勉強しました。だから今日は _____。
   **Kinou takusan benkyou shimashita. Dakara kyou wa _____.**

(8) 朝は食べたけど、昼ご飯は _____ から、おなかがすいた。
   **Asa wa tabeta kedo, hiru-gohan wa _____ kara, onaka ga suita.**

(9) あの監督の映画はたいてい面白いけど、きのうのは _____ ね。
   **Ano kantoku no eiga wa taitei omoshiroi kedo, kinou no wa _____ ne.**

(10) 仕事はふつう大変だが、きのうの仕事はあまり _____ から、早く終わった。
   **Shigoto wa futsuu taihen da ga, kinou no shigoto wa amari _____ kara, hayaku owatta.**

⇨ 5.1.3, 15.1, 22.5, 47.3

**2** ★

In passages (A)–(C), the speaker is making negative remarks about something. Fill in the blanks with the negative form of appropriate words from each list.

(A)

[雰囲気 **fun'iki** 'atmosphere']

> 行く・おいしい・親切だ・いい・飲める
>
> **iku · oishii · shinsetsu da · ii · nomeru**

きのう行ったレストランはひどかった。お酒が ①_____ し、料理もあまり ②_____。ウェーターもあまり ③_____。雰囲気もあまり ④_____ から、⑤_____ 方がいいと思う。

**Kinou itta resutoran wa, hidokatta. O-sake ga ①_____ shi, ryouri mo amari ②_____. Weetaa mo amari ③_____. Fun'iki mo amari ④_____ kara, ⑤_____ hou ga ii to omou.**

(B)

> 食べる・聞く・わかる・帰ってくる・勉強する
>
> **taberu · kiku · wakaru · kaette kuru · benkyou suru**

このごろ子供がよる遅くまで ①_____ ので、心配です。家にいる時もビデオゲームばかりして ②_____。家族と一緒にご飯も ③_____ し、私の言うことは全然 ④_____。何を考えているのか ⑤_____。どうしたらいいでしょうか。

**Konogoro kodomo ga yoru osoku made ①_____ node, shinpai desu. Ie ni iru toki mo bideo geemu bakari shite ②_____. Kazoku to issho ni gohan mo ③_____ shi, watashi no iu koto wa zenzen ④_____. Nani o kangaete iru no ka ⑤_____. Dou shitara ii deshou ka.**

(C)

> できる・ある・おもしろい・行く・出られる
>
> **dekiru · aru · omoshiroi · iku · derareru**

先週の春休みは全然 ①_____。お金が ②_____ ので、どこにも ③_____。それに風邪をひいてしまったので、外にも ④_____。やろうと思っていたことの半分も ⑤_____。

**Senshuu no haru yasumi wa zenzen ①_____. Okane ga ②_____ node, doko ni mo ③_____. Soreni kaze o hiite shimatta node, soto ni mo ④_____. Yarou to omotte ita koto no hanbun mo ⑤_____.**

⇨ 5.1.3, 15.1, 22.2.1, 47.3

**3** ★

Complete these sentences by changing the words in parentheses to their negative forms. Choose **-nakute** or **-naide**, whichever is correct.

> Example: この部屋で （ 食べる ） ください。
> → この部屋で （ 食べないで ） ください。
> **Kono heya de （ taberu ） kudasai.**
> → **Kono heya de （ tabenaide ） kudasai.**

(1) 「帰る」（ だ ）「蛙」だよ。
　　**'Kaeru' （ da ） 'kaeru' da yo.**
　　*I mean 'kaeru' ('frog'), not 'kaeru' ('go home').*
(2) 私のアパートは駅から （ 遠い ） 便利です。
　　**Watashi no apaato wa eki kara （ tooi ） benri desu.**
(3) ここではたばこを （ すう ） ください。
　　**Koko de wa tabako o （ suu ） kudasai.**
(4) 先日は話が （ できる ） 残念でした。
　　**Senjitsu wa hanashi ga （ dekiru ） zannen deshita.**
(5) これは （ 言う ） ほしいんですが。
　　**Kore wa （ iu ） hoshii n desu ga.**
(6) （ 寝る ） 仕事をするのはよくありません。
　　**（ Neru ） shigoto o suru no wa yoku arimasen.**
(7) 何を言っているのか （ わかる ） 困りました。
　　**Nani o itte iru no ka （ wakaru ） komarimashita.**
(8) この夏はアルバイトを （ する ） 夏のコースを取るつもりです。
　　**Kono natsu wa arubaito o （ suru ） natsu no koosu o toru tsumori desu.**

⇨ 12.1, 15.3

**4** ★ ★

The following is an account written by a Japanese teacher. Choose the appropriate adverbs.

ジョーンズさんは最近【① 別に・ぜんぜん】授業に来なくなってしまいました。以前は【② まさか・めったに】授業をサボることもなく、【③ ちっとも・何も】連絡しないで休むことは【④ 決して・別に】ありませんでした。【⑤ ろくに・別に】日本語がきらいになったわけではないようです。【⑥ ぜんぜん・まさか】学校をやめたのではないと思いますが、心配です。

**Joonzu-san wa saikin【① betsuni・zenzen】jugyou ni konaku natte shimaimashita. Izen wa【② masaka・mettani】jugyou o saboru koto mo naku,【③ chittomo・nanimo】renraku shinaide yasumu koto wa【④ kesshite・betsuni】arimasendeshita.【⑤ Roku ni・Betsu ni】Nihongo ga kirai ni natta wake de wa nai you desu.【⑥ Zenzen・Masaka】gakkou o yameta no de wa nai to omoimasu ga, shinpai desu.**

⇨ 15.4

**5** ★

You went to a party. Answer the following questions about it, using **shika** and the words in parentheses.

(1) 先生もいらっしゃいましたか。（学生）
　　**Sensei mo irasshaimashita ka. (gakusei)**
(2) 学生はおおぜい来ましたか。（十人）
　　**Gakusei wa oozei kimashita ka. (juunin)**

(3) いろいろなものが出ましたか。（すし）
**Iroiro na mono ga demashita ka. (sushi)**

(4) おすしは前に何度も食べたことがありましたか。（一度）
**Osushi wa mai ni nando mo tabeta koto ga arimashita ka. (ichido)**

(5) ビールを飲みましたか。（コーラ）
**Biiru o nomimashita ka. (koora)**

(6) 知らない人と話しましたか。（知っている人）
**Shiranai hito to hanashimashita ka. (shitte iru hito)**

⇨ 15.4

**6** ⁑ Fill in the blanks with one of the negative prefixes (無 **mu**, 非 **hi**, 不 **fu**, or 未 **mi**).

(1) （　　）料で使えるソフトがたくさんある。
（　　）**ryou de tsukaeru sofuto ga takusan aru.**

(2) 日本でも郊外に住んでいると、車がないと（　　）便だ。
**Nihon demo kougai ni sunde iru to, kuruma ga nai to** （　　）**ben da.**

(3) 最近は（　　）婚の男女が増えている。
**Saikin wa** （　　）**kon no danjo ga fuete iru.**

(4) （　　）規則な生活は体によくない。
（　　）**kisoku na seikatsu wa karada ni yokunai.**

(5) 道にゴミを捨てるのは（　　）常識 (common sense) だ。
**Michi ni gomi o suteru no wa** （　　）**joushiki (common sense) da.**

(6) この研究はまだ（　　）完成です。
**Kono kenkyuu wa mada** （　　）**kansei desu.**

(7) やると言ってやらないのは（　　）責任だ。
**Yaru to itte yaranai no wa** （　　）**sekinin da.**

(8) （　　）景気で仕事のない人が多い。
（　　）**keiki de shigoto no nai hito ga ooi.**

(9) 未来の話は（　　）現実的な話が多い。
**Mirai no hanashi wa** （　　）**genjitsuteki na hanashi ga ooi.**

(10) 古代の歴史を勉強するのは（　　）意味ではない。
**Kodai no rekishi o benkyou suru no wa** （　　）**imi de wa nai.**

⇨ 15.5.2

# 16
# Numbers and classifiers

1 ★ You are helping your little host sister with her homework. In Japanese, read out and answer the following math problems. The '+' sign is read **tasu**, '−' **hiku**, '×' **kakeru**, '÷' **waru**, and '=' **wa** in Japanese.

   Example: 2 + 3 = 5 (**Ni tasu san wa go.**)

(1)   12 + 9 =       (2)   126 ÷ 3 =       (3)   5 × 7 =       (4)   100 − 58 =

⇨  16.1

2 (A)*
Spell out the numbers in hiragana or romaji.

[約 **yaku** 'approximately']

   Example: いちユーロは約（130: ひゃく　さんじゅう）円です。
         **Ichi yuuro wa yaku (130: hyaku sanjuu) en desu.**

(1) いちインチは（2.4:　　　　　　）センチぐらいです。
    **Ichi inchi wa (2.4:　　　　　　) senchi gurai desu.**
(2) ごひゃくキロ（グラム）は（1100:　　　　　　）ポンドぐらいです。
    **Go hyaku kiro (guramu) wa (1100:　　　　　　) pondo gurai desu.**
(3) いちリットルは約（0.26:　　　　　）ガロンです。
    **Ichi rittoru wa yaku (0.26:　　　　　) garon desu.**
(4) ろくフィートは約（183:　　　　　）センチです。
    **Roku fiito wa yaku (183:　　　　　) senchi desu.**
(5) せんマイルは約（1,609:　　　　　）キロ（メートル）です。
    **Sen mairu wa yaku (1,609:　　　　　) kiro (meetoru) desu.**
(6) いちねんは（365:　　　　　）日あります。
    **Ichi nen wa (365:　　　　　) nichi arimasu.**
(7) 富士山の高さは約（3,776　　　　　）メートルです。
    **Fujisan no takasa wa yaku (3776:　　　　　) meetoru desu.**

(B)**
Say the following numbers in Japanese.

(1) 日本の人口 **Nihon no jinkou**: Approximately 126,650,000
(2) 中国語を話す人の数 **Chuugokugo o hanasu hito no kazu**: Approximately 1,213,000,000
(3) サラリーマンの平均年収 **sarariiman no heikin nenshuu** (average annual income): Approximately ¥4,090,000
(4) 一戸建て平均価格 **ikko-date heikin kakaku** (average price of a single family home): Approximately ¥38,810,000

⇨  16.1

**3** ＊ What time is it now? Spell out the time in hiragana or romaji.

(1) [3:15]     (2) [4:20]     (3) [12:30]     (4) [8:40 am]

(5) [9:09]     (6) [6:36]     (7) [7:57 am]     (8) [11:05 pm]

⇨ 16.1

**4** ＊ You are a grocery store manager. Tell your part-time employees to come to work two days each next month. Spell out the dates in hiragana or romaji.

> Example: 1ˢᵗ & 2ⁿᵈ → 来月は ＿＿ついたちとふつか＿＿ にバイトに入ってください。
> **Raigetsu wa <u>tsuitachi to futsuka</u> ni baito ni haitte kudasai.**

(1) 3ʳᵈ & 6ᵗʰ     (2) 8ᵗʰ & 10ᵗʰ     (3) 9ᵗʰ & 12ᵗʰ
(4) 17ᵗʰ & 20ᵗʰ     (5) 24ᵗʰ & 30ᵗʰ

⇨ 16.1

**5** ＊ Your friend just moved into a new apartment and needs various household items. Tell him/her the great prices you found online in Japanese. Transcribe the prices in hiragana or romaji.

(1) 目覚まし時計     **mezamashi dokei**     ¥      899
(2) 炊飯器          **suihanki**           ¥    4,500
(3) ブレンダー      **burendaa**          ¥    6,750
(4) 電子レンジ      **denshi renji**       ¥    8,600
(5) 冷蔵庫          **reizouko**          ¥   23,300
(6) 大型テレビ      **oogata terebi**      ¥  115,200

⇨ 16.1

**6** ＊ You are making a list of supplies for your new semester. Fill in the blanks with appropriate classifiers.

(1) 鉛筆          **enpitsu**          5＿＿＿
(2) 消しゴム      **keshi gomu**      1＿＿＿
(3) ノート        **nooto**           6＿＿＿
(4) スティック糊  **sutikku nori**     1＿＿＿
(5) CD-ROM      **shiidii-romu**     10＿＿＿

⇨ 16.2

**7** ＊ Fill in the blanks with appropriate classifiers.

(A)

[天国 **tengoku** 'heaven'; モルモット **morumotto** 'guinea pig';
セキセイインコ **sekisei inko** 'parakeet']

うちは (a. 八　　) 家族です。祖父母、両親、姉 (b. 三　　) と僕です。そして我が家はペット天国です。今いるペットはモルモット (c. 三　　)、ねこ (d. 五　　)、犬 (e. 二　　)、セキセイインコ (f. 四　　)、金魚 (g. 十　　)、そして馬 (h. 二　　) です。すごいでしょ？

**Uchi wa** (a. hachi　　) **kazoku desu. Sofubo, ryoushin, ane** (b. san　　) **to boku desu. Soshite wagaya wa petto tengoku desu. Ima iru petto wa morumotto** (c. san　　), **neko** (d. go　　), **inu** (e. ni　　), **sekisei inko** (f. yon　　), **kingyo** (g. ju　　), **soshite uma** (h. ni　　) **desu. Sugoi desho?**

(B)
A: ずいぶん買って来たねえ。何を買ったの？
B: 靴を (a. 一　　)、スーツを (b. 二　　)、ぼうしを (c. 一　　)、ポテトチップ
　　を (d. 一　　)、ジュースを (e. 二　　)、かな。

A: **Zuibun katte kita nee. Nani o katta no?**
B: **Kutsu o** (a. **i**　　), **suutsu o** (b. **ni**　　), **boushi o** (c. **hito**　　), **poteto
　　chippu o** (d. **hito**　　), **juusu o** (e. **ni**　　), **kana.**

⇨ | 16.2

**8** *

Spell out the numbers and classifiers in hiragana or romaji.

(A)
You are discussing with your roommate what you'll need for tomorrow's party.

ルームメート：　明日パーティだけど、何が要る？
私：　　　　　　えーとね、まず、ペーパープレート（　a. 10　）、それから
　　　　　　　　ワイン（　b. 3　）とジュース（　　c. 6　）。あと、すいかも
　　　　　　　　（　d. 1　）買おう。

**Ruumumeeto:**　**Ashita paatii da kedo, nani ga iru?**
**Watashi:**　　　**Eeto ne, mazu peepaa pureeto (　a. 10　), sorekara wain
　　　　　　　　（　b. 3　) to juusu (　c. 6　). Ato, suika mo (　d. 1　)
　　　　　　　　kaou.**

(B)
You are calling your host mother while on a trip.

ホストマザー：　朝ご飯食べた？
私：　　　　　　うん、今日はパンケーキ（　a. 3　）と、ゆで卵（　b. 2　）と、
　　　　　　　　バナナ（　c. 1　）食べて、コーヒーを（　d. 3　）も飲んじゃ
　　　　　　　　った。

**Hosuto mazaa:**　**Asa-gohan tabeta?**
**Watashi:**　　　**Un, kyou wa pankeeki (　a. 3　) to, yude tamago
　　　　　　　　（　b. 2　) to, banana (　c. 1　) tabete, koohii o
　　　　　　　　（　d. 3　) mo nonjatta.**

⇨ | 16.2

# 17
# Compounds

Identify the relationship between the two elements (X, Y) in each nominal compound. The relationships may be classified as follows.

(a) Coordinating: 'X and Y' (e.g. X **to** Y)
(b) Subordinating: 'X modifies Y (e.g. X **no** Y or X (=Adj.) Y)
(c) X is the subject of Y: 'X does/is Y' (e.g. X **ga** Y)
(d) X is the object of action Y: '(someone) does Y to X' (e.g. X **o** Y)
(e) Other

      Example 1: _b_   青空 **ao-zora** 'blue sky'
                    (blue + sky)

      Example 2: _d_   絵描き **e-kaki** '(picture) painter'
                    (picture + paint)

      Example 3: _e_   衝動買い **shoudou-gai** 'impulse buying'
                    (impulse + buy)

(1) ___ 雨降り **ame-furi** 'rainy'
       (rain + fall)

(2) ___ 朝日 **asa-hi** 'morning sun'
       (morning + sun)

(3) ___ 円高 **en-daka** 'high yen exchange rate'
       (yen + high)

(4) ___ 田畑 **ta-hata** 'field'
       (rice field + vegetable, etc. field)

(5) ___ 手書き **te-gaki** 'hand-written'
       (hand + write)

(6) ___ 花見 **hana-mi** 'cherry blossom viewing'
       (flower/cherry blossom + view)

(7) ___ 本箱 **hon-bako** 'bookcase'
       (book + box)

(8) ___ 卵焼き **tamago-yaki** 'fried egg'
       (egg + fry)

⇨ 2.3, 17.1, Exercises in 2.2, 2.3

**2** ⋆

Combine the words on the left with those on the right to create adjectival compounds with the meanings provided. If the first sound of the second word is /t/, /k/ or /h/, change this to /d/, /g/ and /b/, respectively. Use each choice just once.

Example: わる（い）**waru(i)** 'bad' + かしこい **kashikoi** 'clever'
→ わるがしこい **waru-gashikoi** 'sly, cunning'

| | |
|---|---|
| 気 **ki** 'feeling' | いい **ii** 'good' |
| 気持ち **kimochi** 'feeling' | かゆい **kayui** 'itchy' |
| 心 **kokoro** 'heart' | くらい **kurai** 'dark' |
| 根 **ne** 'root' | つよい **tsuyoi** 'strong' |
| 歯 **ha** 'tooth' | ほそい **hosoi** 'thin' |
| うす（い）**usu(i)** 'thin' | らくな **raku na** 'comfortable' |

(1) 'dimly-lit' _____
(2) 'deep-rooted' _____
(3) 'pleasant' _____
(4) 'frustrating' _____
(5) 'easy-going' _____
(6) 'forlorn, insecure' _____

⇨ 2.3, 17.2

**3** ⋆

Match the verbal compounds with their English equivalents.

| | | | |
|---|---|---|---|
| a. | 書き直す **kaki-naosu** | e. | 書き終える **kaki-oeru** |
| b. | 書き写す **kaki-utsusu** | f. | 書き上げる **kaki-ageru** |
| c. | 書き始める **kaki-hajimeru** | g. | 書きかける **kaki-kakeru** |
| d. | 書き上がる **kaki-agaru** | h. | 書き続ける **kaki-tsuzukeru** |

(1) 'begin writing' _____
(2) 'almost/about to write' _____
(3) 'continue writing' _____
(4) 'complete (by writing)' _____
(5) 'finish writing' _____
(6) 're-write' _____
(7) 'be completed' _____
(8) 'copy (by writing)' _____

⇨ 17.3

# 18
## Formal nouns

Fill in the blanks with **no**, **koto** or **mono**.

(A)*
Ms Das, a graduate student, is talking to her host father.

[楽器 **gakki** 'musical instrument']

ホストファーザー：　ダスさん、趣味は何ですか。
ダス：　そうですね、本を読んだり音楽を聞いたりする（ ① ）が好き
です。
ホ：　そうですか。何か楽器、やりますか。
ダス：　いえ、子供の時、ピアノを習った（ ② ）がありますが、すぐ
やめてしまいました。そう言えば、この間お父さんがギターを
ひいてる（ ③ ）を見ましたけど。
ホ：　え、本当？今はめったにやらないけど、若いころは一日中ひい
てた（ ④ ）ですよ。
ダス：　じゃ、コンサートなんかによくいらっしゃるんですか。
ホ：　まぁ、たまに行く（ ⑤ ）はありますけど、そういう時間を見
つける（ ⑥ ）が大変でねぇ。

| Hosuto faazaa: | Dasu-san, shumi wa nan desu ka. |
|---|---|
| Dasu: | Sou desu ne, hon o yondari ongaku o kiitari suru ( ① ) ga suki desu. |
| Ho: | Sou desu ka. Nani ka gakki, yarimasu ka. |
| Dasu: | Ie, kodomo no toki, piano o naratta ( ② ) ga arimasu ga, sugu yamete shimaimashita. Sou ieba, kono aida Otousan ga gitaa o hiite ru ( ③ ) o mimashita kedo. |
| Ho: | E, honto? Ima wa metta ni yaranai kedo, wakai koro wa ichinichijuu hiite ta ( ④ ) desu yo. |
| Dasu: | Ja, konsaato nanka ni yoku irassharu n desu ka. |
| Ho: | Maa, tama ni iku ( ⑤ ) wa arimasu kedo, sou iu jikan o mitsukeru ( ⑥ ) ga taihen de nee. |

(B)**
Mr Mori has decided to get married soon, and is asking his **senpai** (senior) to serve as the MC at their wedding.

[式を挙げる **shiki o ageru** 'to have a wedding'; 披露宴 **hirouen** 'reception'; 司会 **shikai** 'MC'; 後悔 **koukai** 'to regret'; 秘訣 **hiketsu** 'secret'; 見習う **minarau** 'to follow (someone's) example']

森： あのう、実は、今度結婚する（ ① ）になりました。
先輩： え？それはおめでとう。で、いつ？
森： 来年の春です。相手は2年ぐらい付き合ってる人なんですが、やっぱり式を挙げる（ ② ）にしました。あのう、それで、披露宴の司会をお願いしたいんですが …
先輩： えっ？そんなこと、やった（ ③ ）ないんだけど、大丈夫かなぁ。
森： ぜひお願いします。
先輩： うん、じゃ、いいよ。でも，歌を歌う（ ④ ）はやめとくね。「司会を頼んだ（ ⑤ ）の、大失敗だった」なんて後悔されたらいけないから。
森： ありがとうございます！よろしくお願いします。幸せな結婚の秘訣は、お互いを尊敬し合う（ ⑥ ）だって聞いています。先輩ご夫妻を見習って、がんばります！

Mori: Anou, jitsu wa, kondo kekkon suru（ ① ）ni narimashita.
Senpai: E? Sore wa o-medetou. De, itsu?
Mori: Rainen no haru desu. Aite wa ninen gurai tsukiatte ru hito na n desu ga, yappari shiki o ageru（ ② ）ni shimashita. Anou, sore de, hirouen no shikai o o-negai shitai n desu ga . . .
Senpai: E? Sonna koto, yatta（ ③ ）nai n da kedo, daijoubu kanaa.
Mori: Zehi o-negai shimasu.
Senpai: Un, ja, ii yo. Demo, uta o utau（ ④ ）wa yametoku ne. 'Shikai o tanonda（ ⑤ ）no, dai-shippai datta' nante koukai saretara ikenai kara.
Mori: Arigatou gozaimasu! Yoroshiku o-negai shimasu. Shiawase na kekkon no hiketsu wa, o-tagai o sonkei shi-au（ ⑥ ）da tte kiite imasu. Senpai go-fusai o mi-naratte, ganbarimasu!

⇨ 18.1, 18.2.1, 18.3, 26.1

**2** ★★★ Choose an appropriate formal noun. Mr Ou (Wang), a student at a university in Hiroshima, is visiting his friend Jun's home.

[スマート sumaato 'slender']

王： ごめん下さい。あのう、ジュン君は …
母： あ、王さん。ジュンは今帰って来た【① ところ・だけ】。ちょっと待ってて。
王： はい、おじゃまします。
母： お茶をどうぞ。王さんはいつ見てもスマートねぇ。健康には注意しているんですか。
王： はい、毎日運動をして、なるべく野菜を食べる【② こと・よう】にしています。
母： あ、それはいいわね。ジュンも最近はあまり肉を食べない【③ こと・よう】になったみたい。

Ou: Gomen kudasai. Anou, Jun-kun wa . . .
Haha: A, Ou-san. Jun wa ima kaette kita【① tokoro・dake】. Chotto matte te.
Ou: Hai, o-jama shimasu.
Haha: O-cha o douzo. Ou-san wa itsu mite mo sumaato nee. Kenkou ni wa chuui shite iru n desu ka.
Ou: Hai, mainichi undou o shite, narubeku yasai o taberu【② koto・you】ni shite imasu.
Haha: A, sore wa ii wa ne. Jun mo saikin wa amari niku o tabenai【③ koto・you】ni natta mitai.

[原爆病 **genbaku-byou** 'radiation sickness'; 治療 **chiryou** 'treatment']

母： ところで、王さんは留学にどうして広島を選んだの？

王： あ、僕、将来医者になる【④ はず・つもり】なんですけど、原爆病の治療について学びたい【⑤ ん・もん】です。国に帰ったら共同研究に参加する【⑥ こと・よう】になってます。

母： そうですか。

Haha: Tokoro de, Ou-san wa ryuugaku ni doushite Hiroshima o eranda no?

Ou: A, boku, shourai isha ni naru【④ hazu・tsumori】na n desu kedo, genbaku-byou no chiryou ni tsuite manabi-tai【⑤ n・mon】desu. Kuni ni kaettara, kyoudou kenkyuu ni sanka suru【⑥ koto・you】ni natte masu.

Haha: Sou desu ka.

[意欲 **iyoku** 'enthusiasm'; 水をさす **mizu o sasu** 'put a damper']

母： あ、そうだ。私ね、来年中国に行くんだけど、その【⑦ ため・よう】に中国語を勉強しようかなって思ってるの。王さん、ちょっと教えてくれない？

ジュン： だめ、だめ。王さん、やめといた方がいいよ。

母： なんでそんな【⑧ こと・もの】言うの？

ジュン： だって、母さんの【⑨ こと・もん】だから、すぐやめるに決まってるんだ【⑩ こと・もん】。せっかくの意欲に水をさす【⑪ はず・つもり】はないけどさ。

母： なによ。こんな良い機会、めったにないんだから、途中でやめる【⑫ こと・わけ】ないでしょ？

ジュン： 分かった、分かった。ごめん。

Haha: A, sou da. Atashi ne, rainen Chuugoku ni iku n da kedo, sono【⑦ tame・you】ni Chuugokugo o benkyou shiyou kana tte omotte ru no. Ou-san, chotto oshiete kurenai?

Jun: Dame, dame. Ou-san, yametoita hou ga ii yo.

Haha: Nan de sonna【⑧ koto・mono】iu no?

Jun: Datte, Kaasan no【⑨ koto・mon】da kara, sugu yameru ni kimatte ru n da【⑩ koto・mon】. Sekkaku no iyoku ni mizu o sasu【⑪ hazu・tsumori】wa nai kedo sa.

Haha: Nani yo. Konna ii kikai, metta ni nai n da kara, tochuu de yameru【⑫ koto・wake】nai desho?

Jun: Wakatta, wakatta. Gomen.

⇨ 18.1, 18.2.2, 18.3–8, 18.9.2–3

**3** ⁑ Fill in the blanks so that the resulting sentence corresponds to the italicized English equivalents.

(A)
Surprisingly, Tomoko sees her friend Takashi studying very hard.

友子： どうしたの？

孝志： あした大事な試験があるんだよぉ。これにパスしないと、卒業できないんだって。

友子： ああ、それでそんなに ＿＿＿＿＿＿ わけだ。手伝おうか。
*Oh, I see, that's why you are studying so hard.*

Tomoko:   Dou shita no?
Takashi:  Ashita daiji na shiken ga aru n da yoo. Kore ni pasu shinai to, sotsugyou dekinai n da tte.
Tomoko:   Aa, sore de sonna ni _____ wake da. Tetsudaou ka.

(B)
Kyoko is talking to her classmate Hiroshi, who drives a nice sports car.

京子:     宏君のうちって _____ の？ *(Is it that) your family is rich?*
宏:      いや、それほどでもないよ。

Kyouko:  Hiroshi-kun no uchi tte _____ no?
Hiroshi:  Iya, sorehodo demo nai yo.

(C)
Two colleagues, Ms Sasaki and Ms Boku (Park), are chatting over lunch.

[大統領 **daitouryou** 'the President'; 記者会見 **kisha kaiken** 'press conference']

佐々木:  今日は大統領、風邪でダウンしてるそうですね。
朴:      ああ、それで記者会見が _____ わけですね。
       *I see. No wonder the press conference was canceled.*
佐々木:  あれ？朴さん、今日はあまり食べませんねぇ。
朴:      ええ、ちょっと _____ んです。*(It is that) I have a little toothache.*

Sasaki:  Kyou wa daitouryou, kaze de daun shite ru sou desu ne.
Boku:    Aa, sore de kisha kaiken ga _____ wake desu ne.
Sasaki:  Are? Boku-san, kyou wa amari tabemasen nee?
Boku:    Ee, chotto _____ n desu.

(D)
Neighbors Mr Abe and Mr Bando play tennis together every week.

阿部:     来週一週間休みをとって温泉に行ってきます。
坂東:     えっ、ということは、_____ わけですね。
       *That means we won't be able to play tennis together?*

Abe:      Raishuu isshuukan yasumi o totte onsen ni itte kimasu.
Bandou:  E, to iu koto wa, _____ wake desu ne.

⇨ 18.2.2, 18.6, 47.2

**4** ⁂ Shouta and Yui are getting married. The following is a wedding speech given by Shouta's close friend Sugimoto Kazuki. Fill in the blanks with appropriate formal nouns chosen from the box.

> こと・の・よう・もの・ばかり・だけ・ところ・ため
> **koto・no・you・mono・bakari・dake・tokoro・tame**

翔太君、結衣さん、ご結婚おめでとうございます！

僕は、お二人とは大学のサークル仲間だった杉本一樹と言います。翔太とは飲み友達で、学生時代はよく一緒に飲みに行った（ ① ）です。今日は新郎新婦のエピソードをお話しします。

Shouta-kun, Yui-san, go-kekkon o-medetou gozaimasu!

Boku wa, o-futari to wa daigaku no saakuru nakama datta Sugimoto Kazuki to iimasu. Shouta towa nomi-tomodachi de, gakusei jidai wa yoku issho ni nomi ni itta（①）desu. Kyou wa shinrou shinpu no episoodo o o-hanashi shimasu.

大学時代、翔太も僕も語学は大の苦手。英語の授業はサボりまくり、出席してもただ座っている（②）。宿題も他の人のをいつも写していました。

Daigaku jidai, Shouta mo boku mo gogaku wa dai no nigate. Eigo no jugyou wa sabori-makuri, shusseki shite mo tada suwatte iru（②）. Shukudai mo hoka no hito no o itsumo utsushite imashita.

さて、二人の出会いですが、大学に入った（③）の翔太が何か面白いサークルはないかと探していた（④）に、結衣さんが現れたのです。そして、何と彼を英会話サークルに誘ったのです。翔太は結衣さんが英語を優雅に話す（⑤）を見て、すっかり憧れてしまいました。しかし、入会する（⑥）に決めた（⑦）の、一人では心細かったのでしょう。英会話なんて興味のなかった僕も頼まれ、サークルに入会する（⑧）になったのです。その日から僕たち二人の人生が変わりました。英語の授業にはまじめに出席し、宿題も自分達でする（⑨）になったのです。

Sate futari no deai desu ga, daigaku ni haitta（③）no Shouta ga nani ka omoshiroi saakuru wa nai ka to sagashite ita（④）ni, Yui-san ga arawareta no desu. Soshite, nan to kare o Eikawa Saakuru ni sasotta no desu. Shouta wa Yui-san ga Eigo o yuuga ni hanasu（⑤）o mite, sukkari akogarete shimaimashita. Shikashi, nyuukai suru（⑥）ni kimeta（⑦）no, hitori de wa kokoro-bosokatta no deshou. Eikaiwa nante kyoumi no nakatta boku mo tanomare, saakuru ni nyuukai suru（⑧）ni natta no desu. Sono hi kara boku-tachi futari no jinsei ga kawarimashita. Eigo no jugyou ni wa majime ni shusseki shi, shukudai mo jibun-tachi de suru（⑨）ni natta no desu.

そして、ある日、翔太は結衣さんが将来外資系の会社を目指しているという（⑩）を聞いて、一大決心。彼女と同じ会社に就職する（⑪）に、あらゆる努力を払いました。飲み会にも来なくなって。愛の力ってすごいですね。英会話で結ばれた二人はめでたく同じ会社に就職。そして今日この日を迎える（⑫）となったのです。

翔太君、結衣さん、これからも 末永くお幸せに！

Soshite, aru hi, Shouta wa Yui-san ga shourai gaishikei no kaisha o mezashite iru to iu（⑩）o kiite, ichidai-kesshin. Yui-san to onaji kaisha ni shuushoku suru（⑪）ni, arayuru doryoku o haraimashita. Nomikai ni mo konaku natte. Ai no chikara tte, sugoi desu ne. Eikaiwa de musubareta futari wa medetaku onaji kaisha ni shuushoku. Soshite kyou kono hi o mukaeru（⑫）to natta no desu.

Shouta-kun, Yui-san, kore kara mo sue nagaku o-shiawase ni!

# 19
# Auxiliary verbs

Choose the appropriate alternatives from the choices below.

(A)
Two friends are talking about opening the window in a room.

A: ちょっと、部屋の空気悪くない？
B: そう？さっきまで、窓があけて【① あった・いた】んだけど、寒いから
【② しめ・しまっ】ちゃった。
A: またあけてもいい？
B: いいよ。じゃあ、私はセーターをとって【③ 行く・来る】。
A: あ、僕が取って来て【④ あげる・くれる】よ。
B: ありがとう。

A: **Chotto, heya no kuuki waruku nai?**
B: **Sou? Sakki made, mado ga akete【① atta・ ita】n da kedo, samui
kara【② shime・shimat】chatta.**
A: **Mata aketemo ii?**
B: **Ii yo. Jaa, watashi wa seetaa o totte【③ iku・kuru】.**
A: **A, boku ga totte kite【④ ageru・kureru】yo.**
B: **Arigatou.**

(B)
Two acquaintances are talking about exercising.

C: 私、最近、スポーツクラブに通い【① 始めた・出した】んです。
D: え〜、本当ですか。
C: ええ。このところ、外食が多くて、食べ【② すぎた・おわった】せいで、
5キロも【③ 太り・太って】しまって。
D: そうなんですか。私も人ごとじゃないなあ。
C: どうですか、一緒にやって【④ みませんか・きませんか】。
D: そうですね。今度行く時、誘ってください。今担当しているプロジェクトを
やり【⑤ あげたら・こんだら】、しばらく暇になるので。
C: じゃあ、ぜひ、一緒に行きましょう。

C: **Watashi, saikin, supootsu kurabu ni kayoi【① hajimeta・dashita】
n desu.**
D: **Ee, hontou desu ka.**
C: **Ee. Kono tokoro, gaishoku ga ookute, tabe【② sugita・owatta】sei de,
go kiro mo【③ futori・futotte】shimatte.**
D: **Sou na n desu ka. Watashi mo hitogoto ja nai naa.**
C: **Dou desu ka, issho ni yatte【④ mimasen ka・kimasen ka】.**

D: Sou desu ne. Kondo iku toki, sasotte kudasai. Ima tantou shite iru purojekuto o yari 【⑤ agetara · kondara】, shibaraku hima ni naru node.

C: Jaa, zehi, issho ni ikimashou.

⇨ 19.2, 19.3

**2** ∗

Write out what you need to do before going on a vacation, using the auxiliary verb **oku** and the words provided below.

> 航空券・ホテル・観光地・予約する・調べる・買う
>
> **koukuuken · hoteru · kankouchi · yoyaku suru · shiraberu · kau**

(1) _____

(2) _____

(3) _____

⇨ 19.2.4

# 20
# The causative construction

**1** ★ You are a grade school teacher. Complete the list of things you will have your students do in the coming week by filling in the blanks with the words provided. Conjugate the verbs appropriately.

> Example: 運動会の練習を ＿＿＿＿＿＿＿。（する）
> → 運動会の練習をさせる。
> **Undoukai no renshuu o ＿＿＿＿＿＿. (suru)**
> → **Undoukai no renshuu o saseru.**

[かけ算 **kakezan** 'multiplication'; 校庭 **koutei** 'schoolyard'; 委員 **iin** 'committee member'; 空き箱 **akibako** 'empty box']

(1) 作文を ＿＿＿＿＿＿＿。（書く）
**Sakubun o ＿＿＿＿＿＿. (kaku)**
(2) 教科書を ＿＿＿＿＿＿＿。（読む）
**Kyoukasho o ＿＿＿＿＿＿. (yomu)**
(3) 校歌を ＿＿＿＿＿＿＿。（歌う）
**Kouka o ＿＿＿＿＿＿. (utau)**
(4) かけ算を ＿＿＿＿＿＿＿。（覚える）
**Kakezan o ＿＿＿＿＿＿. (oboeru)**
(5) 校庭を ＿＿＿＿＿＿＿。（走る）
**Koutei o ＿＿＿＿＿＿. (hashiru)**
(6) 机を ＿＿＿＿＿＿＿。（ふく）
**Tsukue o ＿＿＿＿＿＿. (fuku)**
(7) 新しい委員を ＿＿＿＿＿＿＿。（決める）
**Atarashii iin o ＿＿＿＿＿＿. (kimeru)**
(8) 家から空き箱を ＿＿＿＿＿＿＿。（もってくる）
**Ie kara akibako o ＿＿＿＿＿＿. (motte kuru)**

⇨ 20.1

**2** ★★ Re-write the following sentences using the causative construction so that the resulting sentences express your feelings of responsibility about what has happened.

(1) ペットの金魚が死んでしまった。→
**Petto no kingyo ga shinde shimatta.**
(2) 友人のカップルが別れてしまった。→
**Yuujin no kappuru ga wakarete shimatta.**
(3) 両親が苦しんでいる。→
**Ryoushin ga kurushinde iru.**

⇨ 20.3

**3**

Read the following paragraphs and choose the most appropriate statement for each paragraph.

(1)
高校の時、留学したいと思っていたので、両親に相談した。両親はやる気があるなら行ってもいいと言った。そこで、高校2年生の時、1年間オーストラリアに留学した。

**Koukou no toki, ryuugaku shitai to omotte ita node, ryoushin ni soudan shita. Ryoushin wa yaruki ga aru nara itte mo ii to itta. Sokode, koukou ninensei no toki, ichinenkan Oosutoraria ni ryuugaku shita.**

(a) （　）私は高校の時オーストラリアに留学させられた。
  **Watashi wa koukou no toki Oosutoraria ni ryuugaku saserareta.**
(b) （　）私は高校の時オーストラリアに留学させてもらった。
  **Watashi wa koukou no toki Oosutoraria ni ryuugaku sasetemoratta.**
(c) （　）高校の時、両親は私をオーストラリアに留学させた。
  **Koukou no toki, ryoushin wa watashi o Oosutoraria ni ryuugaku saseta.**

(2)
弟はロックグループでギターを弾いている。たまにライブハウスでライブをしているらしい。ただ、なかなかチケットが売れず、苦労しているようだ。昨夜は、ケーキを買って来て、お願いがあると言った。来週のライブのチケットがあまっているので、何枚でもいいから、買ってくれと言う。仕方がないので、5枚買った。

**Otouto wa rokku guruupu de gitaa o hiite iru. Tama ni raibu hausu de raibu o shite iru rashii. Tada, nakanaka chiketto ga urezu, kurou shite iru you da. Sakuya wa, keeki o katte kite, o-negai ga aru to itta. Raishuu no raibu no chiketto ga amatte iru node, nanmai demo ii kara, katte kure to iu. Shikata ga nai node, gomai katta.**

(a) （　）私は弟にチケットを買わされた。
  **Watashi wa otouto ni chiketto o kawasareta.**
(b) （　）私は弟にチケットを買わせてあげた。
  **Watashi wa otouto ni chiketto o kawasete ageta.**
(c) （　）私は弟にチケットを買わせてもらった。
  **Watashi wa otouto ni chiketto o kawasete moratta.**

(3)
経済の授業が受けたかったが、もういっぱいで、登録できなかった。どうしてもあきらめきれず、担当の教授に頼みに行った。この教授の授業は前にも受けたことがあり、その時の成績は良かった。教授は、また前回と同じように頑張るのならと言って、特別に許可してくれた。おかげで、経済の授業が受けられることになった。

**Keizai no jugyou ga uketakatta ga, mou ippai de, touroku dekinakatta. Dou shitemo akiramekirezu, tantou no kyouju ni tanomi ni itta. Kono kyouju no jugyou wa mae ni mo uketa koto ga ari, sono toki no seiseki wa yokatta. Kyouju wa, mata zenkai to onaji you ni ganbaru no nara to itte, tokubetsu ni kyoka shite kureta. O-kage de, keizai no jugyou ga ukerareru koto ni natta.**

**The causative construction**

(a) （　）私は教授に経済の授業を受けさせられた。
   **Watashi wa kyouju ni keizai no jugyou o ukesaserareta.**
(b) （　）教授は私に経済の授業を受けさせてくださった。
   **Kyouju wa watashi ni keizai no jugyou o ukesasete kudasatta.**
(c) （　）教授は私に経済の授業を受けさせてさしあげた。
   **Kyouju wa watashi ni keizai no jugyou o ukesasete sashiageta.**

⇨ | 20.1, 20.4, 21.5

# 21
# The passive construction

**1** ★ Rewrite the following sentences using the passive construction.

(1) 母親は子どもをしかりました。→
**Hahaoya wa kodomo o shikarimashita.**
(2) 教師は学生たちに多くの課題を出しました。→
**Kyoushi wa gakusei tachi ni ooku no kadai o dashimashita.**
(3) ルームメイトが私に「しずかにして！」と言いました。→
**Ruumumeito ga watashi ni 'Shizuka ni shite!' to iimashita.**
(4) 遠藤周作がこの本を書きました。→ **Ni-yotte** passive
**Endou Shuusaku ga kono hon o kakimashita.**
(5) いたずらを注意したら、子どもが泣きました。
**Itazura o chuui shitara, kodomo ga nakimashita.** → Adversative passive
(6) 雨が降って、私はぬれてしまいました。
**Ame ga futte, watashi wa nurete shimaimashita.** → Adversative passive

⇨ 21.2, 21.3, 21.4

**2** ★ Fill in the blanks with the passive form of the verbs.

[～やつ **yatsu** 'the one ~'; 飲み放題 **nomi-houdai** 'all you can drink';
追加 **tsuika** 'additional'; 散々 **sanzan** 'terrible'; 災難 **sainan** 'disaster']

A: この間のパーティー、どうだった？
B: あの、一郎に（　① よぶ　）て、行ったやつ？
B: そうそう。
A: あれは、（　② だます　）よ。
B: なんで？
A: 飲み放題って聞いてたのに、酒は1本だけ。あとは追加料金を（　③ 払わせる　）。
しかも、まずい天ぷらを（　④ 食べさせる　）て、お腹はこわすし。散々だった。
B: それは災難だったね。

A: **Kono aida no paatii, dou datta?**
B: **Ano, Ichirou ni（　① yobu　）te, itta yatsu?**
B: **Sou sou.**
A: **Are wa,（　② damasu　）yo.**
B: **Nande?**
A: **Nomi-houdai tte kiite ta noni, sake wa ippon dake. Ato wa
tsuika ryoukin o（　③ harawaseru　）. Shikamo, mazui tenpura o
（　④ tabesaseru　）te, onaka wa kowasu shi. Sanzan datta.**
B: **Sore wa sainan datta ne.**

⇨ 21.1, 21.5

**3** **☆☆** The following is a journal entry about a bad day. Fill in the blanks with appropriate words from the box in the passive or causative-passive form. Use each word only once.

> やる・しかる・降る・汚す・踏む・当てる・呼ぶ・走る・食べる
>
> **yaru · shikaru · furu · yogosu · fumu · ateru · yobu · hashiru · taberu**

[当てる **ateru** 'to call on someone'; 思いっきり **omoikkiri** 'with all one's strength'; 職員室 **shokuinshitsu** 'teachers' office'; 後片付け **ato-katazuke** 'clean up']

今日は最低だった。まず、朝、駅に向かう途中、雨に ①_____。そして、電車の中では、足を思いっきり ②_____。やっと学校に着いたら、職員室に ③_____ て、数学のテストのことで ④_____。授業中も難しい問題ばかり ⑤_____。サッカー部の部活では、グラウンドを10周も ⑥_____。後片付けも一人で ⑦_____。帰ってきて、おやつのケーキを食べようと思っていたのに、トイレに行っている間に、弟に ⑧_____。今日はもう寝る。あ、ネコにベッドを ⑨_____ ！

**Kyou wa saitei datta. Mazu, asa, eki ni mukau tochuu, ame ni ①_____.
Soshite, densha no naka de wa, ashi o omoikkiri ②_____. Yatto gakkou
ni tsuitara, shokuinshitsu ni ③_____ te, suugaku no tesuto no koto
de ④_____. Jugyou-chuu mo muzukashii mondai bakari ⑤_____.
Sakkaabu no bukatsu de wa, guraundo o jusshuu mo ⑥_____.
Ato-katazuke mo, hitoride ⑦_____. Kaette kite, oyatsu no keeki o
tabeyou to omotte ita noni, toire ni itte iru aida ni, otouto ni ⑧_____.
Kyou wa mou neru. A, neko ni beddo o ⑨_____!**

⇨ 21.1, 21.4

**4** **☆** Using causative-passive verbs, list three things that you have been forced/pressured to do against your will. Be sure to add where and/or when; e.g. 'at the hospital,' 'when I was in high school.'

⇨ 21.5

# 22
# Conjunctions and connectives

**1** ★ Choose the most appropriate particle/phrase.

(1) 母は45歳【と・で・や】父は48歳です。
    Haha wa yonjuugo-sai 【to・de・ya】 chichi wa yonjuuhas-sai desu.

(2) 今日は雨だ【が・のに・から】もうすぐ大会がある【が・のに・から】ランニング をするつもりだ。
    Kyou wa ame da 【ga・noni・kara】 mou sugu taikai ga
    aru 【ga・noni・kara】 ranningu o suru tsumori da.

(3) 私は昨日部屋を掃除【して・すると・すれば】買い物に【行ったり・行って・ 行けば】料理を作った。
    Watashi wa kinou heya o souji 【shite・suruto・sureba】 kaimono
    ni 【ittari・itte・ikeba】 ryouri o tsukutta.

(4) 今日は頭が痛い【と・ので・し】、ちょっと熱もある【けど・し・のに】、 アルバイトは休もうと思っている。
    Kyou wa atama ga itai 【to・node・shi】, chotto netsu mo
    aru 【kedo・shi・noni】, arubaito wa yasumou to omotte iru.

(5) 明日も仕事がある【し・のに・とか】飲みすぎてしまった。
    Ashita mo shigoto ga aru 【shi・noni・toka】 nomi-sugite shimatta.

(6) 会社に行く前に、髪をとかす【とか・や・と】、ひげを剃る【とか・ので・し】 するのはあたりまえだ。
    Kaisha ni iku mae ni, kami o tokasu 【toka・ya・to】, hige o
    soru 【toka・node・shi】 suru no wa atarimae da.

(6) 努力しなくてもうまくいくときも【あれば・あるとか・あっても】、がんばって もだめなときもある。
    Doryoku shinakutemo umaku iku toki mo 【areba・arutoka・attemo】,
    ganbatte mo damena toki mo aru.

➪ 22.1, 22.2

**2** ★ Choose the correct form preceding the conjunctive particle.

(1) まだ学生【な・だ・で】ので、お金がありません。
    Mada gakusei 【na・da・de】 node, o-kane ga arimasen.

(2) せっかくの休み【な・だ・で】のに、何も面白いことがない。
    Sekkaku no yasumi 【na・da・de】 noni, nanimo omoshiroi koto ga nai.

(3) 1つ違いの兄弟【な・だ・で】から、子供のころはよくけんかした。
    Hitotsu chigai no kyoudai 【na・da・de】 kara, kodomo no koro wa
    yoku kenka shita.

(4) 今日は【暇な・暇だ・暇】し、他にやることもないから、掃除しよう。
    Kyou wa 【hima na・hima da・hima】 shi, hoka ni yaru koto mo nai
    kara, souji shiyou.

(5) この辺は今は【にぎやかな・にぎやかだ・にぎやか】けど、昔は人があまりいな
かった。

**Kono hen wa ima wa【nigiyaka na・nigiyaka da・nigiyaka】kedo, mukashi wa hito ga amari inakatta.**

(6) 三回も電話【した・して・する】のに、相手は出なかった。

**San-kai mo denwa【shita・shite・suru】noni, aite wa denakatta.**

(7) 家族に紹介【したい・したくて・したかった】ので、ぜひ家に遊びに来てくださ
い。

**Kazoku ni shoukai【shitai・shitakute・shitakatta】node, zehi uchi ni asobi ni kite kudasai.**

(8) ケータイが【あった・あって・あり】から、すぐ連絡ができました。

**Keitai ga【atta・atte・ari】kara, sugu renraku ga dekimashita.**

➪ 22.2, 22.4, 22.5, 39, 47.3

**3** ★ Two men in their 30s, A and B, who are close friends, are talking about voting. Fill in the blanks with appropriate conjunctions or connectives from the box.

> から・けど・のに・それに
>
> **kara・kedo・noni・sore ni**

[参院選 **san'insen** 'upper house election'; 投票 **touhyou** 'to vote'; 義務 **gimu** 'obligation'; 選挙 **senkyo** 'election']

A: 明日の参院選、投票に行く？
B: ちょっと用事がある ①_____ 、やめとく。
A: えー？投票は国民の義務な ②_____ 、行かないの？
B: うーん、実は久しぶりにいい天気になりそうだ ③_____ 、ゴルフに行く約束し
ちゃったんだよね。
A: え、そうなのか。朝早いの？
B: いや、スタートは午後なんだ ④_____ 、ちょっと遠くだ ⑤_____ 、早目に出な
きゃって思ってさ。
A: 俺も明日の選挙はパスしようかな。いくら選挙やっても政治は変わんないし、
⑥_____ 、たまった仕事もあるし。
B: いや、そりゃだめだよ。じゃ、俺も出かける前に投票に行く ⑦_____ 、お前も
行けよな。

A: **Ashita no san'insen, touhyou ni iku?**
B: **Chotto youji ga aru ①_____ , yametoku.**
A: **Ee? Touhyou wa kokumin no gimu na ②_____ , ikanai no?**
B: **Uun, jitsu wa hisashiburi ni ii tenki ni nari sou da ③_____ , gorufu ni iku yakusoku shichatta n da yo ne.**
A: **E, sou na no ka. Asa hayai no?**
B: **Iya, sutaato wa gogo na n da ④_____ , chotto tooku da ⑤_____ , hayame ni denakya tte omotte sa.**
A: **Ore mo ashita no senkyo wa pasu shiyou kana. Ikura senkyo yatte mo seiji wa kawannai shi, ⑥_____ , tamatta shigoto mo aru shi.**
B: **Iya, sorya dame da yo. Ja, ore mo dekakeru mae ni touhyou ni iku ⑦_____ , omae mo ike yona.**

➪ 22.4, 22.5, 39, 47.3

**4** ★ Emma Brown wrote a letter to her future host family introducing herself, but the sentences seem a little 'choppy'. Revise the letter by connecting the underlined sentences with conjunctive particles 'and,' 'but,' 'so,' etc. in Japanese.

はじめまして。私の名前はエマ・ブラウンです。(1)大学生です。19歳です。(2)専攻は美術です。日本語も勉強しています。(3)日本語は難しいです。クラスは楽しいです。(4)九月に日本に行きます。漢字もたくさん勉強しています。

(5)私はよく水泳をします。料理もします。いろいろなことに興味があります。(6)よく図書館に行きます。本を借ります。DVDも借ります。(7)外国の映画を見るのが大好きです。日本の映画もよく見ます。

(8)まだ日本語は上手に話せません。みなさんに会うのを楽しみにしています。どうぞよろしくお願いします。

では、九月に会いましょう。

エマ・ブラウン

---

**Hajimemashite. Watashi no namae wa Ema Buraun desu.** (1)**Daigaku-sei desu. Juukyuu-sai desu.** (2)**Senkou wa bijutsu desu. Nihongo mo benkyou shite imasu.** (3)**Nihongo wa muzukashii desu. Kurasu wa tanoshii desu.** (4)**Kugatsu ni Nihon ni ikimasu. Kanji mo takusan benkyou shite imasu.**

(5)**Watashi wa yoku suiei o shimasu. Ryouri mo shimasu.** Iroirona koto ni kyoumi ga arimasu. (6)**Yoku toshokan ni ikimasu. Hon o karimasu.** DVD mo karimasu. (7)**Gaikoku no eiga o miru no ga daisuki desu. Nihon no eiga mo yoku mimasu.**

(8)**Mada Nihongo wa jouzu ni hanasemasen. Mina-san ni au no o tanoshimi ni shite imasu.** Douzo yoroshiku o-negai shimasu.

**Dewa, kugatsu ni aimashou.**

**Ema Buraun**

⇨ 22.1, 22.4, 22.5, 39, 47.3

# 23
# Temporal clauses

1 * Add a **toki** 'when' clause expressing the meaning given in English.

Example: セーターを着ます。**Seetaa o kimasu.** (cold)
→ 寒い時はセーターを着ます。**Samui toki wa seetaa o kimasu.**

(1) 塾に行きました。(junior high student)
**Juku ni ikimashita.**
(2) ご飯を食べるのを忘れます。(busy)
**Gohan o taberu no o wasuremasu.**
(3) 喫茶店で友達と話をします。(have free time)
**Kissaten de tomodachi to hanashi o shimasu.**
(4) 日本語を話しました。(be in Japan)
**Nihongo o hanashimashita.**
(5) ビールを飲みます。(tired)
**Biiru o nomimasu.**
(6) これは銀座で買いました。(go to Japan)
**Kore wa Ginza de kaimashita.**
(7) クレジットカードを使います。(do shopping on the Internet)
**Kurejittokaado o tsukaimasu.**
(8) レストランで食べません。(do not have much money)
**Resutoran de tabemasen.**

⇨ 23.1, 27.4.2.2, Exercises in 27

# 24
# Conditional clauses

1 * Fill in the blanks with the appropriate conditional forms.

| | tara | nara | ba | to |
|---|---|---|---|---|
| 食べる **taberu** 'eat' | 食べたら **tabetara** | (1) | 食べれば **tabereba** | (2) |
| 読む **yomu** 'read' | (3) | 読むなら **yomu nara** | (4) | (5) |
| する **suru** 'do' | (6) | (7) | (8) | すると **suru to** |
| くる **kuru** 'come' | きたら **kitara** | (9) | (10) | (11) |
| 見る **miru** 'see' | (12) | 見るなら **miru nara** | (13) | (14) |
| 行く **iku** 'go' | (15) | (16) | (17) | 行くと **iku to** |
| 医者 **isha** 'doctor' | (18) | 医者なら **isha nara** | | (19) |
| 高い **takai** 'expensive' | (20) | (21) | 高ければ **takakereba** | (22) |
| 簡単 **kantan** 'easy' | (23) | (24) | | 簡単だと **kantan da to** |

⇨ 24, 12.1

2 * Choose appropriate conditional expressions.

(1) ここは毎年三月に【① なると　② なれば】暖かくなる。
   **Koko wa maitoshi sangatsu ni 【① naru to　② nareba】 atatakaku naru.**
(2) 寒いですか。【① 寒いと　② 寒かったら】、窓を閉めてください。
   **Samui desu ka. 【① samui to　② samukattara】 mado o shimete kudasai.**
(3) 日本に【① 行くなら　② 行ったら】温泉に入りたいです。
   **Nihon ni 【① iku nara　② ittara】 onsen ni hairitai desu.**
(4) この薬を【① 飲めば　② 飲むなら】すぐよくなるよ。
   **Kono kusuri o 【① nomeba　② nomu nara】 sugu yoku naru yo.**

(5) 北海道に【① 行けば　② いく（ん）なら】夏がいいですよ。
   **Hokkaidou ni【① ikeba　② iku (n) nara】natsu ga ii desu yo.**

(6) 私はお酒を【① 飲むと　② 飲めば】すぐ顔が赤くなってしまうんですよ。
   **Watashi wa o-sake o【① nomu to　② nomeba】sugu kao ga akaku natte shimau n desu yo.**

(7) 昨日家に【① 帰ったら　② 帰れば】合格通知がきていた。
   **Kinoo ie ni【① kaettara　② kaereba】goukaku tsuuchi ga kite ita.**

(8) これちょっと高いですねえ。もうちょっと【① 安いと　② 安ければ】買うんですが。
   **Kore chotto takai desu nee. Mou chotto【① yasui to　② yasukereba】kau n desu ga.**

⇨ 24, 55.1

**3** ＊ Your mother asks you to do some chores around the house. How would you reply in the following situations, using one of the conditional forms?

(1) You will do it when you finish your homework.
(2) You will do it if you have free time.
(3) You will do it if (and only if) your mother gives you some money for it.
(4) You will do it if it is washing clothes.
(5) You will do it if it is a task you can finish in half an hour.

⇨ 24.2, 24.3, 24.4, Exercises in chapter 55.

# 25

# Relative (noun-modifying) clauses

1 ✦ Combine two sentences into one using the first sentence as the relative (noun-modifying) clause. Change **wa** to **ga**, if any, in the relative clause.

> Example: 私はきのう映画を見ました。その映画は面白かったです。
> → （私が）きのう見た映画は面白かったです。
> **Watashi wa kinou eiga o mimashita. Sono eiga wa omoshirokatta desu.**
> **→ (Watashi ga) kinou mita eiga wa omoshirokatta desu.**

(1) 私はスポーツをします。そのスポーツはゴルフです。
**Watashi wa supootsu o shimasu. Sono supootsu wa gorufu desu.**

(2) きのう喫茶店でケーキを食べました。そのケーキはおいしかったです。
**Kinou kissaten de keeki o tabemashita. Sono keeki wa oishikatta desu.**

(3) きのう人に会いました。その人は出版社に勤めています。
**Kinou hito ni aimashita. Sono hito wa shuppan-sha ni tsutomete imasu.**

(4) 人が部長と話しています。あの人はだれですか。
**Hito ga buchou to hanashite imasu. Ano hito wa dare desu ka.**

(5) スポーツは日本で人気があります。そのスポーツの一つは野球です。
**Supootsu wa Nihon de ninki ga arimasu. Sono supootsu no hitotsu wa yakyuu desu.**

(6) 駅の前に喫茶店があります。その喫茶店で友達に会いました。
**Eki no mae ni kissaten ga arimasu. Sono kissaten de tomodachi ni aimashita.**

(7) 田中さんは京都で写真をとりました。その写真を見せてもらいました。
**Tanaka-san wa Kyouto de shashin o torimashita. Sono shashin o misete moraimashita.**

(8) 先生は本をお書きになりました。その本を授業で使っています。
**Sensei wa hon o o-kaki ni narimashita. Sono hon o jugyou de tsukatte imasu.**

(9) 作家がベストセラーを書きました。その作家の講演を聞きに行きました。
**Sakka ga besutoseraa o kakimashita. Sono sakka no kouen o kiki ni ikimashita.**

(10) 大学時代に先生にお世話になりました。その先生にお礼を言いたいです。
**Daigaku jidai ni sensei ni o-sewa ni narimashita. Sono sensei ni o-rei o iitai desu.**

⇨ 7.2.3, 25.1

**2** ⋆⋆ The following are accounts by two Japanese native speakers. Bracket the parts of the sentences that modify the underlined words.

(A)

[面倒 **mendou** 'troublesome'; 習慣 **shuukan** 'custom'; 美容院 **biyouin** 'beauty salon']

アメリカで私が面倒だと思う<u>習慣</u>₁の一つにチップの習慣がある。ホテルに泊まると部屋に荷物を運んでくれる<u>ベルボーイ</u>₂にチップ、美容院で髪を切ってくれる<u>美容師さん</u>₃にチップ、ピザを家まで届けてくれる<u>人</u>₄にチップと、いろいろなところで払わなければならない。

**Amerika de watashi ga mendou da to omou <u>shuukan</u>₁ no hitotsu ni chippu no shuukan ga aru. Hoteru ni tomaru to heya ni nimotsu o hakonde kureru <u>berubooi</u>₂ ni chippu, biyouin de kami o kitte kureru <u>biyoushi-san</u>₃ ni chippu, piza o ie made todokete kureru <u>hito</u>₄ ni chippu to, iroiro na tokoro de harawanakereba naranai.**

(B)

[塾 **juku** 'cram school'; 呪文 **jumon** 'magic words'; 不思議 **fushigi** 'mysterious'; 最適 **saiteki** 'most suitable'; 環境 **kankyou** 'environment']

私が英語の勉強が楽しいと感じたのは中学二年生の時でした。そのころ行っていた<u>塾</u>₁で英会話のクラスに参加しました。イギリスから来た<u>先生</u>₂の英語はまるで呪文のようで、とても不思議に聞こえました。でも、これをきっかけに、それまで好きではなかった<u>英語</u>₃が急に面白く思えるようになりました。そして、大学でも英語を専攻することにしました。大学では、母語話者の先生が英語だけで教える<u>授業</u>₄をたくさん取ることができて、英語を学ぶには最適な環境でした。

**Watashi ga Eigo no benkyou ga tanoshii to kanjita no wa chuugaku ninensei no toki deshita. Sono koro itte ita <u>juku</u>₁ de Eikaiwa no kurasu ni sanka shimashita. Igirisu kara kita <u>sensei</u>₂ no Eigo wa marude jumon no you de, totemo fushigi ni kikoemashita. Demo, kore o kikkake ni, sore made suki de wa nakatta <u>Eigo</u>₃ ga kyuuni omoshiroku omoeru you ni narimashita. Soshite, daigaku demo Eigo o senkou suru koto ni shimashita. Daigaku de wa, bogo-washa no sensei ga Eigo dake de oshieru <u>jugyou</u>₄ o takusan toru koto ga dekite, Eigo o manabu ni wa saiteki na kankyou deshita.**

⇨ 25.1

**3** ⋆⋆ Explain the following words using relative clauses.

Example: 先生 = 何かを教えてくれる人
     **sensei = nanika o oshiete kureru hito**

(1) 誕生日 **tanjoubi**  (2) 敬語 **keigo**  (3) 入学試験 **nyuugaku shiken**
(4) お年玉 **o-toshidama**  (5) お歳暮 **o-seibo**  (6) フリーター **furiitaa**

⇨ 25.1

**4** ⁑  Translate the following into Japanese.

(1) We are looking for someone who has done editing work.
(2) Those who want to stay in Japan for a year need to get a visa.
(3) I want to take my friend, who is visiting Japan on a business trip, for an over-night trip. Do you know a good place near Tokyo?
(4) This is a thank-you gift for helping me <u>move</u> (house) (**hikkoshi**).
(5) I heard the sound of someone opening the door.
(6) I cannot read the document (you) kindly attached to (your) mail because <u>it is garbled</u> (= **mojibake shite iru**).

➪  25.1, 25.2

# 26
# Complement clauses

The following passage explains how to protect your computer from harmful viruses. Change the underlined verbs into the appropriate forms.

[乗っ取る **nottoru** 'to hack, highjack'; 〜対策 **~taisaku** 'anti~, countermeasure'; 不用意に **fuyoui ni** 'carelessly; 防ぐ **fusegu** 'to prevent']

パソコンが他人に (1)<u>乗っ取られます</u>のを防ぐにはどうすればいいでしょうか。まずはウイルス対策ソフトを (2)<u>入れます</u>ことです。それから、不用意にソフトのダウンロードを (3)<u>しません</u>ことも大事です。完全に防ぐことは (4)<u>難しいです</u>と思いますが、気をつけるようにしましょう。

**Pasokon ga tanin ni** (1)<u>**nottoraremasu**</u> **no o fusegu ni wa dou sureba ii deshou ka. Mazu wa uirusu taisaku sofuto o** (2)<u>**iremasu**</u> **koto desu. Sorekara, fuyoui ni sofuto no daunroodo o** (3)<u>**shimasen**</u> **koto mo daiji desu. Kanzen ni fusegu koto wa** (4)<u>**muzukashii desu**</u> **to omoimasu ga, ki o tsukeru you ni shimashou.**

▷ 12.1, 13.1.1, 26.1, 26.2

Fill in the blanks with **no**, **koto** or **to**. Also, choose the appropriate particles where alternatives are given.

(1) 問題【が・は】、誰も経験【が・は】ない（　　）です。
**Mondai 【ga・wa】, daremo keiken 【ga・wa】 nai (　　) desu.**

(2) 来週なら会議に出席できる（　　）思います。
**Raishuu nara kaigi ni shusseki dekiru (　　) omoimasu.**

(3) 学校の帰りに妹【が・は】スポーツカーに乗っている（　　）を見た。
**Gakkou no kaeri ni imouto 【ga・wa】 supootsu kaa ni notte iru (　　) o mita.**

(4) 同僚【が・は】会社の書類を家に持ち帰る（　　）を止めた。
**Douryou 【ga・wa】 kaisha no shorui o ie ni mochikaeru (　　) o tometa.**
*I stopped my colleague from taking company documents home.*

(5) 最も大事なの【が・は】皆【が・は】力を合わせる（　　）です。
**Mottomo daiji na no 【ga・wa】 minna 【ga・wa】 chikara o awaseru (　　) desu.**

(6) 母は帰りが遅くなる（　　）言っていた。
**Haha wa kaeri ga osoku naru (　　) itte ita.**

(7) 両親【が・は】言い争う（　　）を聞くのは嫌なものだ。
**Ryoushin 【ga・wa】 ii-arasou (　　) o kiku no wa iyana mono da.**

(8) 考えても分からないから、考える（　　）をやめた。
**Kangaete mo wakaranai kara, kangaeru (　　) o yameta.**

(9) 誰かが「助けてくれ！」（　　）叫ぶ（　　）を聞きました。
**Dareka ga 'Tasukete kure!' （　　）sakebu （　　）o kikimashita.**

(10) 授業で米にはいろいろな種類がある（　　）を習った。
**Jugyou de kome ni wa iroirona shurui ga aru （　　）o naratta.**

⇨ 26.1, 26.2

**3** ∗

Combine the sentences into one by embedding the question in the main clause.

(1) 首相 (prime minister) はどこに住んでいますか。知りません。
**Shushou (prime minister) wa doko ni sunde imasu ka. Shirimasen.**

(2) 漢字はどうやってできたのですか。習いたいです。
**Kanji wa dou yatte dekita no desu ka. Naraitai desu.**

(3) 今日、早く帰れますか。まだ分かりません。
**Kyou, hayaku kaeremasu ka. Mada wakarimasen.**

(4) どうして嘘をつきましたか。友達にたずねました。
**Doushite uso o tsukimashita ka. Tomodachi ni tazunemashita.**

⇨ 12.1, 26.3

**4** ∗

A husband and wife are talking about their vacation plans. Fill in the blanks using embedded questions.

妻：　哲郎さん、来月はお休み取れるの？
夫：　うーん、まだ (1)＿＿＿＿＿＿＿＿＿＿＿＿＿ 分からないなあ。
　　　そっちは？
妻：　金土日、続けてお休みが (2)＿＿＿＿＿＿＿＿＿＿＿＿＿ 課長に聞いて
　　　みたんだけど、大丈夫そうだよ。
夫：　そうか。じゃあ、俺も休みがもらえるように頑張るよ。どこに
　　　(3)＿＿＿＿＿＿＿＿＿＿＿＿＿ 考えといて。

Tsuma:　Tetsurou-san, raigetsu wa o-yasumi toreru no?
Otto:　Uun, mada (1)＿＿＿＿＿＿＿＿＿＿＿ wakaranai naa. Sotchi wa?
Tsuma:　Kin dou nichi, tsuzukete o-yasumi ga (2)＿＿＿＿＿＿＿＿＿＿ kachou ni kiite mita n da kedo, daijoubu sou da yo.
Otto:　Sou ka. Jaa, ore mo yasumi ga moraeru you ni ganbaru yo. Doko ni (3)＿＿＿＿＿＿＿＿＿＿ kangaetoite.

⇨ 26.3

# 27
# Tense and aspect

Complete the following dialogues with the appropriate forms of verbs or adjectives (nonpast or past, affirmative or negative). The cues are given in random order.

(1)
A and B are strangers waiting for a bus. [come, be late]

A: 10番のバスはもう ①＿＿＿＿＿ か。
B: いいえ、まだです。このバスはよく ②＿＿＿＿＿ んですよ。
A: [after 5 minutes] あ、③＿＿＿＿＿ よ。

A: **10 ban no basu wa mou** ①＿＿＿＿＿ **ka.**
B: **Iie, mada desu. Kono basu wa yoku** ②＿＿＿＿＿ **n desu yo.**
A: [after 5 minutes] **A,** ③＿＿＿＿＿ **yo.**

(2)
A and B are close friends. A wants to invite B out for lunch to a new Italian restaurant, but B has just eaten. B had to have lunch early because she has a meeting during lunch time. [eat, be built, exist, think]

A: もうお昼、①＿＿＿＿＿ ？
B: うん、今 ②＿＿＿＿＿ ところ。
A: それは残念。駅の前に新しいイタリア料理の店が ③＿＿＿＿＿ から、いっしょにどうかなと ④＿＿＿＿＿ んだけど。
B: 本当に残念。ごめんね。今日はお昼の時間に会議が ⑤＿＿＿＿＿ から、少し早めに ⑥＿＿＿＿＿ の。
A: じゃ、今度またね。

A: **Mou ohiru** ①＿＿＿＿＿ ？
B: **Un, ima** ②＿＿＿＿＿ **tokoro.**
A: **Sore wa zannen. Eki no mae ni atarashii Itaria ryouri no mise ga**
   ③＿＿＿＿＿ **kara, isshoni dou kana to** ④＿＿＿＿＿ **n da kedo.**
B: **Hontou ni zannen. Gomen ne. Kyou wa o-hiru no jikan ni kaigi ga**
   ⑤＿＿＿＿＿ **kara, sukoshi hayame ni** ⑥＿＿＿＿＿ **no.**
A: **Ja, kondo mata ne.**

(3)

Keiko and Akira are meeting for dinner after work. Keiko is about to leave her office, but Akira is in the middle of responding to an e-mail, which he promises to finish as quickly as possible. [leave, be finished, do, write]

景子：　もしもし、今オフィスを ①＿＿＿＿＿ ところなんだけど、そっちはどう？
明：　　うん、今メールの返事を ②＿＿＿＿＿ ところだけど、あと十分ぐらいで
　　　　③＿＿＿＿＿ と思うよ。
景子：　そう、じゃ、二十分ぐらいしたら、いつものところで。
明：　　うん、なるべく急いで仕事 ④＿＿＿＿＿ から。

**Keiko:** Moshi moshi, ima ofisu o ①＿＿＿＿＿ tokoro na n da kedo, sotchi wa dou?
**Akira:** Un, ima meeru no henji o ②＿＿＿＿＿ tokoro da kedo, ato juppun gurai de ③＿＿＿＿＿ to omou yo.
**Keiko:** Sou, ja, nijuppun gurai shitara, itsumo no tokoro de.
**Akira:** Un, narubeku isoide shigoto ④＿＿＿＿＿ kara.

⇨ 12.1, 18.2.2, 27.2, 27.4.2.3

**2** ★ The following is a diary entry. Fill in the blanks with the appropriate words in the appropriate forms (affirmative or negative, nonpast or past).

私は普通毎日ジョギングを【① do 】が、きのうは気分が【② bad 】ので、ジョギングを【③ do 】。でも、気分はもうだいぶよく【④ become 】ので、あしたはジョギングが【⑤ can do 】と思う。あしたクラスのプロジェクトの原稿を【⑥ hand in 】ことになっているので、今晩は徹夜【⑦ do 】かもしれない。プロジェクトのためのリサーチはもう【⑧ is finished 】のだが、まだ原稿は【⑨ has written 】のだ。がんばろう。

**Watashi wa futsuu mainichi jogingu o 【① do 】 ga, kinou wa kibun ga 【② bad 】 node, jogingu o 【③ do 】. Demo, kibun wa mou daibu yoku 【④ become 】 node, ashita wa jogingu ga 【⑤ can do 】 to omou. Ashita kurasu no purojekuto no genkou o 【⑥ hand in 】 koto ni natte iru node, konban wa tetsuya 【⑦ do 】 kamoshirenai. Purojekuto no tame no risaachi wa mou 【⑧ is finished 】 no da ga, mada genkou wa 【⑨ has written 】 no da. Ganbarou.**

⇨ 12.1, 12.6, 19.2.1, 27.1, 27.2

**3** ★ Choose the appropriate tense form in each set.

(1) 私はいつも母の【作る・作った】おべんとうを食べます。
**Watashi wa itsumo haha no 【tsukuru・tsukutta】 o-bentou o tabemasu.**

(2) 公園で犬を連れて【いる・いた】人を大勢みかけました。
**Kouen de inu o tsurete 【iru・ita】 hito o oozei mikakemashita.**

(3) きのうここに【来る・来た】人はあしたもまた来るそうです。
**Kinou koko ni 【kuru・kita】 hito wa ashita mo mata kuru sou desu.**

(4) 人の家を【訪ねる・訪ねた】時は、何か持って行った方がいい。
**Hito no ie o 【tazuneru・tazuneta】 toki wa, nanika motte itta hou ga ii.**

(5) 先生が私の【書く・書いた】論文を直してくださったので、今度【会う・会った】時にお礼を言います。
**Sensei ga watashi no 【kaku・kaita】 ronbun o naoshite kudasatta node, kondo 【au・atta】 toki ni o-rei o iimasu.**

(6) 家に帰って【来る・来た】人は家族に「ただいま」と言う。
    **Ie ni kaette 【kuru・kita】 hito wa kazoku ni 'tadaima' to iu.**

(7) ご飯を【食べる・食べた】前に勉強をしました。
    **Gohan o 【taberu・tabeta】 mae ni benkyou o shimashita.**

(8) バスを【おりる・おりた】時ステップに気をつけてください。
    **Basu o 【oriru・orita】 toki suteppu ni ki o tsukete kudasai.**

(9) 話を【読む・読んだ】あとで感想を書いてください。
    **Hanashi o 【yomu・yonda】 ato de kansou o kaite kudasai.**

(10) 飛行機の中で日本に【行く・行った】人と話をしました。その人は日本は初め
     てだと言っていました。
     **Hikouki no naka de Nihon ni 【iku・itta】 hito to hanashi o
     shimashita. Sono hito wa Nihon wa hajimete da to itte imashita.**

⇨ 27.4

# 28
# Evidential markers

A and B, who came to visit their friend, are now talking in front of the house. Change the form of the underlined words to fit the context.

[電源 **dengen** 'power'; 雷 **kaminari** 'thunder']

A: おかしいなあ。(1)<u>だれもいません</u> ようです。
B: そうですね。いちおうチャイムを押してみましょう。ああ、(2)<u>こわれています</u> ようです。音がしません。
A: じゃあ、ケータイに電話してみましょう。… 出ませんね。ケータイの 電源 (power) が (3)<u>入っていません</u> ようです。
B: どうしましょうか。天気予報によると、午後は (4)<u>雷です</u> そうですよ。
A: ええ、(5)<u>そうです</u> らしいですね。
B: もうすぐ雨が (6)<u>ふりだします</u> そうだし。
A: じゃあ、あと5分待って、だめなら帰りましょう。

A: **Okashii naa.** (1)**<u>Daremo imasen</u> you desu.**
B: **Sou desu ne. Ichiou chaimu o oshite mimashou. Aa,** (2)**<u>kowarete imasu</u> you desu. Oto ga shimasen.**
A: **Jaa, keitai ni denwa shite mimashou. . . . Demasen ne. Keitai no dengen (power) ga** (3)**<u>haitte imasen</u> you desu.**
B: **Dou shimashou ka. Tenki yohou ni yoru to, gogo wa** (4)**<u>kaminari desu</u> sou desu yo.**
A: **Ee,** (5)**<u>sou desu</u> rashii desu ne.**
B: **Mousugu ame ga** (6)**<u>furi-dashimasu</u> sou da shi.**
A: **Jaa, ato gofun matte, dame nara kaerimashou.**

⇨ 12.1, 19.2.1, 28

What would you say in the following situations? Choose the most appropriate phrase in each set.

(1) You are standing in front of a pastry shop and see a great-looking cake:
うわー、【おいしそうだ・おいしいようだ・おいしいらしい】ね。でも、ちょっと【あま・あまい】そう。
**Uwaa, 【oishi sou da · oishii you da · oishii rashii】 ne. Demo, chotto 【ama · amai】 sou.**
(2) You have heard a rumor that Mr. Tanaka is leaving the company. You talk with another colleague about him:
田中さん、今度会社を【やめそう・やめるらしい・やめるよう】ですね。
**Tanaka-san, kondo kaisha o 【yame-sou · yameru rashii · yameru you】 desu ne.**

(3) You stop by your friend's house, but all the lights are off and the door is locked. You say to yourself:

今は【留守そうだ・留守だそうだ・留守のようだ】。

**Ima wa 【rusu sou da · rusu da sou da · rusu no you da】.**

⇨ 12.1, 13.1, 28.5

**3** ⋆

Respond to each situation below using **sou**, **you** or **rashii**.

(1) You run into an acquaintance. She is carrying a big bag that looks heavy, which you remark upon.

(2) You read about how to roast coffee beans at home with a special kit, which sounds like a lot of work, so you tell your friend who is thinking about it: [to roast coffee: コーヒーまめを煎る **koohii mame o iru**]

(3) Your friend Yoko failed her exam despite studying extra hard. Since then she seems to be really depressed, and has been skipping her tennis practice. You have tried to cheer her up many times, but to no avail. You go to her tennis coach and say: [to be depressed: おちこんでいる **ochikonde iru**]

(4) You often hear your colleague Ms. Taniguchi talk about her pets. You tell an acquaintance what you've inferred:

(5) You haven't met your neighbor yet, but from what you have observed, such as birds chirping, cats chasing each other, and dogs barking, your neighbor has a lot of pet animals. You tell your friend:

⇨ 13.1, 19.2.1, 28.5

# 29
# Honorifics (*keigo*)

1 *
Mark the following descriptions true (○) or false (×).

a.　( ) Exalting words are primarily used for one's out-group members, and humbling words for oneself and one's in-group members.
b.　( ) The polite prefix **o-** is always attached to Japanese native words, and **go-** to words of Chinese origin, but neither is attached to loan words from Western languages.
c.　( ) Speaking to one's teacher and one's superiors at work, it is common to switch from formal style (e.g. **sou desu ka**) to informal style (e.g. **sou ka**) when they become close after years of acquaintance.
d.　( ) With beautifying words, **o-** and **go-** are used even when referring to one's own belongings and actions.
e.　( ) One type of humbling verb implies that the speaker's action involves the addressee(s) or another social superior (e.g. **mooshi-ageru** 'say'), while the other type (e.g. **moosu** 'say') does not.
f.　( ) From the speaker's perspective, the in-group/out-group membership of a referent does not change no matter whom the addressee may be.
g.　( ) The exalting form, **-(r)areru**, is popular especially among young people nowadays.

➪ 29.1, 29.2, 29.5, 29.6, 29.7

2 *
(A)
Write exalting expressions for the following in the **-(r)areru** form.

① はなす **hanasu** 'talk' _____;　② くる **kuru** 'come' _____;
③ する **suru** 'do' _____;　④ まつ **matsu** 'wait' _____;
⑤ でる **deru** 'leave' _____;　⑥ はらう **harau** 'pay' _____;
⑦ けんきゅうする **kenkyuu suru** 'research' _____

(B)
Write the exalting expression in the **o-** (or **go-**) verb **ni naru** form.

① はなす **hanasu** 'talk' _____;　② きく **kiku** 'listen' _____;
③ かりる **kariru** 'borrow' _____;　④ まつ **matsu** 'wait' _____;
⑤ とる **toru** 'take' _____;　⑥ うける **ukeru** 'receive' _____;
⑦ しゅっせきする **shusseki suru** 'attend' _____

(C)
Write the special exalting form.

① いう **iu** 'say' _____;　② ねる **neru** 'sleep, go to bed' _____;
③ する **suru** 'do' _____;　④ くる **kuru** 'come' _____;

⑤ いる **iru** 'be, stay' _____;    ⑥ くれる **kureru** 'give (me)' _____;
⑦ 知っている **shitte iru** 'know' _____です **desu**

⇨ 29.3

**3** ⋆

You will be reporting to your department colleagues how Chief Yamada is doing in the hospital. Change the underlined words to honorific forms attaching a polite prefix to nouns and adjectives, and using the -(r)areru or special forms of verbs.

> 皆さん、おはようございます。えー、山田部長はだいぶ ①元気に ②なったそうですので、③安心下さい。昨夜はぐっすり ④寝、今朝は少し ⑤歩いたり、新聞を ⑥読んだりしたそうです。私が伺った時は、音楽を聞いて ⑦いました。皆さんによろしくと ⑧言っていました。以上です。

> **Minasan, ohayou gozaimasu. Ee, Yamada Buchou wa daibu ①genki ni ②natta sou desu node, ③anshin kudasai. Sakuya wa gussuri ④ne, kesa wa sukoshi ⑤aruitari shinbun o ⑥yondari shita sou desu. Watashi ga ukagatta toki wa, ongaku o kiite ⑦imashita. Minasan ni yoroshiku to ⑧itte imashita. Ijou desu.**

⇨ 29.3

**4** ⋆

(A)
Write humbling expressions in the **o-** (or **go-**) verb **suru** form.

① もつ **motsu** 'carry, take' _____;    ② かえす **kaesu** 'return' _____;
③ かりる **kariru** 'borrow' _____;    ④ みせる **miseru** 'show' _____;
⑤ あける **akeru** 'open' _____;    ⑥ きく **kiku** 'ask' _____;
⑦ そうだんする **soudan suru** 'consult' _____

(B)
Write the humbling expressions in the verb-**(s)asete itadaku** form.
① うたう **utau** 'sing' _____;    ② する **suru** 'do' _____;
③ やめる **yameru** 'quit' _____;    ④ くる **kuru** 'come' _____;
⑤ かえる **kaeru** 'return' _____;    ⑥ しめる **shimeru** 'close' _____;
⑦ ひく **hiku** 'play (instrument)' _____;
⑧ せつめいする **setsumei suru** 'explain' _____

(C)
Write the special humbling form.

① いう **iu** 'say' _____;    ② いく **iku** 'go' _____;
③ する **suru** 'do' _____;    ④ いる **iru** 'be, stay' _____;
⑤ きく **kiku** 'ask' _____;
⑥ たべる **taberu** 'eat,' のむ **nomu** 'drink,' もらう **morau** 'receive' _____

⇨ 29.4

**5** ★

Below is an e-mail message written by Chris Evert to his/her former professor asking for a recommendation letter. Write non-honorific equivalents of the underlined honorific expressions.

[在学中 **zaigaku-chuu** 'when I was a student'; 転職 **tenshoku** 'change jobs'; 志望動機 **shibou douki** 'reason for applying'; 恐縮 **kyoushuku** 'I feel bad']

---

鈴木先生、
　①いかが ②お過ごしでいらっしゃいますか。
長い間ご無沙汰して ③おりまして ④申し訳ございません。
2年前に○○大学を卒業しましたクリス・エバートです。
在学中は大変お世話になりましてありがとうございました。
　実は今日はお願いがありまして、⑤ご連絡させて頂いております。大学卒業以来ABCという会社に勤務しているのですが、近く日本企業に転職を考えています。その際、推薦状が必要になるのですが、先生に ⑥お願いしてもよろしいでしょうか。
　⑦お引き受けいただける ようでしたら、志望動機などの書類を大至急 ⑧送らせて頂きます。
　ご多忙のところを恐縮ですが、ご返信を ⑨お待ちしております。
　どうぞよろしくお願い ⑩致します。

クリス・エバート

---

Suzuki Sensei,
　①ikaga ②o-sugoshi de irasshaimasu ka.
Nagai aida go-busata shite ③orimashite ④moushiwake gozaimasen.
Ninen mae ni ○○ Daigaku o sotsugyou shimashita Kurisu Ebaato desu.
Zaigaku-chuu wa taihen o-sewa ni narimashite arigatou gozaimashita.
　Jitsu wa kyou wa o-negai ga arimashite, ⑤go-renraku sasete itadaite orimasu. Daigaku sotsugyou irai ABC to iu kaisha ni kinmu shite iru no desu ga, chikaku Nihon kigyou ni tenshoku o kangaete imasu. Sono sai, suisenjou ga hitsuyou ni naru no desu ga, sensei ni ⑥o-negai shitemo yoroshii deshou ka.
　⑦O-hikiuke itadakeru you deshitara, shibou douki nado no shorui o daishikyuu ⑧okurasete itadakimasu.
　Go-tabou no tokoro o kyoushuku desu ga, go-henshin o ⑨o-machi shite orimasu.
　Douzo yoroshiku o-negai ⑩itashimasu.

Kurisu Ebaato

---

①_____ ; ②_____ ; ③_____ ; ④_____ ; ⑤_____ ;

⑥_____ ; ⑦_____ ; ⑧_____ ; ⑨_____ ; ⑩_____

⇨ 29.3, 29.4

## Part B

# Functions

# 30
# Social interaction

1

Yuri is talking to her friend Daisuke, who recently came back from studying abroad in Canada. Read the dialogue, and then answer the questions.

[繰り返し **kuri-kaeshi** 'repetition'; 自信 **jishin** 'confidence'; 満ちる **michiru** 'full of...']

| | |
|---|---|
| 由利： | 久しぶり！ |
| 大介： | あ、由利。1年ぶりだよね。元気？ |
| 由利： | まあね。でも、毎日同じことの繰り返しで、ちょっとつまんない、みたいな…。カナダはどうだったー？ |
| 大介： | すっごい良かった（由利：ほーんとー）。あっちの授業ってディスカッションばっかだからー（由利：うん）、けっこう大変だったんだけどー、特に最初ね？（由利：うん）まぁ、そのおかげでー（由利：うん）、自分の意見とか英語で言えるようになったって感じ。 |
| 由利： | ふーん、良かったねー。あのさー、そう言えばなんか、大ちゃん、一回り大きくなったような気がする。自信に満ちてるってゆうか。 |
| 大介： | あ、カロリーの多いものよく食べてたんで。 |
| 由利： | またそんなこと言っちゃってー。でも、いいなぁ。どっか留学したいなー、あたしも。 |

Yuri: **Hisashiburi!**
Daisuke: **A, Yuri. Ichinen-buri da yo ne. Genki?**
Yuri: **Maa ne. Demo, mainichi onaji koto no kurikaeshi de, chotto tsumannai, mitai na ... Kanada wa dou dattaa?**
Daisuke: **Suggoi yokatta (Yuri: Hoontoo). Atchi no jugyou tte disukasshon bakka da karaa (Yuri: Un), kekkou taihen datta n da kedoo, toku ni saisho ne? (Yuri: Un). Maa, sono o-kagedee (Yuri: Un), jibun no iken toka Eigo de ieru you ni natta tte kanji.**
Yuri: **Fuun, yokatta nee. Ano saa, sou ieba nanka, Dai-chan, hito-mawari ookiku natta you na ki ga suru. Jishin ni michite ru tte yuu ka.**
Daisuke: **A, karorii no ooi mono, yoku tabete ta n de.**
Yuri: **Mata sonna koto itchattee. Demo, ii naa. Dokka ryuugaku shitai naa, atashi mo.**

(A)
In this dialogue, find at least one example each of the following features of spoken language, especially casual style speech.

① Incomplete sentences (omission of subject, verb, etc.)
② Omission of the particles **wa**, **ga**, **o**, and **ni**

③ Interactive particles
④ Listener responses (**aizuchi**)
⑤ Fillers
⑥ Hedges (words and particles used to lessen the impact of an utterance)
⑦ Sound changes; e.g. contractions, vowel elongation, consonant doubling
⑧ Postposing (sentences with words appearing after the main predicate/verb)

(B)
Supposing that you are Yuri, complete the journal entry below. Note that diary entries are customarily written in plain style. The first sentence is an example.

---

9月9日（水）晴れ
　　1年ぶりに大介君に　__会った__　。カナダ留学は①_____ とのこと。自信に満ちた彼は②_____ 感じがした。英語も
③_____ らしい。それに比べて、私の生活はどうだろう。毎日が
④_____ ではないか。いつか自分も⑤_____ と思うが、夢で終わるかもしれない。

---

**Kugatsu Kokonoka (sui) Hare**
　　**Ichinen-buri ni Daisuke-kun ni** __atta__ **. Kanada ryuugaku wa**
①_____ **to no koto. Jishin ni michita kare wa**
②_____ **kanji ga shita. Eigo mo** ③_____ **rashii.**
**Sore ni kurabete, watashi no seikatsu wa dou darou. Mainichi ga**
④_____ **de wa nai ka. Itsuka jibun mo** ⑤_____
**to omou ga, yume de owaru kamo shirenai.**

---

⇨ 5.1.1, 6.1, 6.2, 30.1

**2** ⋆

Paying attention to the context, write appropriate greetings or expressions.

(1) [A and B are colleagues, but are not very close]
　　A: おはようございます。**Ohayou gozaimasu.**
　　B: _____
　　　　今日はいい天気ですね。**Kyou wa ii tenki desu ne.**
　　A: _____

(2) [A and B are neighbors]
　　A: 久しぶりですね。お変わりありませんか。
　　　　**Hisashiburi desu ne. O-kawari arimasen ka.**
　　B: ええ、_____
　　　　**Ee,** _____

(3) [A is a professor, and B her/his former student]
　　A: あぁ、○○さん、久しぶりですね。**Aa, ○○-san, hisashiburi desu ne.**
　　B: はい、_____ 申し訳ありません。
　　　　**Hai,** _____ **moushiwake arimasen.**

(4) [A is leaving work for the day while her/his boss B stays]
　　A: お先に失礼します。**O-saki ni shitsurei shimasu.**
　　B: _____

(5) [A is leaving home temporarily while B stays]
　　A: _____
　　B: 行ってらっしゃい。**Itte rasshai.**

(6) [A returns home, and B welcomes her/him back]
　　A: ただいま。**Tadaima.**
　　B: _____

(7) [A congratulates B for getting married]
　　A: _____
　　B: ありがとうございます。**Arigatou gozaimasu.**

⇨ 5.1.1, 6.2, 10.4, 30.2

**3** ★

You are starting your internship for a Japanese company today. Introduce yourself including: ① an opening phrase; ② name; ③ affiliation (e.g. X University in City Y); ④ major; ⑤ hobbies; and ⑥ a concluding phrase.

_____

_____

_____

_____

_____

_____

⇨ 5.1.1, 5.2, 6.2, 30.2, 30.3

**4** ★

You are introducing a business acquaintance, Kaoru Miyazaki, to your boss Yuko Tanabe. Ms. Tanabe (in her late 40s) is your department chief, and Mr/Ms Miyazaki (much younger than she) works for a company called アニメワークス **Anime Waakusu.** Fill in the blanks with appropriate phrases.

| あなた： | 部長、こちら、宮崎さんです。 |
|---|---|
| **Anata:** | **Buchou, kochira, Miyazaki-san desu.** |
| 宮崎 **Miyazaki:** | ① _____。 |
| | ② _____。 |
| | ③ _____。 |
| 田辺 **Tanabe:** | 田辺 **Tanabe** ④ _____。 |
| | ⑤ _____。 |

⇨ 5.2, 30.2, 30.3, 30.4

**5** ★

Carl Schmidt works in Japan. He has been invited to the home of a colleague, a man several years older than he. With a small gift in his hand, he rings the doorbell. Complete dialogues (A) and (B) choosing appropriate expressions from the lists below. Use each expression once only. The dots '. . .' indicate that some time has elapsed.

(A)

> a. あがって下さい・b. いただきます・c. いらっしゃい・
> d. おかまいなく・e. おじゃまします・f. けっこうです・
> g. ごめん下さい・h. これ、よかったら、どうぞ。・
> i. たいしたものじゃないんです・j. 悪いね
>
> a. agatte kudasai・b. itadakimasu・c. irasshai・d. o-kamai naku・
> e. o-jama shimasu・f. kekkou desu・g. go-men kudasai・
> h. kore, yokattara, douzo・i. taishita mono ja nai n desu・j. warui ne

[玄関で] ピンポン！

カール： ___①___ 。
同僚： あ、カールさん、___②___ 。 どうぞ ___③___ 。
カール： ありがとうございます。___④___ 。
　　　　 あのう、___⑤___ 。この間実家から送って来たんです。
同僚： ああ、___⑥___ 。そんな気を使わなくてもよかったのに。
カール： いえ、本当に ___⑦___ 。
同僚： そう？どうもありがとう。じゃ、こっちの方へ。せまい所だけど。

[リビングで]

同僚： ちょっと失礼。お茶、入れて来るから。
カール： あ、どうぞ、___⑧___ 。
同僚： いや、いや、やっぱり。… さ、どうぞ。
カール： ありがとうございます。じゃ、___⑨___ 。
同僚： … もう一杯、どうですか。
カール： あ、___⑩___ 。
同僚： そう？えんりょはしないようにね。

[Genkan de] Pinpon!

Kaaru: ___①___ .
Douryou: A, Kaaru-san, ___②___ . Douzo ___③___ .
Kaaru: Arigatou gozaimasu. ___④___ .
　　　　 Anou, ___⑤___ . Kono aida jikka kara okutte kita n desu.
Douryou: Aa, ___⑥___ . Sonna ki o tsukawanakute mo yokatta noni.
Kaaru: Ie, hontou ni ___⑦___ .
Douryou: Sou? Doumo arigatou. Ja, kotchi no hou e. Semai tokoro
　　　　 da kedo.

[Ribingu de]

Douryou: Chotto shitsurei. O-cha, irete kuru kara.
Kaaru: A, douzo ___⑧___ .
Douryou: Iya, iya, yappari. . . . Sa, douzo.
Kaaru: Arigatou gozaimasu. Ja, ___⑨___ .
Douryou: . . . Mou ippai dou desu ka.
Kaaru: A, ___⑩___ .
Douryou: Sou? Enryo wa shinai you ni ne.

(B)

> a. ありがとうございます・b. ありがとうございました・c. 感激・
> d. えんりょなく・e. おいしそうですね・f. おかげさまで・
> g. おかわり・h. ごちそうさまでした・i. 失礼します・j. そろそろ …
>
> a. **arigatou gozaimasu**・b. **arigatou gozaimashita**・c. **kangeki**・
> d. **enryo naku**・e. **oishisou desu ne**・f. **o-kage-sama de**・g. **o-kawari**・
> h. **go-chisou-sama deshita**・i. **shitsurei shimasu**・j. **sorosoro** . . .

[夕食時]

| | |
|---|---|
| 同僚： | いやぁ、たいしたものは作れないんだけどね、たくさん食べてって下さい。 |
| カール： | ありがとうございます。わぁ、___①___！じゃ、___②___、いただきます。 |
| 同僚： | … ごはんとかみそ汁の ___③___ はどう？ |
| カール： | あ、お願いします。どれもこれもおいしくて ___④___ です！ |

[いとまごい 'leave taking']

| | |
|---|---|
| カール： | あ、もうこんな時間。じゃ、___⑤___。 |
| 同僚： | そんなこと言わず、もっとゆっくりして行ったら？ |
| カール： | いえ、本当に。今日は ___⑥___。 |
| 同僚： | いや、とんでもない。だけど、時間の経つのがあっと言う間だったねぇ。 |
| カール： | 本当ですね。今日は ___⑦___、日本の味を満喫 ('fully enjoy') することができました。仕事のこともいろいろ教えていただいて、すごく勉強になったし。本当に ___⑧___。 |
| 同僚： | どういたしまして。また来て下さい。 |
| カール： | はい、___⑨___。じゃ、___⑩___。 |

[夕食時 Yuushoku-ji]

| | |
|---|---|
| **Douryou:** | Iyaa, taishita mono wa tsukurenai n da kedo ne, takusan tabete tte kudasai. |
| **Kaaru:** | Arigatou gozaimasu. Waa, ___①___! Ja, ___②___. |
| **Douryou:** | . . . Go-han toka misoshiru no ___③___ wa dou? |
| **Kaaru:** | A, o-negai shimasu. Dore mo kore mo oishikute ___④___ desu. |

[Itoma-goi 'leave taking']

| | |
|---|---|
| **Kaaru:** | A, mou konna jikan. Ja, ___⑤___. |
| **Douryou:** | Sonna koto iwazu, motto yukkuri shite ittara? |
| **Kaaru:** | Ie, hontou ni. Kyou wa ___⑥___. |
| **Douryou:** | Iya, tondemo nai. Dakedo, jikan no tatsu no ga a tto iu ma datta nee. |
| **Kaaru:** | Hontou desu ne. Kyou wa ___⑦___, Nihon no aji o mankitsu ('fully enjoy') suru koto ga dekimashita. Shigoto no koto mo iroiro oshiete itadaite, sugoku benkyou ni natta shi. Hontou ni ___⑧___. |
| **Douryou:** | Dou itashimashite. Mata kite kudasai. |
| **Kaaru:** | Hai, ___⑨___. Ja, ___⑩___. |

⇨ 5.2, 6.2, 6.3, 12.7, 29.1, 29.2, 29.3, 30.6, 30.7

**6** ***

You (Terry Castle) work for the Apple Bank, and are calling to speak with
Mr Oshiro at the Honmaru Bank in Japan. He is not in the office, so you leave
a message for him to return your call. Choose an appropriate phrase.

[プルルル、プルルル …]

受付 ： はい、本丸銀行でございます。いつも大変お世話になっております。

あなた ： あ、もしもし、こちらアメリカのアップル銀行のテリー・キャッス
ルと【① 申します・申し上げます】が、大城さん、【② おります・
おられます】でしょうか。

受付 ： 申し訳ございません、【③ 大城・大城さん】はただいま出かけており
ますが。

あなた ： そうですか。何時ごろ【④ もどれ・もどられ】ますか。

受付 ： あ、ちょっと分かりかねますが。申し訳ございません。何かお言付け、
おありでしょうか。

あなた ： はい、では、明朝私の方にお電話を【⑤ 下さる・いただく】
ように【⑥ お伝えして・お伝え】下さいますか。

受付 ： はい、かしこまりました。

あなた ： あのう、時差がありますので、日本時間で朝の10時【⑦ まで・までに】
かけていただけるとありがたいんですが。

受付 ： はい、そのように申し伝えます。恐れ入りますが、そちらのお電話番号
を【⑧ お聞きになっても・お聞きしても】よろしいでしょうか。

あなた ： はい、えー、こちらアメリカで、234-567-8901です。

受付 ： はい、お電話番号が234-567-8901、アップル銀行様のテリー・キャッス
ル様でいらっしゃいますね。

あなた ： はい、じゃ、よろしくお願いします。

[Purururu, purururu . . .]

Uketsuke: Hai, Honmaru Ginkou de gozaimasu. Itsumo taihen o-sewa ni
natte orimasu.

Anata: A, moshimoshi, kochira Amerika no Appuru Ginkou no
Terii Kyassuru to 【① moushimasu・moushi-agemasu】 ga,
Ooshiro-san, 【② orimasu・oraremasu】 deshou ka.

Uketsuke: Moushiwake gozaimasen, 【③ Ooshiro・Ooshiro-san】 wa
tadaima dekakete orimasu ga.

Anata: Sou desu ka. Nanji goro 【④ modore・modorare】 masu ka.

Uketsuke: A, chotto wakari-kanemasu ga. Moushiwake gozaimasen. Nani
ka o-kotozuke, o-ari deshou ka.

Anata: Hai, dewa, myouchou wata(ku)shi no hou ni o-denwa
o 【⑤ kudasaru・itadaku】 you ni 【⑥ o-tsutae shite・
o-tsutae】 kudasaimasu ka.

Uketsuke: Hai, kashikomarimashita.

Anata: Anou, jisa ga arimasu node, Nihon jikan de asa no
juuji 【⑦ made・made ni】 kakete itadakeru to arigatai
n desu ga.

Uketsuke: Hai, sono you ni moushi-tsutaemasu. Osore irimasu ga, sochira
no o-denwa bangou o 【⑧ o-kiki ni natte mo・o-kiki shite mo】
yoroshii deshou ka.

Anata:      Hai, ee, kochira Amerika de, nii san yon no goo roku nana no hachi kyuu zero ichi desu.

Uketsuke:   Hai, o-denwa bangou ga nii san yon no goo roku nana no hachi kyuu zero ichi, Appuru Ginkou-sama no Terii Kyassuru-sama de irasshaimasu ne.

Anata:      Hai, ja, yoroshiku o-negai shimasu.

⇨  29.3, 29.4, 30.11

# 31
# Basic communication strategies

1 ⋆ Write down what you would say, in the blanks (a)–(p).

(A)

Two women, Yoko and Aya, are seniors in college and are close friends.

洋子： 　(1) _____ (Get Aya's attention)
亜矢： 　(2) _____ (Respond)
洋子： 　心理学の先生の名前、何だったっけ？
亜矢： 　綾部先生のこと？
洋子： 　あ、そうそう。(3) _____
　　　　(Ask how to write 'Ayabe' in kanji)
亜矢： 　(4) _____ (a filler) こうだと思うけど。
洋子： 　ああ、そうか。ありがとう。
亜矢： 　ううん、でも、なんで綾部先生に用があるの？
洋子： 　(5) _____
　　　　(Say 'I want to ask her about graduate schools')
亜矢： 　(6) _____ (Show excitement) どこの大学院？
洋子： 　(7) _____
　　　　(Mention hesitantly the University of Tokyo and Keio University)
亜矢： 　(8) _____
　　　　(Say you couldn't hear and want her to repeat)
洋子： 　東京大学とか慶応大学とか…、無理かも、っていうか、たぶん無理だけど。
亜矢： 　そんなこと、やってみなきゃわからないよ。
洋子： 　まあね。(9) _____
　　　　(Change the topic and ask if Aya can take over your part-time job
　　　　next week)
亜矢： 　(10) _____ (Express reluctance)
洋子： 　そこをなんとか、お願い！
亜矢： 　(11) _____ (Reluctantly accept) 今回だけだからね。

**Youko:** (1) _____ (Get Aya's attention)
**Aya:** (2) _____ (Respond)
**Youko:** **Shinrigaku no sensei no namae, nan datta kke?**
**Aya:** **Ayabe-sensei no koto?**
**Youko:** **A, sou sou.** (3) _____
　　　　(Ask how to write 'Ayabe' in kanji)
**Aya:** (4) _____ (a filler) **kou da to omou kedo.**
**Youko:** **Aa, sou ka. Arigatou.**

Aya: Uun, demo, nande Ayabe-sensei ni you ga aru no?
Youko: (5) _____
(Say 'I want to ask her about graduate schools')
Aya: (6) _____ (Show excitement)
**Doko no daigakuin?**
Youko: (7) _____
(Mention hesitantly the University of Tokyo and Keio University)
Aya: (8) _____
(Say you couldn't hear and want her to repeat)
Youko: **Toukyou daigaku toka Keiou daigaku toka, murikamo, tte iu ka, tabun muri da kedo.**
Aya: **Sonna koto, yatte minakya wakaranai yo.**
Youko: **Maane.** (9) _____
(Change the topic and ask if Aya can take over your part-time job next week)
Aya: (10) _____ (Express reluctance)
Youko: **Soko o nantoka, o-negai!**
Aya: (11) _____ (Reluctantly accept) **Konkai dake dakara ne.**

(B)
Taro is lost, so he goes into a store, and asks a sales clerk for directions.

太郎： (1) _____ (Get the sales clerk's attention)
店員： (2) _____ (Respond)
太郎： (3) _____ (Hesitation phrase) 山田歯科医院という歯医者を探し
ているんですが…
店員： (4) _____
(Ask Taro to repeat the name of the dentist)
太郎： 山田歯科です。
店員： ああ、山田歯科ですね。(5) _____
(Say 'Go straight,' then add 'about 5 minutes' as an afterthought)
太郎： ここをまっすぐ行けばいいんですね。ありがとうございました。

Tarou: (1) _____ (Get the sales clerk's attention)
Ten'in: (2) _____ (Respond)
Tarou: (3) _____ (Hesitation phrase) **Yamada shika iin to iu haisha o sagashite iru n desu ga . . .**
Ten'in: (4) _____
(Ask Taro to repeat the name of the dentist)
Tarou: **Yamada shika desu.**
Ten'in: **Aa, Yamada shika desu ne.** (5) _____
(Say 'Go straight,' then add 'about 5 minutes' as an afterthought)
Tarou: **Koko o massugu ikeba ii n desu ne. Arigatou gozaimashita.**

⇨ 31.1, 31.4.2, 31.7, 31.8, 31.10, 31.12, 31.15

**2** ✯✯ The following is a transcript of Sachi's class presentation about environmental issues. Fill in the blanks with appropriate expressions from the box. You may use each phrase once.

(A)

> a. 次に・b. 話したいと思います・c. 最後に・d. 最初に
>
> a. tsugi ni・b. hanashitai to omoimasu・c. saigo ni・d. saisho ni

今日は環境問題について(1)＿＿。皆さんの生活の中で、どんなことが環境問題に関係があると思いますか。この発表では、(2)＿＿ ゴミの問題について、(3)＿＿ 大気汚染について、(4)＿＿ 地球温暖化について話します。

Kyou wa kankyou mondai ni tsuite (1)____. Minasan no seikatsu no naka de, donna koto ga kankyou mondai ni kankei ga aru to omoimasu ka. Kono happyou de wa, (2)____ gomi no mondai ni tsuite, (3)____ taiki osen ni tsuite, (4)____ chikyuu ondanka ni tsuite hanashimasu.

(B)

> e. つまり・f. はじめに・g. ですから・h. まず第一に
>
> e. tsumari・f. hajime ni・g. desukara・h. mazu daiichi ni

(5)＿＿、ゴミの問題ですが、日本では1日に1人976gのゴミを出しているそうです。(6)＿＿1年では人口一人あたり356.24kgのゴミが捨てられるということです。これは大変な量です。それだけのゴミを焼却したり埋めたりしなければならないのですから、簡単なことではありません。(7)＿＿、ゴミの問題を解決するには (8)＿＿ 一人一人が出すゴミの量を減らすことが大事だと思います。

(5)____, gomi no mondai desu ga, Nihon de wa ichinichi ni hitori 976 guramu no gomi o dashite iru sou desu. (6)____ ichinen de wa jinkou hitori atari 356.24 kiro guramu no gomi ga suterareru to iu koto desu. Kore wa taihen na ryou desu. Sore dake no gomi o shoukyaku shitari umetari shinakereba naranai no desu kara, kantan na koto de wa arimasen. (7)____, gomi no mondai o kaiketsu suru ni wa (8)____ hitori hitori ga dasu gomi no ryou o herasu koto ga daiji da to omoimasu.

(C)

> i. いくつか例をあげてみましょう・j. では・k. 第一に・
> l. では次に・m. 第二には・n. それに対して
>
> i. ikutsuka rei o agete mimashou・j. dewa・k. daiichi ni・
> l. dewa tsugi ni・m. daini ni wa・n. sore ni taishite

(9)＿＿、大気汚染の問題に移りますが、大気汚染の原因には、個人の責任によるものと公共の責任によるものがあります。(10)＿＿。個人レベルのものは、たとえば、自家用車の排気ガスや家庭でゴミを燃やした時に出る煙などです。(11)＿＿ 大小の工場の排気ガスなどは公共の責任によるものでしょう。(12)＿＿、大気汚染を減らすために何ができるでしょうか。(13)＿＿、なるべく車を使わないなど、ガソリンに頼らない移動方法を考えることです。(14)＿＿、企業に工場の排気ガスをきれいにしてから外に出すよう義務づけることだと思います。

(9)____, taiki osen no mondai ni utsurimasu ga, taiki osen no gen'in ni wa, kojin no sekinin ni yoru mono to koukyou no sekinin ni yoru mono ga arimasu. (10)____. Kojin reberu no mono wa, tatoeba, jikayousha no haiki gasu ya katei de gomi o moyashita toki ni deru kemuri nado desu. (11)____ daishou no koujou no haiki gasu nado wa koukyou no sekinin ni yoru mono deshou. (12)____, taiki osen o herasu tame ni nani ga dekiru deshou ka. (13)____, narubeku kuruma o tsukawanai nado, gasorin ni tayoranai idou houhou o kangaeru koto desu. (14)____, kigyou ni koujou no haiki gasu o kirei ni shite kara soto ni dasu you gimuzukeru koto da to omoimasu.

(D)

> o. たとえば・p. その結果・q. では最後に
>
> o. **tatoeba**・p. **sono kekka**・q. **dewa saigo ni**

(15)____ 温暖化の問題について、少し説明したいと思います。温暖化によって自然界のバランスがくずれ、色々な影響が出てきます。(16)____、海面が上昇したり、異常気象が多発したりすると言われています。(17)____、住居や食料生産にも問題が出てくるでしょう。しかし温暖化の原因はとても複雑でまだまだ分かっていないことが多いそうです。

(15)____ ondanka no mondai ni tsuite, sukoshi setsumei shitai to omoimasu. Ondanka ni yotte shizenkai no baransu ga kuzure, iroiro na eikyou ga dete kimasu. (16)____, kaimen ga joushou shitari, ijou kishou ga tahatsu shitari suru to iwarete imasu. (17)____, juukyo ya shokuryou seisan ni mo mondai ga dete kuru deshou. Shikashi ondanka no gen'in wa totemo fukuzatsu de madamada wakatte inai koto ga ooi sou desu.

(E)

> r. ご清聴ありがとうございました・s. 結論をいうと・t. 以上で
>
> r. **go-seichou arigatou gozaimashita**・s. **ketsuron o iu to**・t. **ijou de**

このように環境問題にはいろいろな側面がありますが、(18)____、一つだけ解決しても、環境問題は改善できないということです。環境の複雑な仕組みを研究して、問題に対処することが大切なのではないでしょうか。(19)____ 私の発表は終わります。(20)____。

**Kono you ni kankyou mondai ni wa iroirona sokumen ga arimasu ga, (18)____, hitotsu dake kaiketsu shitemo, kankyou mondai wa kaizen dekinai to iu koto desu. Kankyou no fukuzatsu na shikumi o kenkyuu shite, mondai ni taisho suru koto ga taisetsu na no de wa nai deshou ka. (19)____ watashi no happyou wa owarimasu. (20)____.**

31.5

# 32
# Questions

1 * Complete the questions in both formal and informal styles.

(1) You want to know if your addressee is going to the party tonight.
今晩パーティーに _____。
**Konban paatii ni (** 　　　　　　　　　　　　　　　　**)**

(2) Seeing your colleague/friend acting in a very happy manner:
何かいいことが _____。
**Nanika ii koto ga (** 　　　　　　　　　　　　　　**)**

(3) You want to find out why your friend is studying Japanese:
どうして日本語を _____。
**Doushite nihongo o (** 　　　　　　　　　　　　　　　　**)**

(4) You want to ask your colleague/friend who went to a movie yesterday if it was interesting:
映画 _____。
**Eiga (** 　　　　　　　　　　　　**)**

(5) You baked a cake for your friend and want to know whether he/she found it tasty:
_____。

(6) You heard that your colleague/friend bought a house. Confirm it with him/her:
家を _____。 **Ie o (** 　　　　　　　　　　　**)**

(7) When you sit down at the doctor's office, your doctor asks:
どう _____。 **Dou (** 　　　　　　　　　**)**

⇨ 12.1, 13.11, 19.2.1, 32.1.1, 32.1.2, 32.2

2 * Fill in the blanks with phrases meaning 'yes' or 'no.'

(1) A: もう食べましたか。 　　　　Mou tabemashita ka.
　　 B: (　　　　) 食べました。 　　(　　　　) tabemashita.

(2) A: お金ないの？ 　　　　　　　Okane nai no?
　　 B: (　　　　) あるよ。 　　　(　　　　) aru yo.

(3) A: その本、おもしろい？ 　　　Sono hon, omoshiroi?
　　 B: (　　　　) 全然。 　　　　(　　　　) zenzen.

(4) A: スミスさんを探しているんだけど、見なかった？
　　　　**Sumisu-san o sagashite iru n da kedo, minakatta?**
　　 B: (　　　　) エレベーターの前で見たよ。
　　　　(　　　　) **erebeetaa no mae de mita yo.**

(5) A: きのうは会社に行かなかったんですか。
　　　　**Kinou wa kaisha ni ikanakatta n desu ka.**
　　 B: (　　　　) 休んでしまいました。
　　　　(　　　　) **yasunde shimaimashita.**

(6) A: 風邪をひいたんじゃありませんか。
**Kaze o hiita n ja arimasen ka.**
B: （　　　　） ひいてしまったようです。せきが出るんです。
（　　　　） **hiite shimatta you desu. Seki ga deru n desu.**
(7) A: あなた、このごろちょっと太ったんじゃない？
**Anata, konogoro chotto futotta n ja nai?**
B: （　　　　） ちょっと太ったみたい。
（　　　　） **chotto futotta mitai.**

⇨ 32.1.3

**3** ⋆⋆ You want to get a part-time job, so you called an English language school. The following are the answers you heard. What kind of questions did you ask?

[対象 **taishou** 'target (students)'; 時給 **jikyuu** 'hourly pay']

(1) あなた：＿＿＿＿＿＿＿＿＿＿＿＿＿＿＿＿＿＿＿＿。
学院：　いいえ、対象は小学生ですが。
(2) あなた：＿＿＿＿＿＿＿＿＿＿＿＿＿＿＿＿＿＿＿＿。
学院：　いいえ、教えた経験はなくても大丈夫です。
(3) あなた：＿＿＿＿＿＿＿＿＿＿＿＿＿＿＿＿＿＿＿＿。
学院：　一週間に三時間ぐらいです。
(4) あなた：＿＿＿＿＿＿＿＿＿＿＿＿＿＿＿＿＿＿＿＿。
学院：　時給は一時間三千円ぐらいです。
(5) あなた：＿＿＿＿＿＿＿＿＿＿＿＿＿＿＿＿＿＿＿＿。
学院：　来週から始めてもらいたいんですが。

(1) Anata: ＿＿＿＿＿＿＿＿＿＿＿＿＿＿＿＿＿＿。
Gakuin: Iie, taishou wa shougakusei desu ga.
(2) Anata: ＿＿＿＿＿＿＿＿＿＿＿＿＿＿＿＿＿＿。
Gakuin: Iie, oshieta keiken wa nakutemo daijoubu desu.
(3) Anata: ＿＿＿＿＿＿＿＿＿＿＿＿＿＿＿＿＿＿。
Gakuin: Isshuukan ni sanjikan gurai desu.
(4) Anata: ＿＿＿＿＿＿＿＿＿＿＿＿＿＿＿＿＿＿。
Gakuin: Jikyuu wa ichijikan sanzen en gurai desu.
(5) Anata: ＿＿＿＿＿＿＿＿＿＿＿＿＿＿＿＿＿＿。
Gakuin: Raishuu kara hajimete moraitai n desu ga.

⇨ 32.2, 44, 52.1

**4** ⋆⋆ You want to find out what your friend Keiko did during the spring break. Ask the following questions. You and Keiko are good friends.

(a) How the spring break was:
(b) Whether she went anywhere:
(c) Whether she went alone or with someone:
(d) Whether she went by Shinkansen:
(e) How much the ticket was:
(f) How long the trip was:
(g) Whether she stayed at a Japanese inn:
(h) How much it was per night:

⇨ 4.3, 4.4, 32.1.1, 32.2

# 33
# Reporting

1 * Change the direct quotations into indirect quotations in the appropriate forms.

① 恵子は（「大阪に出張に行きます」）と言っていました。
   **Keiko wa ('Oosaka ni shutchou ni ikimasu') to itte imashita.**
② 課長に（「明日までに書類を見ておいてください」）と言われました。
   **Kachou ni ('Ashita made ni shorui o mite oite kudasai') to iwaremashita.**
③ カナダ人の友達は（「英語を教えてあげます」）と言いました。
   **Kanada-jin no tomodachi wa ('Eigo o oshiete agemasu') to iimashita.**
④ 新聞によると（「首相は中国を訪問します」）そうです。
   **Shinbun ni yoruto ('Shushou wa Chuugoku o hoomon shimasu')
   sou desu.**
⑤ ホストファミリーのお母さんに（「どんな食べ物が好きですか」）と聞かれた。
   **Hosuto famirii no o-kaasan ni ('Donna tabemono ga suki desu ka')
   to kikareta.**
⑥ 友達に（「京都に行ったことがありますか」）聞きました。
   **Tomodachi ni ('Kyouto ni itta koto ga arimasu ka') kikimashita.**
⑦ 両親に（「勉強しなさい」）とよく言われた。
   **Ryoushin ni ('Benkyou shinasai') to yoku iwareta.**
⑧ ルームメイトに（「静かにしてください」）ように頼んだ。
   **Ruumumeeto ni ('Shizuka ni shite kudasai') you ni tanonda.**
⑨ 先生に（「授業中は携帯電話を使わないでください」）ように注意された。
   **Sensei ni ('Jugyou-chuu wa keitai denwa o tsukawanaide kudasai')
   you ni chuui sareta.**

⇨ 12.1, 13.2.1, 33.2, 33.3, 33.4.2

2 ** The following is a conversation between you and a detective (**keiji**). Write 4–5 sentences about it in your diary. The first sentence is given as an example.

[強盗 **goutou** 'robbery'; 聞き込み **kiki-komi** 'information gathering, legwork';
犯人 **hannin** 'perpetrator']

刑事：　きのうご近所で強盗があったので、聞き込みをしているんですが、きのう
　　　　は家におられましたか。
あなた：はい、おりました。
刑事：　何か音を聞きませんでしたか。あるいは、変な人を見かけたとか。
あなた：いいえ、別に変わったことはありませんでした。
刑事：　そうですか。まだ犯人が見つかっていないので、十分に注意をしてください。

Keiji:    Kinou go-kinjo de goutou ga atta node, kikikomi o shite iru n
           desu ga, kinou wa ie ni oraremashita ka.
Anata:   Hai, orimashita.
Keiji:    Nanika oto o kikimasendeshita ka. Aruiwa, henna hito o
           mikaketa toka.
Anata:   Iie, betsuni kawatta koto wa arimasendeshita.
Keiji:    Sou desu ka. Mada hannin ga mitsukatte inai node, juubun ni
           chuui o shite kudasai.

---

三月八日（水）雨のち曇り
きのう近所で強盗事件があったそうだ。それで、

**Sangatsu youka (sui) Ame nochi kumori**
**Kinou kinjo de goutou jiken ga atta sou da. Sorede,**

---

⇨   33.2, 33.3, 33.4

**3** ⋆

You are looking after your friend Ichiro's house while he is away. You will be
staying at his house. His instructions to you follow below. Tell your other
friend what you were asked to do or not to do, using verbs such as
**tanomareru** 'to be asked' or **iwareru** 'to be told.'

（例：〜ように頼まれた、〜ように言われた、Vてくれと頼まれた）

① 犬を毎日散歩させてください。
   **Inu o mainichi sanpo sasete kudasai.**
② 私の部屋には入らないでください。
   **Watashi no heya ni wa hairanaide kudasai.**
③ 何かあったら携帯に電話してください。
   **Nanika attara keitai ni denwa shite kudasai.**
④ まどを閉めて出かけてください。
   **Mado o shimete dekakete kudasai.**
⑤ 指定日にごみを出してください。
   **Shiteibi ni gomi o dashite kudasai.**

⇨   33.4

# 34
# Asking and giving personal information

1 ★ At a party Carol, who is 20 years old, met Yoshiko, who is in her mid-30s. Complete the following conversation.

よし子：　(1)＿＿＿＿＿＿＿＿＿。阿部よし子 (2)＿＿＿＿＿＿＿＿＿＿。
キャロル：　(3)＿＿＿＿＿＿＿＿＿。キャロル・ジョーンズ (4)＿＿＿＿＿＿＿＿＿。
　　　　　どうぞよろしく。
よし子：　キャロルさんは (5)＿＿＿＿＿＿＿＿＿。
キャロル：　オーストラリアのシドニーです。
よし子：　ああ、いいところですね。今 (6)＿＿＿＿＿＿＿＿＿。
キャロル：　はい、大学四年生です。六ヵ月間東京の〇〇電気という会社でインターンをすることになって、先週日本に来ました。
よし子：　そうですか。じゃあ大学では工学を (7)＿＿＿＿＿＿＿＿＿。
キャロル：　いいえ、(8)＿＿＿＿＿＿＿＿＿は経済なので、事務関係の仕事だと思います。よし子さんは (9)＿＿＿＿＿＿＿＿＿。
よし子：　私は雑誌の編集の仕事をしています。
キャロル：　そうですか。面白そうですね。(10)＿＿＿＿＿＿＿＿＿。
よし子：　はい、一人います。
キャロル：　(11)＿＿＿＿＿＿＿＿＿＿＿＿。
よし子：　五歳になります。
キャロル：　じゃあ、仕事と家庭と両方で大変ですね。
よし子：　まあ、何とかやってます。キャロルさんは

　　　　　(12)＿＿＿＿＿＿＿＿＿。
キャロル：　はい、姉が二人います。私が日本にいる間に遊びに来てくれるはずです。
よし子：　それは楽しみですね。ところで、キャロルさん

　　　　　(13)＿＿＿＿＿＿＿＿＿。
キャロル：　私はテニスをするのが好きなんです。
よし子：　私もテニスが大好きなんですよ。今度一度いっしょにやりませんか。
キャロル：　ええ、(14)＿＿＿＿＿＿＿＿＿。

**Yoshiko:**　(1)＿＿＿＿＿＿＿＿＿. Abe Yoshiko (2)＿＿＿＿＿＿＿＿＿.
**Kyaroru:**　(3)＿＿＿＿＿＿＿＿＿. Kyaroru Joonzu (4)＿＿＿＿＿＿＿＿＿. **Douzo yoroshiku.**
**Yoshiko:**　Kyaroru-san wa (5)＿＿＿＿＿＿＿＿＿.
**Kyaroru:**　Oosutoraria no shidonii desu.
**Yoshiko:**　Aa, ii tokoro desu ne. Ima (6)＿＿＿＿＿＿＿＿＿.
**Kyaroru:**　Hai, daigaku yonensei desu. Rokkagetsukan Toukyou no 〇〇Denki to iu kaisha de intaan o suru koto ni natte, senshuu Nihon ni kimashita.

| | |
|---|---|
| Yoshiko: | Sou desu ka. Jaa daigaku de wa kougaku o (7)_____. |
| Kyaroru: | Iie, (8)_____ wa keizai na node, jimu kankei no shigoto da to omoimasu. Yoshiko-san wa (9)_____. |
| Yoshiko: | Watashi wa zasshi no henshuu no shigoto o shite imasu. |
| Kyaroru: | Sou desu ka. Omoshiro-sou desu ne. (10)_____. |
| Yoshiko: | Hai, hitori imasu. |
| Kyaroru: | (11)_____。 |
| Yoshiko: | Gosai ni narimasu. |
| Kyaroru: | Jaa, shigoto to katei to ryouhou de taihen desu ne. |
| Yoshiko: | Maa, nantoka yattemasu. Kyaroru-san wa (12)_____. |
| Kyaroru: | Hai, ane ga futari imasu. Watashi ga Nihon ni iru aida ni asobi ni kite kureru hazu desu. |
| Yoshiko: | Sore wa tanoshimi desu ne. Tokorode, Kyaroru-san (13)_____ |
| Kyaroru: | Watashi wa tenisu o suru no ga suki na n desu. |
| Yoshiko: | Watashi mo tenisu ga daisuki na n desu yo. Kondo ichido issho ni yarimasen ka. |
| Kyaroru: | Ee, (14)_____. |

⇨ | 30.3, 34, 74.4.1

**2** ★

You are going to Japan to study and will stay with a Japanese family. To introduce yourself, write a letter which includes the following information. (Modify the model answer to fit your own situation.)

- Your name
- Year in school
- Your major
- Your nationality
- Where you were born
- Where you currently live
- Your family
- Your hobby

⇨ | 6.1, 6.2, 34

**3** ★★

The following is information about an applicant for a job. Answer the questions below about her.

| | |
|---|---|
| 氏名 | 山田花子（女） |
| 生年月日 | 昭和62年1月15日（満26才） |
| 現住所 | 神奈川県藤沢市海岸○○丁目○○番地 |
| 学歴 | 平成17年4月　南西大学経済学部入学 |
| | 平成21年3月　南西大学経済学部卒業 |
| 職歴 | 平成21年4月　平和銀行人事課入社 |
| | 現在に至る |
| 特技 | 日本舞踊 |
| 趣味 | 料理 |

(1) 山田花子さんはいつ生まれましたか。
**Yamada Hanako-san wa itsu umaremashita ka.**
(2) 山田さんはどこに住んでいますか。
**Yamada-san wa doko ni sunde imasu ka.**
(3) 大学を卒業したのは何年ですか。
**Daigaku o sotsugyou shita no wa nannen desu ka.**
(4) 大学で何を専攻しましたか。
**Daigaku de nani o senkou shimashita ka.**
(5) 今何をしていますか。
**Ima nani o shite imasu ka.**
(6) 山田さんは何をするのが好きですか。
**Yamada-san wa nani o suru no ga suki desu ka.**
(7) 山田さんは何をするのが上手ですか。
**Yamada-san wa nani o suru no ga jouzu desu ka.**

⇨ | 34, 62

# 35
# Identifying

**1 ★** You are playing golf with your business friends Ms Kimura and Mr Taniguchi, who are meeting each other for the first time. Choose appropriate phrases in the dialogue. Either or both choices may be correct.

[初心者 **shoshinsha** 'beginner'; また謙遜ばかり **Mata kenson bakari** 'You're being modest as usual']

あなた： 谷口さん、【① これ・こちら】は木村さんです。
木村： はじめまして。木村恵美子と【② 言います・申します】。どうぞよろしくお願いします。
谷口： トヨサン【③ の・で】谷口です。こちらこそよろしくお願いします。
あなた： 木村さんは実家が札幌（さっぽろ）【④ な・だ】そうですよ。
谷口： そうですか。私も北海道なんですよ。ところで【⑤ これ・ここ】はなかなかいいコースですねぇ。
木村： ええ、でも、難しそうですね。私、初心者【⑥ な・いる】ので、ちょっと心配ですけど …。
あなた： また謙遜ばかり。谷口さん、この【⑦ 人・かた】、実はすごく上手なんですよ。あ、それ、新しいクラブ【⑧ です・あります】ね。
谷口： え？まあ …。

Anata: Taniguchi-san, 【① kore · kochira】 wa Kimura-san desu.
Kimura: Hajimemashite. Kimura Emiko to 【② iimasu · moushimasu】 Douzo yoroshiku o-negai shimasu.
Taniguchi: Toyosan 【③ no · de】 Taniguchi desu. Kochira koso yoroshiku o-negai shimasu.
Anata: Kimura-san wa jikka ga Sapporo 【④ na · da】 sou desu yo.
Taniguchi: Sou desu ka. Watashi mo Hokkaidou na n desu yo. Tokoro de 【⑤ kore · koko】 wa nakanaka ii koosu desu nee.
Kimura: Ee, demo, muzukashi-sou desu ne. Watashi, shoshin-sha 【⑥ na · iru】 node, chotto shinpai desu kedo ...
Anata: Mata kenson bakari! Taniguchi-san, kono 【⑦ hito · kata】, jitsu wa sugoku jouzu na n desu yo. A, sore, atarashii kurabu 【⑧ desu · arimasu】 ne?
Taniguchi: E? Maa ...

⇨ 7.2.1, 28.4, 30.3, 30.4, 35.2, 35.3

# 36
# Telling the time, dates, etc.

Your friend Miho e-mailed you the following message. Based on the contents of this email, complete the following dialogue between you and Yuki, another friend of yours.

[ささやかな **sasayaka na** 'small'; 参加 **sanka** 'to participate']

---

皆様、
　　毎日春らしい日が続いていますが、お変わりありませんか。
　　さて、もうすぐ私も30歳の誕生日を迎えることになりました。それで、親しい方を招いて、ささやかな誕生会を自宅で持ちたいと思っています。お忙しいこととは思いますが、是非おいで下さい。誕生日は六月三日ですが、誕生会は二日早い六月一日（土曜日）の6時を予定しています。
　　すみませんが、ご参加になれるかどうかメールでお返事いただけますか。久しぶりに会ってお話するのを楽しみにしています！

　　　　　　　　　　　　　　　　　　　　　　　　　　　　　　　美穂

---

Minasama,
　　Mainichi haru rashii hi ga tsuzuite imasu ga, o-kawari arimasen ka.
　　Sate, mousugu watashi mo sanjussai no tanjoubi o mukaeru koto ni narimashita. Sorede, shitashii kata o maneite, sasayaka na tanjou-kai o jitaku de mochitai to omotte imasu. O-isogashii koto to wa omoimasu ga, zehi o-ide kudasai. Tanjoubi wa rokugatsu mikka desu ga, tanjou-kai wa futsuka hayai rokugatsu tsuitachi (doyoubi) no rokuji o yotei shite imasu.
　　Sumimasen ga go-sanka ni nareru ka dou ka meeru de o-henji itadakemasu ka. Hisashiburi ni atte o-hanashi suru no o tanoshimi ni shite imasu!

　　　　　　　　　　　　　　　　　　　　　　　　　　　　　　　Miho

[The following day you meet your friend Yuki, who also knows Miho.]

あなた： きのう、久しぶりに美穂からメールがあったよ。
ゆき： へえ。何だって？
あなた： ①_____ って。
ゆき： え、本当？30歳になるの？誕生日はいつ？
あなた： ②_____。
ゆき： あ、そう。何かお祝いするの？
あなた： うん、美穂の家で ③_____ らしい。
　　　　 ねえ、ゆきも一緒に行かない？
ゆき： え？いつ？
あなた： ④_____。
ゆき： それって、何曜日？
あなた： ⑤_____。会社、休みでしょう？
ゆき： うん、行ってもいいけど。
あなた： じゃあ、美穂に聞いてみるね。

Anana: Kinou, hisashiburi ni Miho kara meeru ga atta yo.
Yuki: Hee. Nan da tte?
Anata: ①_____ tte.
Yuki: E, honto? Sanjussai ni naru no? Tanjoubi wa itsu?
Anata: ②_____.
Yuki: A, sou. Nani ka o-iwai suru no?
Anata: Un, Miho no uchi de ③_____ rashii.
　　　　 Nee, Yuki mo issho ni ikanai?
Yuki: E? Itsu?
Anata: ④_____.
Yuki: Sorette, nanyoubi?
Anata: ⑤_____. Kaisha, yasumi deshou?
Yuki: Un, itte mo ii kedo.
Anata: Jaa, Miho ni kiite miru ne.

⇨ 6, 26.2, 32.2, 36.2

**2** ★★ Today is March the 3ʳᵈ. Your friend invites you to a movie. Check your schedule below and complete the following conversation. Accept her/his invitation if you are available for the time suggested. Ask her/him a couple of questions as well.

| 3/1 月<br>getsu | 3/2 火<br>ka | 3/3 水<br>sui<br>レポート<br>repooto | 3/4 木<br>moku | 3/5 金<br>kin | 3/6 土<br>do<br>母来る<br>haha<br>kuru | 3/7 日<br>nichi<br>アルバイト<br>arubaito<br>3:00~10:00 |
|---|---|---|---|---|---|---|
| 3/8 月<br>getsu<br>面接<br>mensetsu | 3/9 火<br>ka<br>試験<br>shiken | 3/10 水<br>sui | 3/11 木<br>moku | 3/12 金<br>kin | 3/13 土<br>do<br>アルバイト<br>arubaito<br>12:00~5:00 | 3/14 日<br>nichi |

| 友達： | 今週の土曜日、映画、見に行かない？ |
|---|---|
| あなた： | 土曜日？ ① _____。 |
| 友達： | じゃあ、日曜日は？ |
| あなた： | 日曜日は ② _____。 |
| 友達： | 何時から何時まで？ |
| あなた： | ③ _____。 |
| 友達： | じゃあ、来週の土曜日はどう？ |
| あなた： | ④ _____。 |
| 友達： | アルバイト、何時まで？ |
| あなた： | ⑤ _____。 |
| 友達： | じゃあ、バイトが終わってからは？ |
| あなた： | ⑥ _____。 |
| 友達： | 良かった！ |
| あなた： | ⑦ _____？ |
| 友達： | 7時15分に始まるみたい。 |
| あなた： | ⑧ _____？ |
| 友達： | そうだなあ …6時半はどう？駅の前で。 |

| Tomodachi: | Konshuu no doyoubi, eiga, mi ni ikanai? |
|---|---|
| Anata: | Doyoubi? ① _____. |
| Tomodachi: | Jaa, nichiyoubi wa? |
| Anata: | Nichiyoubi wa ② _____. |
| Tomodachi: | Nanji kara nanji made? |
| Anata: | ③ _____. |
| Tomodachi: | Jaa, raishuu no doyoubi wa dou? |
| Anata: | ④ _____. |
| Tomodachi: | Arubaito, nanji made? |
| Anata: | ⑤ _____. |
| Tomodachi: | Jaa, baito ga owatte kara wa? |
| Anata: | ⑥ _____. |
| Tomodachi: | Yokatta! |
| Anata: | ⑦ _____? |
| Tomodachi: | Shichi-ji juugo-fun ni hajimaru mitai. |
| Anata: | ⑧ _____? |
| Tomodachi: | Sou da naa . . . Rokuji han wa dou? Eki no mae de. |

⇨ 6, 32.2, 36.1, 36.2

# 37
# Describing people, places, states and conditions

★ Paying attention to the context, write a question that would elicit each response below.

(A)
[The class is finished and students are gathering their things to leave the room.]

先生 : ①_____。
学生 : いいえ、それは私の本です。リンさんのじゃないです。
先生 : ②_____。
学生 : リンさんのはこれだと思います。

**Sensei:** ①_____.
**Gakusei:** Iie, sore wa watashi no hon desu. Rin-san no ja nai desu.
**Sensei:** ②_____.
**Gakusei:** Rin-san no wa kore da to omoimasu.

(B)
You just got off the airport bus from Narita to Shinjuku. Stop at the **kouban** ('police box') for directions.

あなた : すみません、①_____。
おまわりさん : 新宿ホテルですか？えーと、新宿ホテルは…あ、あの赤い建物です。
あなた : あそこに大きい建物がありますよね。
　　　　　②_____。
おまわりさん : ああ、あれは郵便局です。
あなた : ありがとうございました。

**Anata:** Sumimasen, ①_____.
**O-mawari-san:** Shinjuku Hoteru desu ka? Eeto, Shinjuku Hoteru wa . . . A, ano akai tatemono desu.
**Anata:** Asoko ni ookii tatemono ga arimasu yo ne.
②_____.
**O-mawari-san:** Aa, are wa yuubinkyoku desu.
**Anata:** Arigatou gozaimashita.

(C)

[Ms Honda and Ms Kawasaki have stopped for coffee after a PTA meeting.]

本田：　　あ～あ、今日の集まりも疲れましたねぇ。ところで、
　　　　　① ＿＿＿＿＿＿＿＿＿＿＿＿＿＿＿＿＿＿＿＿＿＿＿。

川崎：　　私の出身は青森です。　（出身 'where one is from'）

本田：　　そうですか。② ＿＿＿＿＿＿＿＿＿＿＿＿＿＿＿＿＿＿＿。

川崎：　　ちょっと寒いけど、いい所ですよ。

本田：　　③ ＿＿＿＿＿＿＿＿＿＿＿＿＿＿＿＿＿＿＿＿＿＿＿。

川崎：　　いえ、最近は忙しくて、あまり帰れないんです。あ、でも、去年のお
　　　　　正月は家族で④ ＿＿＿＿＿＿＿＿＿＿＿＿＿＿＿＿＿＿＿＿＿。

**Honda:**　Aaa, kyou no atsumari mo tsukaremashita nee. Tokoro de,
① ＿＿＿＿＿＿＿＿＿＿＿＿＿＿＿＿＿＿＿＿＿＿＿.

**Kawasaki:**　Watashi no shusshin wa Aomori desu. (**shusshin** 'where one is from')

**Honda:**　Sou desu ka. ② ＿＿＿＿＿＿＿＿＿＿＿＿＿＿＿＿＿＿＿＿.

**Kawasaki:**　Chotto samui kedo, ii tokoro desu yo.

**Honda:**　③ ＿＿＿＿＿＿＿＿＿＿＿＿＿＿＿＿＿＿＿＿＿.

**Kawasaki:**　Ie, saikin wa isogashikute, amari kaerenai n desu. A, demo,
kyonen no o-shougatsu wa kazoku de ④ ＿＿＿＿＿＿＿＿＿＿＿.

(D)

You just got off the train in Sendai, and realize that you left your purse on the train. Go to the **o-wasure-mono sentaa** ('lost and found').

あなた：　　あのう、バッグを電車に忘れちゃったんですけど … 。

駅の人：　　え？そうですか。① ＿＿＿＿＿＿＿＿＿＿＿＿＿＿＿＿＿。

あなた：　　いえ、そんなに大きくないです。このぐらいです。

駅の人：　　② ＿＿＿＿＿＿＿＿＿＿＿＿＿＿＿＿＿＿＿。

あなた：　　茶色です。

駅の人：　　うーん、③ ＿＿＿＿＿＿＿＿＿＿＿＿＿＿＿＿。

あなた：　　筒型なんですけど。（つつがた 'cylindrical'）

駅の人：　　④ ＿＿＿＿＿＿＿＿＿＿＿＿＿＿＿＿。

あなた：　　いえ、ビニールです。（ビニール 'vinyl'）

駅の人：　　じゃ、ここに名前と住所とケータイの番号を書いて下さい。

**Anata:**　Anou, baggu o densha ni wasurechatta n desu kedo . . .

**Eki-in:**　E? Sou desu ka. ① ＿＿＿＿＿＿＿＿＿＿＿＿＿＿＿＿.

**Anata:**　Ie, sonna ni ookiku nai desu. Kono gurai desu.

**Eki-in:**　② ＿＿＿＿＿＿＿＿＿＿＿＿＿＿＿＿＿＿.

**Anata:**　Cha-iro desu.

**Eki-in:**　Uun, ③ ＿＿＿＿＿＿＿＿＿＿＿＿＿.

**Anata:**　Tsutsu-gata na n desu kedo. (**tsutsu-gata** 'cylindrical')

**Eki-in:**　④ ＿＿＿＿＿＿＿＿＿＿＿＿＿＿＿.

**Anata:**　Ie, biniiru desu. (**biniiru** 'vinyl')

**Eki-in:**　Ja, koko ni namae to juusho to keetai no bangou o kaite
kudasai.

(E)

A crime suspect (**yougisha**) is being interrogated by a detective (**keiji**).

刑事　　： ゆうべの11時ごろ ① _____。
容疑者　： 家でテレビを見ていました。
刑事　　： じゃ、② _____ んですね。
容疑者　： はい、出かけませんでした。
刑事　　： テレビで ③ _____ んですか。
容疑者　： オリンピックの水泳を見ていました。
刑事　　： 本当ですか。近所の人は一晩中電気が消えていたと言ってますよ。
容疑者　： 電気を消して、見ていたんです！
刑事　　： なるほど。じゃ、水泳では ④ _____。
容疑者　： いや、あのう、そのう、アメリカのチームが勝ったと思いますけど…。
刑事　　： ⑤ _____ んですか。
容疑者　： はい、よく覚えていません。途中で寝てしまったので。
刑事　　： ふ～ん。じゃ、車は ⑥ _____。
容疑者　： 家の前に止めてありました。
刑事　　： 近所の人は車がいつもの所になかったと言うんですがねぇ。
　　　　　 車を ⑦ _____ とか？
容疑者　： そうです！昨日は妹に貸してたんです。本当です！

Keiji:      Yuube no juuichiji goro ① _____.
Yougisha:   Ie de terebi o mite imashita.
Keiji:      Ja, ② _____ n desu ne?
Yougisha:   Hai, dekakemasendeshita.
Keiji:      Terebi de ③ _____ n desu ka.
Yougisha:   Orinpikku no suiei o mite imashita.
Keiji:      Hontou desu ka. Kinjo no hito wa hitoban-juu denki ga kiete
            ita to itte masu yo.
Yougisha:   Denki o keshite, mite ita n desu!
Keiji:      Naruhodo. Ja, suiei de wa ④ _____.
Yougisha:   Iya, anou, sonou, Amerika no chiimu ga katta to omoimasu
            kedo . . .
Keiji:      ⑤ _____ n desu ka.
Yougisha:   Hai, yoku oboete imasen. Tochuu de nete shimatta node.
Keiji:      Fuun. Ja, kuruma wa ⑥ _____.
Yougisha:   Ie no mae ni tomete arimashita.
Keiji:      Kinjo no hito wa kuruma ga itsumo no tokoro ni nakatta to
            iu n desu ga nee. Kuruma o ⑦ _____
            toka?
Yougisha:   Sou desu! Kinou wa imouto ni kashite ta n desu. Hontou
            desu!

⇨   12, 37.2~11

**2** ★  You recently moved to the area, and are attending a neighborhood association meeting with Kikuchi-san. Looking at the picture, fill in the blanks with appropriate phrases. Be sure to include particles.

田中
Tanaka

山田
Yamada

佐藤
Sato

鈴木
Suzuki

あなた： ずいぶん人が来てますねぇ。あ、あの、
① _____ 人はだれですか。

菊池： あの人は田中さんです。着物ってやっぱりいいですねぇ。

あなた： ええ、本当に。ぼうし ② _____ 人もいま
すね。あの、かみ ③ _____ 人。あの人は？

菊池： ああ、あれは山田さんです。シンガーソングライターらしいですよ。

あなた は〜ん。鈴木さんって ④ _____ 人ですか。
山田さんと ⑤ _____ 人ですか。

菊池： いや、あれは佐藤さんです。鈴木さんはあの、めがね
⑥ _____ 人です。

あなた： ああ、あの、ネクタイ ⑦ _____ て、
めがね ⑧ _____ 人ですね。

菊池： ええ、そうです。

あなた： あ、菊池さん、顔にケチャップ ⑨ _____
ますよ。

菊池： え？あ、ほんとだ。ハハハ …

Anata: **Zuibun hito ga kite masu nee. A, ano,**
① _____ **hito wa dare desu ka.**

Kikuchi: **Ano hito wa Tanaka-san desu. Kimono tte yappari ii desu nee.**

Anata: **Ee, hontou ni. Boushi** ② _____ **hito mo
imasu ne. Ano, kami** ③ _____ **hito.
Ano hito wa?**

Kikuchi: **Aa, are wa Yamada-san desu. Shingaa songu raitaa rashii
desu yo.**

Anata: **Haan. Suzuki-san tte** ④ _____ **desu ka.
Yamada-san to** ⑤ _____ **hito desu ka.**

Kikuchi: **Iya, are wa Satou-san desu. Suzuki-san wa ano, megane**
⑥ _____ **hito desu.**

Anata: **Aa, ano, nekutai** ⑦ _____ **te, megane**
⑧ _____ **hito desu ne.**

Kikuchi: **Ee, sou desu.**

Anata: **A, Kikuchi-san, kao ni kechappu** ⑨ _____
**masu yo.**

Kikuchi: **E? A, honto da. Hahaha . . .**

⇨ 19.2.1, 37.1, 37.6, 37.11

**3** ★★★ The following is an e-mail message from a Japanese man to his wife. Mark the following descriptions true (○) or false (×).

幸子、元気でやってるかい？

　小生、ニューヨークに来て早4週間、こちらの生活にもだいぶ慣れて来た。仕事は思ったより大変だが、来週から長期滞在用ホテルに移るので、少し落ち着けると思う。

　ニューヨークは「眠らない街」と呼ばれるらしいが、実に活気に満ちている。世界の商業、文化、ファッション、そして国際政治にまで多大な影響を及ぼす都市として、確かに唯一無二だと言える。

　ニューヨークの街を歩いていて驚くのは、これほどの大都市でありながら、緑が多いことだ。セントラルパークはとてつもない広さで、一歩中に入ると、都会の喧噪を忘れさせてくれる。この街は美術館や博物館が多いので、退屈することはなさそうだ。メトロポリタン美術館はいつもにぎわっているが、個人的には近代美術館が一番気に入っている。君に見せたい絵や彫刻もたくさんある。

　そちらは一人で子供達の面倒をみていて大変だろうが、無理をしないように。体にはくれぐれも気を付けてほしい。

またみんなとスカイプをするのを楽しみにしている。

それでは、

秀樹拝

Sachiko, genki de yatte ru kai?

　Shousei, Nyuuyooku ni kite haya yonshuukan, kochira no seikatsu ni mo daibu narete kita. Shigoto wa omotta yori taihen da ga, raishuu kara chouki taizai-you hoteru ni utsuru node, sukoshi ochitsukeru to omou.

　Nyuuyooku wa 'Nemuranai machi' to yobareru rashii ga, jitsu ni kakki ni michite iru. Sekai no shougyou, bunka, fasshon, soshite kokusai seiji ni made tadai na eikyou o oyobosu toshi to shite, tashika ni yuiitsu muni da to ieru.

　Nyuuyooku no machi o aruite ite odoroku no wa, kore hodo no dai-toshi de ari nagara, midori ga ooi koto da. Sentoraru Paaku wa totetsu mo nai hirosa de, ippo naka ni hairu to, tokai no kensou o wasuresasete kureru. Kono machi wa bijutsukan ya hakubutsukan ga ooi node, taikutsu suru koto wa nasa-sou da. Metoroporitan Bijutsukan wa itsumo nigiwatte iru ga, kojin-teki ni wa Kindai Bijutsukan ga ichiban ki ni itte iru. Kimi ni misetai e ya choukoku mo takusan aru.

　Sochira wa hitori de kodomo-tachi no mendou o mite ite taihen darou ga, muri o shinai you ni. Karada ni wa kuregure mo ki o tsukete hoshii.

Mata minna to Sukaipu o suru no o tanoshimi ni shite iru.

Sore dewa,

Hideki hai

a. ( ) 秀樹は約1ヶ月前にニューヨークに着いた。
b. ( ) 現在、長期滞在用ホテルに暮らしている。
c. ( ) 日本を出る前は、仕事が今ほど大変になるとは想像していなかった。
d. ( ) 秀樹はセントラルパークが気に入っている。
e. ( ) ニューヨークで一番好きな美術館はメトロポリタン美術館だ。
f. ( ) もしニューヨークに美術館や博物館がこれほどなかったら、秀樹はたぶん
　　　　退屈するだろうと思う。
g. ( ) 秀樹は、ニューヨークは商業や文化などの分野で世界的に大きい影響力を
　　　　持っているユニークな街だという考えに同感だ。
h. ( ) 秀樹は家族とは前にスカイプをしたことがない。

a. ( ) Hideki wa yaku ikkagetsu mae ni Nyuuyooku ni tsuita.
b. ( ) Genzai, chouki taizai you hoteru ni kurashite iru.
c. ( ) Nihon o deru mae wa, shigoto ga ima hodo taihen ni naru to wa
　　　　souzou shite inakatta.
d. ( ) Hideki wa Sentoraru Paaku ga ki ni itte iru.
e. ( ) Nyuuyooku de ichiban suki na bijutsukan wa Metoroporitan
　　　　Bijutsukan da.
f. ( ) Moshi Nyuuyooku ni bijutsukan ya hakubutsukan ga kore hodo
　　　　nakattara, Hideki wa tabun taikutsu suru darou to omou.
g. ( ) Hideki wa, Nyuuyooku wa shougyou ya bunka nado no bun'ya de
　　　　sekaiteki ni ookii eikyouryoku o motte iru yuniiku na machi da to
　　　　iu kangae ni doukan da.
h. ( ) Hideki wa kazoku to wa mae ni Sukaipu o shita koto ga nai.

⇨ 37.2

# 38
# Comparisons

**1** A colleague, Mr Watanabe, arrived from Japan six months ago with his family. It is December now, and you live in Michigan.

(A)

[ゆううつ **yuuutsu** 'depressing'; 地球温暖化 **chikyuu ondanka** 'global warming']

| | |
|---|---|
| 渡辺： | 12月に入ったら、寒くなりましたねぇ。 |
| あなた： | ええ、でも、【① 1月はもっと寒いです・1月の方が寒いです】よ。 |
| 渡辺： | そうでしょうねぇ。ミシガンとミネソタではどっちのほう【② が・は】寒いですか。 |
| あなた： | あ、ミネソタの方【③ が・は】ずっと寒いです。でも、あっちは晴れの日が多いので、ミシガン【④ より・ほど】ゆううつにならないそうです。 |
| 渡辺： | そうなんですか … 。 |
| あなた： | ええ、でも、ミシガンでも地球温暖化のせいか、最近は昔【⑤ より・ほど】雪が少なくなりました。 |

| | |
|---|---|
| Watanabe: | Juunigatsu ni haittara, samuku narimashita nee. |
| Anata: | Ee, demo, 【① ichigatsu wa motto samui desu · ichigatsu no hou ga samui desu】 yo. |
| Watanabe: | Sou deshou nee. Mishigan to Minesota de wa dotchi no hou 【② ga · wa】 samui desu ka. |
| Anata: | A, Minesota no hou 【③ ga · wa】 zutto samui desu. Demo, atchi wa hare no hi ga ooi node, Mishigan 【④ yori · hodo】 yuuutsu ni naranai sou desu. |
| Watanabe: | Sou na n desu ka... |
| Anata: | Ee, demo, Mishigan demo chikyuu ondanka no sei ka, saikin wa mukashi 【⑤ yori · hodo】 yuki ga sukunaku narimashita. |

⇨ 38.1

(B)

[迷惑をかける **meiwaku o kakeru** 'to make oneself OR be a nuisance']

| | |
|---|---|
| あなた： | アメリカは暮らしにくいと思いますか。 |
| 渡辺： | いえ、いえ、いい所ですよ。他人に迷惑【① まで・さえ】かけなければ、自由な生き方ができるし、古い考え【② に・で】しばられなくていいし。アメリカも日本も、どちら【③ か・も】便利な点・不便な点があって、何とも言えませんけどねぇ。 |
| あなた： | そうですねぇ。渡辺さんは今までアメリカ国内、あちこち旅行していらっしゃるようですけど、どこ【④ が・は】一番面白いと思いましたか。 |
| 渡辺： | そうですねぇ。私にとってはどこ【⑤ か・も】みんな面白いです。 |

Anata: Amerika wa kurashi nikui to omoimasu ka.
Watanabe: Ie, ie, ii tokoro desu yo. Tanin ni meiwaku 【① made · sae】 kakenakereba, jiyuu na ikikata ga dekiru shi, furui kangae 【② ni · de】 shibararenakute ii shi. Amerika mo Nihon mo, dochira 【③ ka · mo】 benri na ten, fuben na ten ga atte, nan to mo iemasen kedo nee.
Anata: Sou desu nee. Watanabe-san wa ima made Amerika kokunai achikochi ryokou shite irassharu you desu kedo, doko 【④ ga · wa】 ichiban omoshiroi to omoimashita ka.
Watanabe: Sou desu nee. Watashi ni totte wa doko 【⑤ ka · mo】 minna omoshiroi desu.

⇨ 21.4.1, 38.3, 55.4.1


(C)
あなた： ご家族のみなさんも、こちらに慣れたようですか。
渡辺： はい、おかげさまで。娘は私【① に・で】似て、スポーツが好きなので、家にいないことが多いんです。息子は娘【② から・と】違って、外に出たがらなくて困っていますが。で、妻は他の日本人の奥さん方【③ から・と】同じように、ケーキ作りを楽しんでいるようですね。
あなた： そうですか。今度みんなで一緒にどこかに行きましょう。

Anata: Go-kazoku no minasan mo, kochira ni nareta you desu ka.
Watanabe: Hai, o-kage-sama de. Musume wa watashi 【① ni · de】 nite, supootsu ga suki na node, uchi ni inai koto ga ooi n desu. Musuko wa musume 【② kara · to】 chigatte, soto ni detagaranakute komatte imasu ga. De, tsuma wa hoka no Nihonjin no okusan-gata 【③ kara · to】 onaji you ni, keeki-zukuri o tanoshinde iru you desu ne.
Anata: Sou desu ka. Kondo minna de issho ni dokoka ni ikimashou.

⇨ 38.2, 39.1, 39.2

**2** ∗ Your friend is interested in renting an apartment. Compare the two apartments in terms of the five points mentioned below.

| しろがね荘 | メゾンマツカワ |
|---|---|
| • 築10年 ('10 years old') | • 新築！('newly built') |
| • 1LDK | • 地下鉄の駅から車で15分 |
| • JRの駅から歩いて10分 | • 一ヶ月14万8,000円 |
| • 家賃 月43,000円 | • 3LDK バス・トイレ付き |
| • ショッピングセンターまで車で30分 | • ショッピングセンターまで歩いて5分 |

| Shirogane-sou | Mezon Matsukawa |
|---|---|
| • Chiku juu nen ('10 years old') | • Shinchiku! ('newly built') |
| • Ichi LDK | • Chikatetsu no eki kara kuruma de juugofun |
| • JR no eki kara aruite juppun | • Ikkagetsu juuyonman hassen en |
| • Yachin tsuki yonman sanzen en. | • San LDK basu · toire-tsuki |
| • Shoppingu Sentaa made kuruma de sanjuppun | • Shoppingu Sentaa made aruite gofun |

Examples: Convenience to the shopping mall:

- ショッピングセンターまでは、メゾンマツカワからは歩いて5分ですが、
  しろがね荘からは車で30分かかります。
- メゾンマツカワのほうがしろがね荘より便利です。

- **Shoppingu Sentaa made wa, Mezon Matsukawa kara wa aruite gofun
  desu ga, Shirogane-sou kara wa kuruma de sanjuppun kakarimasu.**
- **Mezon Matsukawa no hou ga Shirogane-sou yori benri desu.**

(1) Distance from the station:

_____

(2) Apartment size:

_____

(3) Years since construction:

_____

(4) Rental fee:

_____

⇨ 38.1, 39

# 39
# Contrast

1 ★

You are looking for a car to buy. You made some notes comparing two cars A and B. Choose the appropriate phrase from each pair.

[中古 **chuuko** 'used'; 手頃 **tegoro** 'reasonable'; 距離 **kyori** 'distance'; 燃費 **nenpi** 'fuel efficiency'; 節約 **setsuyaku** 'save (on something)']

A車は新車だし、色も気に入っている。【① でも・したがって】値段がかなり高い。【② いっぽう・その結果】B車は中古だ【③ から・けど】値段は手頃だ。走行距離も100キロちょっとしかない。【④ しかし・その上】B車は燃費が悪いから、ガソリン代がかなりかかるだろう。【⑤ それゆえ・ぎゃくに】A車はハイブリッドだから、燃費が良くて、ガソリン代を節約できる。【⑥ それに・その反面】ナビもテレビもDVDも付いている。

**A-sha wa shinsha da shi, iro mo ki ni itte iru. 【① Demo · Shitagatte】 nedan ga kanari takai. 【② Ippou · Sono kekka】 B-sha wa chuuko da 【③ kara · kedo】 nedan wa tegoro da. Soukou kyori mo hyakkiro chotto shika nai. 【④ Shikashi · Sono ue】 B-sha wa nenpi ga warui kara, gasorin-dai ga kanari kakaru darou. 【⑤ Sore yue · Gyaku ni】 A-sha wa haiburiddo da kara, nenpi ga yokute, gasorin-dai o setsuyaku dekiru. 【⑥ Sore ni · Sono hanmen】 nabi mo terebi mo DVD mo tsuite iru.**

⇨ 22.5, 39.1, 39.2

2 ★

You are planning a vacation with your friend and you are in charge of finding accommodations. Using the information below, report to your friend by filling in the blanks with the appropriate conjunctions meaning 'but,' 'on the other hand,' etc.

|  | 値段<br>**nedan** | 場所<br>**basho** | プール<br>**puuru** | 温泉<br>**onsen** |
|---|---|---|---|---|
| ホテルA<br>**Hoteru A** | 25,000円<br>25,000 en | 駅から5分<br>eki kara gofun | 有り<br>ari | 有り<br>ari |
| ホテルB<br>**Hoteru B** | 5,000円<br>5,000 en | 駅から30分<br>eki kara sanjuppun | 無し<br>nashi | 有り<br>ari |
| ホテルC<br>**Hoteru C** | 4,000円<br>4,000 en | 海まで3分<br>umi made sanpun | 有り<br>ari | 無し<br>nashi |
| ホテルD<br>**Hoteru D** | 15,000円<br>15,000 en | 海まで0分<br>umi made zerofun | 無し<br>nashi | 無し<br>nashi |

**Contrast**

ホテルAは高い (1)＿＿＿＿、駅から近いし、プールや温泉もある。(2)＿＿＿＿、ホテルB は安い (3)＿＿＿＿、駅から遠いし、プールもない。(4)＿＿＿＿、温泉はある。ホテルCは 一番安くて、海にも近い (5)＿＿＿＿、温泉はない。(6)＿＿＿＿、プールはある。(7)＿＿＿＿、 ホテルDは高いし、プールも温泉もない (8)＿＿＿＿、目の前にビーチがある。

**Hoteru A wa takai** (1)＿＿＿＿, eki kara chikai shi, puuru ya onsen mo aru. (2)＿＿＿＿, hoteru B wa yasui (3)＿＿＿＿, eki kara tooi shi, puuru mo nai. (4)＿＿＿＿, onsen wa aru. Hoteru C wa ichiban yasukute, umi ni mo chikai (5)＿＿＿＿, onsen wa nai. (6)＿＿＿＿, puuru wa aru. (7)＿＿＿＿, hoteru D wa takai shi, puuru mo onsen mo nai (8)＿＿＿＿, me no mae ni biichi ga aru.

⇨ 22.5, 39.1, 39.2

# 40
# Location and distance

1 *

Having just arrived at a town she has never been to, Aoi stops by at a **kouban** (police box) inside the train station to ask for directions. Read the conversation below and identify what A–G on the map are in Japanese.

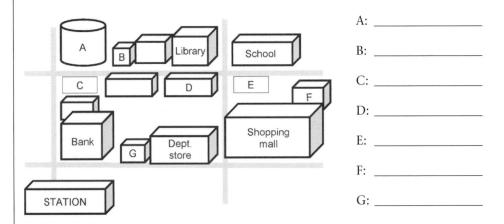

A: _____

B: _____

C: _____

D: _____

E: _____

F: _____

G: _____

[巡査 **junsa** 'policeman'; 市立 **shiritsu** 'municipal'; 交差点 **kousaten** 'intersection'; Xの手前 X **no temae** 'right before X'; 駐車場 **chuushajou** 'parking lot']

| 葵： | すみません、市立病院はどこにありますか。 |
| 巡査： | この道をまっすぐ行くと、次の交差点の手前に公園があります。市立病院は公園の先の丸い建物ですよ。 |
| 葵： | はい。あのう、花咲大学はどこでしょうか。 |
| 巡査： | 病院の隣に喫茶店があって、その近くに図書館があるんですが、花咲大学は図書館のすぐ前です。近くに学校や駐車場がありますから、すぐ分かりますよ。 |
| 葵： | はい。あ、それから、この近くにコンビニありますか。 |
| 巡査： | コンビニはこの銀行とデパートの間にもあるし、あのショッピングセンターの後ろにもありますよ。 |
| 葵： | はい、ありがとうございました。 |

| Aoi: | **Sumimasen, Shiritsu Byouin wa doko ni arimasu ka.** |
| Junsa: | **Kono michi o massugu iku to, tsugi no kousaten no temae ni kouen ga arimasu. Shiritsu Byouin wa kouen no saki no marui tatemono desu yo.** |
| Aoi: | **Hai. Anou, Hanasaka Daigaku wa doko deshou ka.** |

Location and distance

| Junsa: | Byouin no tonari ni kissaten ga atte, sono chikaku ni toshokan ga aru n desu ga, Hanasaka Daigaku wa toshokan no sugu mae desu. Chikaku ni gakkou ya chuushajou ga arimasu kara, sugu wakarimasu yo. |
| Aoi: | Hai. A, sorekara, kono chikaku ni konbini arimasu ka. |
| Junsa: | Konbini wa kono ginkou to depaato no aida ni mo aru shi, ano shoppingu sentaa no ushiro ni mo arimasu yo. |
| Aoi: | Hai, arigatou gozaimashita. |

⇨ 40.1, 40.2, 76.1

**2** *

Ken, a junior high school student, went to visit his friend Ryota one Sunday afternoon. Complete the following conversation in informal style. Note that **Pochi** is a common dog name, and **Tama** a common cat name.

| 賢： | ごめん下さい！僚太君いますか。 |
| 僚太の母： | あ、賢ちゃん。①＿＿＿＿＿＿＿＿＿＿＿＿＿＿＿ けど。 |
| | 'Ryota is in his room' |
| 賢： | あれ？今日は ②＿＿＿＿＿＿＿＿＿＿＿＿＿ の？ |
| | 'Pochi isn't (home)?' |
| 母： | え？③＿＿＿＿＿＿＿＿＿＿＿＿＿？ |
| | 'Isn't (he) under the couch?' |
| 賢： | あ、いる、いる。タマは？ |
| 母： | たぶん ④＿＿＿＿＿＿＿＿＿＿＿＿ と思う。 |
| | '(she) is on top of the refrigerator' |
| 僚太： | よう、賢。 |
| 賢： | ねえ、このボールどうしたの？買ったの？ |
| 僚太： | え？⑤＿＿＿＿＿＿＿＿＿＿＿＿？ |
| | 'where did you find it (Lit. where was (it))?' |
| 賢： | ⑥＿＿＿＿＿＿＿＿＿＿＿。 |
| | 'in the box over there' |

| Ken: | Gomen kudasai! Ryouta-kun imasu ka. |
| Ryouta no haha: | A, Ken-chan. ①＿＿＿＿＿＿＿＿＿＿＿ kedo. |
| | 'Ryota is in his room' |
| Ken: | Are? kyou wa ②＿＿＿＿＿＿＿＿＿ no? |
| | 'Pochi isn't (home)?' |
| Haha: | E? ③＿＿＿＿＿＿＿＿＿？ |
| | 'Isn't (he) under the couch?' |
| Ken: | A, iru, iru. Tama wa? |
| Haha: | Tabun ④＿＿＿＿＿＿＿＿＿ to omou. |
| | '(she) is on top of the refrigerator' |
| Ryouta: | You, Ken. |
| Ken: | Nee, kono booru dou shita no? Katta no? |
| Ryouta: | E? ⑤＿＿＿＿＿＿＿＿？ |
| | 'Where did you find it (Lit. Where was (it))?' |
| Ken: | ⑥＿＿＿＿＿＿＿＿. |
| | 'In the box over there' |

⇨ 40.1, 40.2

**3** ⋆ Choose an appropriate expression.

① 私のホストファミリーの家は駅から10分ぐらい【にあります・の所にあります】。
Watashino hosuto famirii no ie wa eki kara juppun gurai【ni arimasu・no tokoro ni arimasu】.

② 東京の大学までは毎日ちょうど1時間【かかります・の所にあります】。
Toukyou no daigaku made wa mainichi choudo ichi-jikan【kakarimasu・no tokoro ni arimasu】.

⇨ 40.3

**4** ⋆ Terry and her husband are staying in a hotel in Tokyo, and would like to visit the Ghibli Museum. Complete the following conversation between her and a receptionist in formal (**desu/masu**) style according to the cues provided.

テリー： すみません、ジブリ美術館に行きたいんですけど、ここから歩いて行けますか。

受付： そうですね、① _____ から、
'It's (Lit. there is) 5–6 km'
② _____ けど。
'(It)'ll take a little while'

テリー： そうですか。電車だと ③ _____ 。
'How long will it take?'

受付： 電車でしたら、すぐですよ。三鷹駅（みたかえき）からマイクロバスもありますし。でも、駅からは歩いても
④ _____ よ。
'It won't even take 10 minutes'

Terii: **Sumimasen, Ghibli Bijutsukan ni ikitai n desu kedo, koko kara aruite ikemasu ka.**

Uketsuke: **Sou desu ne,** ① _____ **kara,**
'It's (Lit. there is) 5–6 km'
② _____ **kedo.**
'(It)'ll take a little while'

Terii: **Sou desu ka. Densha da to** ③ _____ .
'How long will it take?'

Uketsuke: **Densha deshitara, sugu desu yo. Mitaka-eki kara maikuro basu mo arimasu shi. Demo, eki kara wa aruite mo**
④ _____ **yo.**
'It won't even take 10 minutes'

⇨ 40.3

# 41
# Possession

1 *

A group of people is discussing what they have that may be useful for an upcoming company party. Choose the appropriate item from the alternatives.

山田 ： うちに大きなスピーカー【① に・が・を】あります。
田中 ： 僕はステレオ【② に・が・を】持っています。ちょっと古いですけど。
森田 ： ステレオよりパソコンをスピーカーにつなげたほうがいいんじゃないでしょうか。うち【③ に・が・を】あるパソコンを持ってきますよ。
鈴木 ： あ、お願いします。いすやテーブルは会社の倉庫 (storage room) に【④ ある・もっている】から、あれを使いましょう。

Yamada: **Uchi ni ookina supiikaa 【① ni · ga · o】 arimasu.**
Tanaka: **Boku wa sutereo 【② ni · ga · o】 motte imasu. Chotto furui desu kedo.**
Morita: **Sutereo yori pasokon o supiikaa ni tsunageta hou ga ii n ja nai deshou ka. Uchi 【③ ni · ga · o】 aru pasokon o motte kimasu yo.**
Suzuki: **A, o-negai shimasu. Isu ya teeburu wa kaisha no souko ('storage room') ni 【④ aru · motte iru】 kara, are o tsukaimashou.**

⇨ 5.2.3, 40.1.1, 41.1

2 *

Close friends Michiko and Taro are talking about their families and pets. Choose the most appropriate phrase from the alternatives.

道子 ： 太郎君のうちって、3人家族だっけ？
太郎 ： うん、両親とぼくの3人。でも、ペットがたくさん【① ある・いる・かう】から、にぎやかだよ。
道子 ： へえ、どんなペットを【② もって・いて・かって】いるの？
太郎 ： ネコ2匹と、犬1匹と、うさぎ3匹。

Michiko: **Tarou-kun no uchi tte, sannin kazoku da kke?**
Tarou: **Un, ryoushin to boku no sannin. Demo, petto ga takusan 【① aru · iru · kau】 kara, nigiyaka da yo.**
Michiko: **Hee, donna petto o 【② motte · ite · katte】 iru no?**
Tarou: **Neko nihiki to, inu ippiki to, usagi sanbiki.**

⇨ 41.2

**3** •  Below are descriptions of an imaginary family. Fill in the blanks with the appropriate words in the informal style.

(a) 父は **Chichi wa** _____ (has short hair)
(b) 母は **Haha wa** _____ (has pretty hands)
(c) 姉は **Ane wa** _____ (has long legs)
(d) 弟は **Otouto wa** _____ (has a nice (lit. high) nose)
(e) 私は **Watashi wa** _____ (has a round face)
(f) ねこは **Neko wa** _____ (has big and blue eyes)

⇨  41.3

# 42
## Gifts

1 ★

Akiko is getting married and leaving her current job soon, so her colleagues had a farewell party for her. Below, she is telling her mother about the presents she received. Choose the appropriate phrase from the alternatives.

明子： お母さん、見て、こんなに【① あげちゃった・もらっちゃった】。
母： まあ、申し訳ないわねぇ。
明子： これは山田課長に【② いただいた・くださった】スカーフ。これはさち子達が【③ もらった・くれた】エプロン。料理の練習しなさいって。それから、このティーカップ、佐藤先輩が【④ いただいた・くださった】の。すてきでしょ？
母： ほんと。部長さんも何か【⑤ くださった・いただいた】の？
明子： 小森部長にはこのジュエリーボックスを【⑥ くださった・いただいた】の。
母： じゃ、皆さんに何かお返しを【⑦ やらなきゃ・さしあげなきゃ】ね。

Akiko: O-kaasan, mite, konna ni 【① agechatta · moratchatta】.
Haha: Maa, moushiwake nai wa nee.
Akiko: Kore wa Yamada-kachou ni 【② itadaita · kudasatta】 sukaafu. Kore wa Sachiko-tachi ga 【③ moratta · kureta】 epuron. Ryouri no renshuu shinasai tte. Sorekara, kono tii kappu, Satou-senpai ga 【④ itadaita · kudasatta】 no. Suteki desho?
Haha: Honto. Buchou-san mo nanika 【⑤ kudasatta · itadaita】 no?
Akiko: Komori-buchou ni wa kono juerii bokkusu o 【⑥ kudasatta · itadaita】 no.
Haha: Ja, minasan ni nanika o-kaeshi o 【⑦ yaranakya · sashiagenakya】 ne.

⇨ 12.7, 42.1, 42.2

2 ★★

A magazine is interviewing people about what gifts they have given or received for Father's Day. Express the interviewees' responses in Japanese.

女 **Onna 1:** I gave socks to my father.
女 **Onna 2:** I sent a tie to my father-in-law (義父 **gifu**).
男 **Otoko 1:** I didn't do anything, but my younger sister gave our father a homemade cake.
男 **Otoko 2:** I gave my parents vouchers for a hot-spring inn (温泉旅館の宿泊券 **onsen ryokan no shukuhaku-ken**).
男 **Otoko 3:** I received a golf club from my son.

⇨ 42.1, 42.2, 42.3

# 43
# Kind acts

1 ★ Choose the most appropriate expression in each context.

(1) Taro turned on the light for you when you were reading. You appreciated that.
   a.   太郎が電気をつけました。**Tarou ga denki o tsukemashita.**
   b.   太郎に電気をつけられました。**Tarou ni denki o tsukeraremashita.**
   c.   太郎が電気をつけてくれました。**Tarou ga denki o tsukete kuremashita.**

(2) Taro turned on the light when you were still sleeping. You were annoyed by his action.
   a.   太郎が電気をつけました。**Tarou ga denki o tsukemashita.**
   b.   太郎に電気をつけられました。**Tarou ni denki o tsukeraremashita.**
   c.   太郎が電気をつけてくれました。**Tarou ga denki o tsukete kuremashita.**

(3) Your friend helped you with your homework, and you appreciated that.
   a.   友達が宿題を手伝ってあげました。
        **Tomodachi ga shukudai o tetsudatte agemashita.**
   b.   友達が宿題を手伝わせました。
        **Tomodachi ga shukudai o tetsudawasemashita.**
   c.   友達が宿題を手伝ってくれました。
        **Tomodachi ga shukudai o tetsudatte kuremashita.**

(4) You see an old man carrying heavy-looking luggage. Offer him some help.
   a.   お持ちしましょうか。**O-mochi shimashou ka.**
   b.   持ってあげましょうか。**Motte agemashou ka.**
   c.   持っていただきましょうか。**Motte itadakimashou ka.**

(5) Your colleague gave you a ride home when you missed your train, and you appreciated that.
   a.   同僚に家まで送ってくれた。**Douryou ni ie made okutte kureta.**
   b.   同僚に家まで送ってもらった。**Douryou ni ie made okutte moratta.**
   c.   同僚に家まで送ってやった。**Douryou ni ie made okutte yatta.**

⇨ 19.2.8, 20.2, 21.4, 29.4, 43.1, 43.2

2 ★ John spent a year in Japan, working at a municipal office. He met many people in the community and made many friends. He is making a speech at the end-of-the-year party. Choose the most appropriate phrase.

皆さん、この一年たいへんお世話になりました。皆さんには本当に親切に
して【① ください・いただき・さしあげ】ました。僕が道に迷った時は、
地図を書いて【② くださった・いただいた・さしあげた】り、目的地まで一緒
に行って【③ くださった・いただいた・さしあげた】りしました。

Minasan, kono ichinen taihen o-sewa ni narimashita. Minasan ni wa hontou ni shinsetsu ni shite【① kudasai・ itadaki・sashiage】mashita. Boku ga michi ni mayotta toki wa, chizu o kaite【② kudasatta・itadaita・ sashiageta】ri, mokuteki-chi made issho ni itte【③ kudasatta・itadaita・ sashiageta】ri shimashita.

最初のころは、日本語があまり話せなくて苦労しましたが、皆さんがゆっくり話して【④ くださった・いただいた・さしあげた】ので、理解することができました。また、いろいろな人が僕を家に招待して【⑤ くださり・いただき・さしあげ】、日本の文化や習慣について教えて【⑥ ください・いただき・さしあげ】ました。皆さんに教えて【⑦ くださった・いただいた・さしあげた】ことは、ずっと忘れません。すごいごちそうを作って【⑧ あげた・いただいた・さしあげた】ことも、数えきれないほどあります。

Saisho no koro wa, Nihongo ga amari hanasenakute kurou shimashita ga, minasan ga yukkuri hanashite【④ kudasatta・itadaita・sashiageta】node, rikai suru koto ga dekimashita. Mata, iroiro na hito ga boku o ie ni shoutai shite【⑤ kudasari・itadaki・sashiage】, Nihon no bunka ya shuukan ni tsuite oshiete【⑥ kudasai・itadaki・sashiage】mashita. Minasan ni oshiete【⑦ kudasatta・itadaita・sashiageta】koto wa, zutto wasuremasen. Sugoi go-chisou o tsukutte【⑧ ageta・itadaita・sashiageta】koto mo, kazoe kirenai hodo arimasu.

これから僕がみなさんのためにして【⑨ くだされる・いただける・さしあげられる】ことは、国のみんなにこの町のすばらしさを伝えることだと思います。それから、皆さんが僕の国にいらっしゃったら、いろいろな所に案内して【⑩ くださる・いただく・さしあげる】ことです。

Kore kara boku ga minasan no tame ni shite【⑨ kudasareru・itadakeru・ sashiagerareru】koto wa, kuni no minna ni kono machi no subarashisa o tsutaeru koto da to omoimasu. Sore kara, minasan ga boku no kuni ni irasshattara, iroiro na tokoro ni annaishite【⑩ kudasaru・itadaku・ sashiageru】koto desu.

皆さん、ぜひ僕の国に遊びにきてください。またお会いできる日を楽しみにしています。本当にありがとうございました。

Minasan, zehi boku no kuni ni asobi ni kite kudasai. Mata o-ai dekiru hi o tanoshimi ni shite imasu. Hontou ni arigatou gozaimashita.

⇨ 43.1, 43.2

# 44

# Experience

**1** * You are trying to impress your Japanese friend. How would you say the following? Also write two or three sentences of your own.

(1) You have made sushi many times.
(2) You have been to Japan once.
(3) You have seen many Japanese movies.
(4) You have studied Japanese in Japan for a year.
(5) You have taught Japanese at a summer camp a few times.
(6) (Your own sentences?)

⇨ 18.1, 44.1, 44.2

**2** * You are being interviewed for a job. Say the following in Japanese.

(1) You have worked at a Japanese company as an intern for two months.
(2) You have worked as a Japanese language interpreter as a volunteer.
(3) You have had a part-time job at a convenience store.
(4) You have never been late for work.
(5) You have been studying Japanese for four years.
(6) You have participated in the Japan America Student Conference (**Nichi-Bei Gakusei Kaigi**.)

⇨ 18.1, 44.1, 44.2

# 45
# Intentions and plans

**1** ★ ★  Say the following New Year's resolutions in Japanese.

(1) You intend to do exercise three times a week.
(2) You intend to find a better job.
(3) You intend to quit smoking.
(4) You intend to try not to waste money. (waste money = **mudazukai o suru**)
(5) (State your own resolution.)

➪ 12.1, 16.1, 18.4, 45.1

**2** ★ ★  Complete the dialogues using expressions for stating plans and intentions.

(A)
You (Lee-san) and your teacher are talking about plans for the summer. You had originally planned to work, but the plan failed. So, you are now thinking of taking a summer Japanese course, which will be useful for your study abroad next year.

先生 ： リーさん、夏休みはどうするんですか。
あなた： アルバイトを ①＿＿＿＿＿＿＿ が、急に仕事がなくなってしまったの
　　　　で、日本語のコースを ②＿＿＿＿＿＿＿＿＿
　　　　＿＿＿＿＿＿＿＿＿＿＿＿。
先生 ： そうですか。夏のコースはペースが速くて大変ですよ。
あなた： はい、ですから今から漢字の復習を ③＿＿＿＿＿＿＿＿＿。来年日本に
　　　　④＿＿＿＿＿＿＿＿＿ ので、夏のコースは役に立つと思います。

Sensei: Lii-san, natsuyasumi wa dou suru n desu ka.
Anata: Arubaito o ①＿＿＿＿＿＿＿ ga, kyuu ni shigoto ga naku natte
shimatta node, Nihongo no koosu o ②＿＿＿＿＿＿＿.
Sensei: Sou desu ka. Natsu no koosu wa peesu ga hayakute taihen desu yo.
Anata: Hai, desukara ima kara kanji no fukushuu o ③＿＿＿＿＿＿＿.
Rainen Nihon ni ④＿＿＿＿＿＿＿ node, natsu no koosu wa
yaku ni tatsu to omoimasu.

(B)
You have been invited to your friend's wedding reception. As a gift you are thinking of sending a gift catalogue so that she can select what she wants.

恵子：　来週の週末は何か予定ある？
あなた：　友達の結婚披露宴 ('reception') に ①＿＿＿＿＿＿＿＿。
恵子：　ふーん。で、贈り物はどうするの？
あなた：　日本では現金を持って行くのが普通だと思うんだけど、ギフトカタログを
　　　　　送って、好きなものを ②＿＿＿＿＿＿＿＿ んだけど。
恵子：　ああ、いい考えだね。

Keiko:　**Raishuu no shuumatsu wa nanika yotei aru?**
Anata:　**Tomodachi no kekkon hirouen ('reception') ni ①＿＿＿＿＿＿＿.**
Keiko:　**Fuun. De, okurimono wa dou suru no?**
Anata:　**Nihon de wa genkin o motte iku no ga futsuu da to omou n da kedo, gifuto katarogu o okutte, suki na mono o ②＿＿＿＿＿ n da kedo.**
Keiko:　**Aa, ii kangae da ne.**

⇨　12.1, 45.1, 45.2

(C)
You and your teacher are talking about Yoshida Jiro, who plans to work for a Japanese import-export company after graduation. He does not intend to work there too long as he plans to go to a graduate school in the U.S. in a few years.

先生：　吉田さんは卒業後どうするか知っていますか。
あなた：　彼は ①＿＿＿＿＿＿＿＿ と言っていました。
先生：　そうですか。ずっとその会社で働くつもりなんでしょうか。
あなた：　いや、ずっと ②＿＿＿＿＿＿＿＿ らしいです。数年後アメリカの
　　　　　大学院に ③＿＿＿＿＿＿＿＿ と言っていました。

Sensei:　**Yoshida-san wa sotsugyou-go dou suru ka shitte imasu ka.**
Anata:　**Kare wa ①＿＿＿＿＿＿＿ to itte imashita.**
Sensei:　**Sou desu ka. Zutto sono kaisha de hataraku tsumori na n deshou ka.**
Anata:　**Iya, zutto ②＿＿＿＿＿＿ rashii desu. Suunen-go Amerika no daigakuin ni ③＿＿＿＿＿＿＿ to itte imashita.**

⇨　45.3

# 46
# Temporal relations

1 * The following is a list of Yoshiko's activities last weekend.

| a.m. | | p.m. | |
|---|---|---|---|
| 8:00 | got up | 1:00 | ate lunch while watching TV |
| 8:30 | went for a jog | 3:00 | went to a movie with a friend (The movie lasted for two hours.) |
| 9:30 | ate breakfast | 6:00 | had dinner at a sushi restaurant |
| 10:00 | cleaned my room and did laundry | 8:30 | went to an 'izakaya' (a pub) and talked with friends while drinking sake |
| | | 10:00 | went home and went to bed before it was late |

Write the activities as sentences using the structures expressing *before*, *after*, *while*, etc. You may have to conjugate verbs and/or add some words. Below, the structure of each sentence (or a connective word) is given first, then words to be included are given after the plus (+) sign. The first one is an example.

    (1) 前に＋朝ご飯、ジョギング　**mae ni + asa-gohan, jogingu**
    → 朝ご飯を食べる前に，ジョギングをした。
      **Asa go-han o taberu mae ni, jogingu o shita.**

(2) -てから＋洗濯、テレビ、昼ご飯
    **-te kara + sentaku, terebi, hiru-gohan**
(3) 後で＋昼ご飯、映画　**ato de + hirugohan, eiga**
(4) そして＋映画、終わる、すし屋　**soshite + eiga, owaru, sushiya**
(5) -ながら＋居酒屋、酒、話　**-nagara + izakaya, sake, hanashi**
(6) うちに＋遅くなる、寝る　**uchi ni + osoku naru, neru**

⇨ 46.1.1, 46.1.2, 46.2.1

2 * Choose the more appropriate expression of the two.

(1) 子供が寝ている【間・間に】本を読んでいました。
    **Kodomo ga nete iru 【aida · aida ni】 hon o yonde imashita.**
(2) 子供は食べている【間は・間に】静かです。
    **Kodomo wa tabete iru (aida wa · aida ni) shizuka desu.**
(3) 忘れ【る前に・ないうちに】書いておきます。
    **Wasure 【ru mae ni · nai uchi ni】 kaite okimasu.**

(4) 日本にいる【間・間に】いい友達ができました。

**Nihon ni iru 【aida · aida ni】 ii tomodachi ga dekimashita.**

(5) 建物を【出たら・出て】雨が降っていました。

**Tatemono o 【detara · dete】 ame ga futte imashita.**

(6) 私が電話をしている【間・間に】息子は出かけたようです。

**Watashi ga denwa o shite iru 【aida · aida ni】 musuko wa dekaketa you desu.**

(7) お母さんにしかられ【る前に・ないうちに】やりなさい。

**Okaasan ni shikarare 【ru mae ni · nai uchi ni】 yarinasai.**

(8) 大学を卒業【する前に・しないうちに】旅行をしたい。

**Daigaku o sotsugyou 【suru mae ni · shinai uchi ni】 ryokou o shitai.**

⇨ 46.1.1, 46.2.2, 46.2.3

**3** ✱ The following is what Jason wrote to a Japanese friend.

(A)

Choose appropriate expressions where choices are given.

日本に【① 着いたから・着いてから】いつの間にか一ヵ月経ってしまいました。【② 来た・来る】すぐ後は、日本人の話す日本語が速くて困りましたが、今はだいぶ慣れて来ました。日本に【③ 来る・来た】前に先生にいろいろ日本の習慣や文化について教えてもらっていたので、あまりカルチャーショックはありませんでした。しかし、【④ 来る・来た】前には「です・ます体」しか習わなかったので、自分の話し方がちょっとていねいすぎるということに気がついたのは日本に【⑤ 来て・来た】からでした。今は状況によって話し方を変えなければいけないということがわかり、少しずつ日本語が上手になっていると思います。でも、本当に上手に【⑥ なる後で・ならないうちに】帰国することになるのではないかと心配です。

**Nihon ni 【① tsuita kara · tsuite kara】 itsu no ma ni ka ikkagetsu tatte shimaimashita. 【② Kita · Kuru】 sugu ato wa, Nihonjin no hanasu Nihongo ga hayakute komarimashita ga, ima wa daibu narete kimashita. Nihon ni 【③ kuru · kita】 mae ni sensei ni iroiro Nihon no shuukan ya bunka ni tsuite oshiete moratte ita node, amari karuchaa shokku wa arimasendeshita. Shikashi, 【④ kuru · kita】 mae ni wa 'desu masu-tai' shika narawanakatta node, jibun no hanashi-kata ga chotto teinei sugiru to iu koto ni ki ga tsuita no wa Nihon ni 【⑤ kite · kita】 kara deshita. Ima wa joukyou ni yotte hanashi-kata o kaenakereba ikenai to iu koto ga wakari, sukoshi zutsu Nihongo ga jouzu ni natte iru to omoimasu. Demo, hontou ni jouzu ni 【⑥ naru ato de · naranai uchi ni】 kikoku suru koto ni naru no de wa nai ka to shinpai desu.**

(B)

Mark the statements below with ◯ if they are true, and ✕ if they are false.

(1) ( ) ジェイソンは日本に来る前に日本語を勉強した。

**Jeison wa Nihon ni kuru mae ni Nihongo o benkyou shita.**

(2) ( ) ジェイソンは日本の文化を勉強してから日本に来た。

**Jeison wa Nihon no bunka o benkyou shite kara Nihon ni kita.**

(3) ( ) ジェイソンは日本に来る前に日本語のいろいろな話し方を習った。

**Jeison wa Nihon ni kuru mae ni Nihongo no iroiro na hanashi-kata o naratta.**

(4) (　) ジェイソンは日本に来る前は自分の日本語がていねいすぎるということを
知らなかった。
**Jeison wa Nihon ni kuru mae wa jibun no Nihongo ga teinei-
sugiru to iu koto o shiranakatta.**

(5) (　) ジェイソンは帰国するまでに日本語がぜったいにぺらぺらになるだろうと
思っている。
**Jeison wa kikoku suru made ni Nihongo ga zettai ni perapera ni
naru darou to omotte iru.**

⇨　46.1

# 47
# Explanation, reason and purpose

**1** ★ Choose the appropriate phrases below. Note: There may be more than one correct answer in each set.

(1) 今日は疲れている【ので・から・だから】出かけるつもりはありません。
**Kyou wa tsukarete iru 【node · kara · da kara】 dekakeru tsumori wa arimasen.**

(2) 父は糖尿病【なので・から・だから】食事に気をつけています。
**Chichi wa tounyou-byou 【na node · kara · da kara】 shokuji ni ki o tsukete imasu.** [糖尿病 **tounyoubyou** 'diabetes']

(3) あまり外食はしません。ダイエット中な【ので・から・んです】。
**Amari gaishoku wa shimasen. Daietto-chuu na 【node · kara · n desu】.**

(4) 今日は日曜日だ【ので・から・のに】銀行は閉まっています。
**Kyou wa nichiyoubi da 【node · kara · noni】 ginkou wa shimatte imasu.**

▷ 47.2, 47.3

**2** ★ Choose appropriate phrases from the box, to fill in the blanks below.

---

a. あきちゃったもん **akichatta mon**
b. 母の具合が良くないものですから
   **haha no guai ga yokunai mono desu kara**
c. 遠距離恋愛はしたくなかったから **enkyori ren'ai** (long distance relationship) **wa shitaku nakatta kara**
d. 有休がとれたんです **yuukyuu** (paid vacation) **ga toreta n desu**
e. 朝寝坊したので **asa-nebou shita node**

---

(1) ＿＿＿ 遅刻してしまいました。
    ＿＿＿ **chikoku shite shimaimashita.**
(2) 来週から1週間旅行に出ます。＿＿＿。
    **Raishuu kara isshuukan ryokou ni demasu. ＿＿＿.**
(3) ＿＿＿ 彼と別れた。
    ＿＿＿ **kare to wakareta.**
(4) 今日は早退させていただきます。  ＿＿＿。 [早退 **soutai** 'leave early']
    **Kyou wa soutai sasete itadakimasu.  ＿＿＿.**
(5) もうビデオゲームはしたくない。  ＿＿＿。
    **Mou bideo geemu wa shitaku nai.  ＿＿＿.**

▷ 47.2, 47.3

**3** ⋆

Several students in Korea were interviewed about their purpose in studying Japanese. Fill in the blanks with appropriate expressions.

[字幕 **jimaku** 'subtitles'; 言語学 **gengogaku** 'linguistics'; 選択科目 **sentaku kamoku** 'elective course'; 単位 **tan'i** 'credit'; 通訳 **tsuuyaku** 'interpreter']

インタビュアー： どういう目的で日本語を勉強しているんですか。
学生A： 字幕なしで日本の映画が (1)＿＿＿＿＿＿、勉強しています。
学生B： 将来、仕事で (2)＿＿＿＿＿ です。
学生C： 言語学の研究の (3)＿＿＿＿＿ です。
学生D： 選択科目の単位を (4)＿＿＿＿＿ です。それと、いつか日本に行ってみたいからです。
学生E： 通訳に (5)＿＿＿＿＿ です。

| | |
|---|---|
| Intabyuaa: | Dou iu mokuteki de Nihongo o benkyou shite iru n desu ka. |
| Gakusei A: | Jimaku nashi de Nihon no eiga ga (1)＿＿＿＿＿, benkyou shite imasu. |
| Gakusei B: | Shourai, shigoto de (2)＿＿＿＿＿ desu. |
| Gakusei C: | Gengogaku no kenkyuu no (3)＿＿＿＿＿ desu. |
| Gakusei D: | Sentaku kamoku no tan'i o (4)＿＿＿＿＿ desu. Sore to, itsuka Nihon ni itte mitai kara desu. |
| Gakusei E: | Tsuuyaku ni (5)＿＿＿＿＿ desu. |

⇨ 47.4, 47.5

**4** ⋆

Kenta and Hana have been dating for three years. Hana was not sure about marrying him because she wants to continue to work after getting married and having kids. The following is what Kenta said in his proposal, which convinced her. Choose an appropriate phrase in each set.

[協力 **kyouryoku** 'cooperate; 新居 **shinkyo** 'new home'; 貯金 **chokin** 'savings']

君が仕事を続けられる【① ように・ために】、僕もできるだけ家事をする。子供が生まれても、君が働ける【② ように・ために】、僕の両親にも協力してもらう。健康の【③ ように・ために】ダイエットもするし、運動のかわりに毎日風呂掃除もする。新居を建てる【④ ように・ために】、もう3年前から貯金もしているんだ。ぼくと結婚してくれたら、君を幸せにする【⑤ ように・ために】、何でもする。

Kimi ga shigoto o tsuzukerareru 【① you ni・tame ni】, boku mo dekiru dake kaji o suru. Kodomo ga umarete mo, kimi ga hatarakeru 【② you ni・tame ni】, boku no ryoushin ni mo kyouryoku shite morau. Kenkou no 【③ you ni・tame ni】 daietto mo suru shi, undou no kawari ni mainichi furo-souji mo suru. Shinkyo o tateru 【④ you ni・tame ni】, mou sannen mae kara chokin mo shite iru n da. Boku to kekkon shite kuretara, kimi o shiawase ni suru 【⑤ you ni・tame ni】, nan demo suru.

⇨ 47.5

# 48
## Cause and effect

1 *

Make sentences combining a cause from the left column with an effect from the right column. Use each clause once.

| | |
|---|---|
| (1) 台風で | a. 気持ち悪いです。 |
| (2) 授業をサボりすぎたせいで | b. 出かける時間がありません。 |
| (3) 長い間外国に住んでいると | c. 私はひとりぼっち (all alone) です。 |
| (4) 食べ過ぎて | d. 屋根がとんでしまった。 |
| (5) 忙しくて | e. 卒業できなかった。 |
| (6) 家族が旅行中で | f. 母国語を忘れてしまう。 |

| | |
|---|---|
| (1) **Taifuu de** | a. **kimochiwarui desu.** |
| (2) **Jugyou o sabori sugita sei de** | b. **dekakeru jikan ga arimasen.** |
| (3) **Nagai aida gaikoku ni sunde iru to** | c. **watashi wa hitoribotchi (all alone) desu.** |
| (4) **Tabe-sugite** | d. **yane ga tonde shimatta.** |
| (5) **Isogashikute** | e. **sotsugyou dekinakatta.** |
| (6) **Kazoku ga ryokou-chuu de** | f. **bokokugo o wasurete shimau.** |

⇨ 48.3

2 *

What would you say in the following situations?

(1) Your friend had a fight with her boyfriend. You want to know what caused it:
けんかの ＿＿＿＿＿＿ は何だったの？
**Kenka no ＿＿＿＿＿＿ wa nan datta no?**
(2) Your roommate forgot to wake you up this morning. You want to say that it was his/her fault:
今朝寝坊したのはルームメイトが起こしてくれなかった ＿＿＿＿＿＿ だ。
**Kesa nebou shita no wa ruumumeito ga okoshite kurenakatta ＿＿＿＿＿＿ da.**
(3) You want to say that one of the causes of increase in obesity among children seems to be fast food:
子供の肥満が増加した ＿＿＿＿＿＿ の一つはファーストフードらしいです。
**Kodomo no himan ga zouka shita ＿＿＿＿＿＿ no hitotsu wa faasuto fuudo rashii desu.**
(4) You want to ask how (lit. why) fast food leads to obesity:
ファーストフードが ＿＿＿＿＿＿ 肥満につながるのでしょうか。
**Faasuto fuudo ga ＿＿＿＿＿＿ himan ni tsunagaru no deshou ka.**

⇨ 48.1, 48.2

**Cause and effect**

**3** Combine two clauses into one sentence so that the first clause expresses the cause for the second. Add words and/or change the end of the first clause, as appropriate.

Example: 熱い・飲めない　→　熱くて飲めない。

**atsui · nomenai** → **Atsukute nomenai.**

(1) 足が痛い・歩けない **ashi ga itai · arukenai**
(2) みんなから愛される・幸せです **minna kara ai sareru · shiawase desu**
(3) 事故だ・足を折った **jiko da · ashi o otta**
(4) 雨が降らない・水不足になった **ame ga furanai · mizu busoku ni natta**
(5) うそをついた・信用を失った。 **uso o tsuita · shinyou o ushinatta**

⇨ 48.3

# 49
# Describing procedures

**1** ✱ Mariko does not know how to use an ATM. Describe the procedures for her by rearranging the following statements into the proper order. Insert words such as **mazu**, **saisho ni**, **tsugi ni**, **soshite**, and **saigo ni** where appropriate.

[暗証番号 **anshou bangou** 'PIN (personal identification number)';
入力 **nyuuryoku** 'input'; 画面 **gamen** 'screen'; 引き落とし **hiki-otoshi**
'(bank) withdrawal']

- 暗証番号を入力します。
  **Anshou bangou o nyuuryoku shimasu.**
- ATMにカードを入れます。
  **ATM ni kaado o iremasu.**
- 必要金額を入力すると、お金が出てきます。
  **Hitsuyou kingaku o nyuuryoku suru to, o-kane ga dete kimasu.**
- 画面で引き落としを選びます。
  **Gamen de hiki-otoshi o erabimasu.**

⇨ 31.5.2, 49

**2** ✱ The following are the steps for making **tori no kara-age** 'Japanese style fried chicken.' Put the sentences into the correct order.

[しょうが **shouga** 'ginger'; 片栗粉 **katakuriko** 'potato starch'; まぶす **mabusu**
'to coat']

(A) 次に、しょうゆ、酒、しょうがをまぜて、切った鶏肉をその中につけて、
   一時間おきます。
   **Tsugi ni, shouyu, sake, shouga o mazete, kitta toriniku o sono naka ni tsukete, ichijikan okimasu.**
(B) 最後に180度の油であげます。
   **Saigo ni 180 do no abura de agemasu.**
(C) まず鶏肉を食べやすい大きさに切ります。
   **Mazu toriniku o tabeyasui ookisa ni kirimasu.**
(D) そして、鶏肉の余分な水気をふき、全体に片栗粉をまぶします。
   **Soshite, toriniku no yobun na mizuke o fuki, zentai ni katakuriko o mabushimasu.**

⇨ 31.5.2, 49

# 50
# Changes

1 ★

The following describes Kenji's high school days and his current college days. Describe how he has changed, using 健二は大学に入ってから … なりました。 **'Kenji wa daigaku ni haitte kara . . . narimashita.'**

| *In high school* | *In college* |
|---|---|
| • did not study<br>• could not read Japanese<br>• could not eat sushi<br>• bad at cooking<br>• had lots of free time<br>• had savings (**chokin**) | • studies a lot<br>• can read Japanese<br>• can eat sushi<br>• good at cooking<br>• very busy<br>• does not have savings |

⇨ 50.1, 50.2

2 ★

The following is a conversation between a student 'A' and his/her neighbor 'B.' Complete it using **-te kuru** in the appropriate forms.

A: 先月は寒かったですが、最近 (1)＿＿＿＿＿＿＿＿＿ ね。
B: そうですね。ところで日本語の勉強はどうですか。
A: 日本文化についてたくさん習っているので、(2)＿＿＿＿＿＿＿＿。
　　でも、漢字が (3)＿＿＿＿＿＿＿。
B: そうですか。漢字は日本人にも難しいんですよ。私もこのごろワープロで書いてばかりいるので、難しい漢字が (4)＿＿＿＿＿＿＿。
A: そうですか。やっぱり練習するしかないですね。がんばります。

A: **Sengetsu wa samukatta desu ga, saikin** (1)＿＿＿＿＿＿＿ **ne.**
B: **Sou desu ne. Tokorode Nihongo no benkyou wa dou desu ka.**
A: **Nihon bunka ni tsuite takusan naratte iru node,** (2)＿＿＿＿＿＿＿.
　　**Demo, kanji ga** (3)＿＿＿＿＿＿＿.
B: **Sou desu ka. Kanji wa nihonjin ni mo muzukashii n desu yo.**
　　**Watashi mo konogoro waapuro de kaite bakari iru node, muzukashii kanji ga** (4)＿＿＿＿＿＿＿.
A: **Sou desu ka. Yappari renshuu suru shika nai desu ne. Ganbarimasu.**

⇨ 50.3

3 ★

The following describes some changes which have or have not taken place in Japan in the last 60 years or so. Complete the passages with the appropriate words from the box according to the English equivalents.

(1)

> 味覚・西洋化・変化・食事・若い
>
> **mikaku・seiyouka ・henka・shokuji・wakai**

（　①　）された（　②　）に親しんで来た（　③　）世代の日本人の（　④　）はずいぶん（　⑤　）して来た。

（　①　）**sareta**（　②　）**ni shitashinde kita**（　③　）**sedai no Nihonjin no**（　④　）**wa zuibun**（　⑤　）**shite kita.**

*The preferences (lit. taste) of young people who have become accustomed to western food have changed a lot.*

(2)

> 社会進出・低下・晩婚化
>
> **shakai-shinshutsu・teika・bankonka**

女性の（　①　）と共に（　②　）が進み、それにつれて子供の出生率も（　③　）している。

**Josei no**（　①　）**to tomo ni**（　②　）**ga susumi, sore ni tsurete kodomo no shusseiritsu mo**（　③　）**shite iru.**

*With the advance of women's social status, more women are getting married later, and the birth rate has declined.*

(3)

> 男性・女性・変身・育児・家事・戦後
>
> **dansei・josei・henshin・ikuji・kaji・sengo**

(You will need to use the same word more than once.)

（　①　）、働く（　②　）が増えて、女性は（　③　）、（　④　）そして仕事を全部しなければならなくなった。しかし（　⑤　）や（　⑥　）をする男性はまだ少なく、（　⑦　）が（　⑧　）していないのが問題だ。

（　①　）**, hataraku**（　②　）**ga fuete, josei wa**（　③　）**,**（　④　）**soshite shigoto o zenbu shinakereba naranaku natta. Shikashi**（　⑤　）**ya**（　⑥　）**o suru dansei wa mada sukunaku,**（　⑦　）**ga**（　⑧　）**shite inai no ga mondai da.**

*After the war, the number of working women increased, and these women now have to do all the work, such as housework, child care, and an outside job. However, men who do housework and childcare are still few in number and they have not changed, which is the problem.*

⇨　50.3, 50.4

132

# 51
# Expressing abilities

**1** *

You are interviewing a job candidate and want to find out the following. Ask appropriate questions.

(1) What languages she can speak.
(2) Whether she can write a business letter in English.
(3) Whether she can write a report using Excel.
(4) Whether she can work until late in the evening.
(5) Whether she can <u>get along with others</u> (他の人とうまくやっていく **hoka no hito to umaku yatte iku**).

⇨ 12.6, 51

**2** *

Your friend is going to Tokyo and Kyoto on vacation, and you are making some suggestions about what s/he can do. Complete the sentences with the appropriate verbs in the potential form.

(1) 浅草に行くと、いろいろ日本的なお土産が（　　　　　　　　）。
**Asakusa ni iku to, iroiro Nihonteki na omiyage ga** (　　　　　　　　).

(2) スカイツリーに上ると、東京の町が（　　　　　　　　）。[見渡す]
**Sukai Tsurii ni noboru to, Toukyou no machi ga** (　　　　　　　　).
[miwatasu]

(3) 箱根の旅館に泊まると、温泉に（　　　　　　　　）し、おいしい日本
料理が（　　　　　　　　）。
**Hakone no ryokan ni tomaru to, onsen ni** (　　　　　　　　) **shi, oishii Nihon ryouri ga** (　　　　　　　　).

(4) 秋葉原に行くと、メイド喫茶でメイドさんと（　　　　　　　　）。
**Akihabara ni iku to, meido kissa de meido-san to** (　　　　　　　　).

(5) 地下鉄や電車の線がたくさんあるので、タクシーを使わないでいろいろ
な所に（　　　　　　　　）。
**Chikatetsu ya densha no sen ga takusan aru node, takushii o tsukawanaide iroiro na tokoro ni** (　　　　　　　　).

(6) 東京駅で新幹線に（　　　　　　　　）。
**Toukyou eki de Shinkansen ni** (　　　　　　　　).

(7) 京都では古いお寺や神社がたくさん（　　　　　　　　）。
**Kyouto de wa furui otera ya jinja ga takusan** (　　　　　　　　).

(8) 京都の祇園で舞子さんと写真が（　　　　　　　　）。
**Kyouto no Gion de maiko-san to shashin ga** (　　　　　　　　).

⇨ 12.6, 51.2

**3** ★★

You are going to Japan and making some arrangements about transportation and sightseeing options, talking to a travel agent. What would you say to find out the following? Use the words in parentheses where provided.

(1) whether you can ride the **Nozomi Shinkansen** with a JR pass.
(2) whether you can use a JR pass <u>inside Tokyo</u> (都内 **tonai**).
(3) whether you can sit in reserved seats. (指定席 **shiteiseki**)
(4) what places you can see if you take a <u>sightseeing</u> (観光 **kankou**) bus.
(5) if you can get off the sightseeing bus in the middle of the tour (ツアー **tsuaa**).

⇨ 12.6, 51

**4** ★★

The following is an advertisement for a Japanese inn in Hakone. Describe what guests can do if they stay at this inn.

- 箱根芦ノ湖を一望できる純和風の宿。あざやかな四季の中で安らぎのひとときをお過ごしいただけます。
- 天下の名湯、箱根の湯を心ゆくまで楽しんでいただけます。露天風呂では富士山を眺めながらゆっくりとお体を休めていただけます。
- 新鮮な四季折々のお料理を味わっていただけます。
- 箱根神社まで徒歩5分ですので、散歩なさるのもよろしいかと存じます。
- 芦ノ湖モーターボートで芦ノ湖一周、またゴルフやテニスも近くでお楽しみいただけます。

- Hakone Ashinoko o ichibou dekiru jun-wafuu no yado. Azayaka na shiki no naka de yasuragi no hitotoki o o-sugoshi itadakemasu.
- Tenka no meiyu, Hakone no yu o kokoro yuku made tanoshinde itadakemasu. Roten-buro de wa Fujisan o nagame-nagara yukkuri to o-karada o yasumete itadakemasu.
- Shinsen na shiki oriori no o-ryouri o ajiwatte itadakemasu.
- Hakone Jinja made toho gofun desu node, sanpo nasaru no mo yoroshii ka to zonjimasu.
- Ashinoko mootaabooto de Ashinoko isshuu, mata gorufu ya tenisu mo chikaku de o-tanoshimi itadakemasu.

⇨ 19.2.8, 29.5, 51

# 52
# Needs

**1** ✳

Complete the following sentences with expressions meaning 'need' or 'do not need.' Use the cues provided.

(1) イギリスから日本に観光旅行する時は、＿＿＿＿＿＿＿＿＿。
   **Igirisu kara Nihon ni kankou-ryokou suru toki wa, _____.**
   (visa unnecessary)

(2) 新幹線に乗るには ＿＿＿＿＿＿＿＿＿。
   **Shinkansen ni noru ni wa _____.**
   (ticket for express train necessary)

(3) 成田からリムジンバスに乗るには ＿＿＿＿＿＿＿＿＿。
   **Narita kara rimujin basu ni noru ni wa _____.**
   (reservation unnecessary)

(4) 事業を始めるには ＿＿＿＿＿＿＿＿＿。
   **Jigyou o hajimeru ni wa _____.**   (capital/funds necessary)

▷ 52.1.1, 52.1.2, 52.2

**2** ✳

The following is a list of things you have to do to prepare for an interview with a Japanese company. Say them with **nakute wa** (or **nakereba**) **ikenai** in formal (**desu/masu**) style first. Then, tell your friends the same thing in the informal form.

(1) practice **keigo**
(2) buy a suit
(3) <u>do research</u> (調べる **shiraberu**) on the Internet about the company
(4) organize ideas about why (you) are applying to this company
(5) practice a mock interview

▷ 24.2, 52.1.3, 80.1.2

**3** ✳

Answer the following questions using the expressions provided.

(1) 学生：　　この論文のタイトルを変えた方がいいでしょうか。
   先生：　　（　　　　　　　　　　）と思いますが。（〜には及ばない）
   **Gakusei:  Kono ronbun no taitoru o kaeta hou ga ii deshou ka.**
   **Sensei:  _____ to omoimasu ga. (. . . ni wa oyobanai)**

(2) A:　タクシーに乗りましょうか。
   B:　近いんだから、わざわざ ＿＿＿＿＿＿＿ と思いますが。（〜ことはない）
   A:  **Takushii ni norimashou ka.**
   B:  **Chikai n da kara, wazawaza _____ to omoimasu ga.**
      **(. . . koto wa nai)**

(3) A: このサイトを使うには、会員にならないといけないのかな？

    B: _____ んじゃない？（〜てもいい）

    A: **Kono saito o tsukau ni wa, kai 'in ni naranai to ikenai no kana?**

    B: **_____ n ja nai? (. . . te mo ii)**

(4) A: 家まで送ってもらったお礼をした方がいいでしょうか。

    B: 特に _____ と思うけど。（〜までもない）

    A: **Uchi made okutte moratta o-rei o shita hou ga ii deshou ka.**

    B: **Toku ni _____ to omou kedo. (. . . made mo nai)**

(5) A: スミスさんの家で集まるそうですけど、何か作って行った方が
いいんでしょうか。

    B: 別に _____ んじゃないでしょうか。私は何か買って行
くつもりです。（〜てもいい）

    A: **Sumisu-san no ie de atsumaru sou desu kedo, nanika tsukutte itta hou ga ii n deshou ka.**

    B: **Betsu ni _____ n ja nai deshou ka. Watashi wa nanika katte iku tsumori desu. (. . . te mo ii)**

⇨ 52.2

# 53
# Possibility and probability

1 ★

The following is the weather forecast for a December day in five cities in Japan. Temperatures are given in centigrade. Complete the following description by filling in the blanks. The first two sentences are given as examples.

| | 天気<br>Tenki | 降水確率<br>Kousui<br>kakuritsu | 最高気温<br>Saikou<br>kion | 最低気温<br>Saitei<br>kion | 風<br>Kaze |
|---|---|---|---|---|---|
| 札幌<br>Sapporo | | 80 | 1 | −4 | strong wind |
| 東京<br>Toukyou | | 0 | 10 | 2 | no wind |
| 大阪<br>Oosaka | | 50 | 12 | 6 | weak wind |
| 広島<br>Hiroshima | | 70 | 14 | 5 | weak wind |
| 那覇<br>Naha | | 0 | 22 | 17 | no wind |

あしたは札幌は （ ① 雪 ）でしょう。風が強く、気温は （ ② 低い ）でしょう。
東京は （ ③ ）でしょう。風は （ ④ ）、おだやかな日となるでしょう。
大阪は （ ⑤ ）ですが、雨が降る （ ⑥ ）。気温は平年並みですが、日中は
（ ⑦ ）でしょう。広島は朝のうちは曇りですが、午後から （ ⑧ ）でしょう。
那覇は （ ⑨ ）でしょう。風はなく、日中は （ ⑩ ）かもしれません。

**Ashita wa Sapporo wa （ ① yuki ） deshou. Kaze ga tsuyoku, kion wa
（ ② hikui ） deshou. Toukyou wa （ ③ ） deshou. Kaze wa （ ④ ），
odayaka na hi to naru deshou. Oosaka wa （ ⑤ ） desu ga, ame ga furu
（ ⑥ ）. Kion wa heinen nami desu ga, nitchuu wa （ ⑦ ） deshou.
Hiroshima wa asa no uchi wa kumori desu ga, gogo kara （ ⑧ ） deshou.
Naha wa （ ⑨ ） deshou. Kaze wa naku, nitchuu wa （ ⑩ ） kamo
shiremasen.**

⇨ 37.3, 53.1.3, 53.2.1

**2** ★

What might be the reasons for the following situations? Give possible reasons using **(no) kamo shiremasen**.

(1) 友達の家に贈り物を郵便で送りましたが、届いていません。
  **Tomodachi no ie ni okurimono o yuubin de okurimashita ga, todoite imasen.**

(2) ポケットに入れたと思った財布がありません。
  **Poketto ni ireta to omotta saifu ga arimasen.**

(3) 友達と待ち合わせをしているのですが、30分待っても来ません。
  **Tomodachi to machiawase o shite iru no desu ga, sanjuppun mattemo kimasen.**

(4) 東京の電車は時間通り来るのが普通だが、今日は遅れている。
  **Toukyou no densha wa jikan-doori kuru no ga futsuu da ga, kyou wa okurete iru.**

(5) 今日本では、少子化、つまり生まれる子供の数が少なくなっていることが問題になっています。原因は何なのでしょうか。（「からかもしれません」を使って答えてください。）
  **Ima Nihon de wa, shoushika, tsumari umareru kodomo no kazu ga sukunaku natte iru koto ga mondai ni natte imasu. Gen'in wa nan na no deshou ka. ('Kara kamoshiremasen' o tsukatte kotaete kudasai.)**

⇨ 18.2, 53.1.3

**3** ★

Fill in the blanks with appropriate expressions from this list, using no expression more than once.

| | | |
|---|---|---|
| (a) でしょう | (b) かもしれない | (c) あり得ない |
| (d) 可能性がある | (e) 不可能だ | (f) 無理だ |
| (a) **deshou** | (b) **kamo shirenai** | (c) **ari-enai** |
| (d) **kanousei ga aru** | (e) **fukanou da** | (f) **muri da** |

(1) 田中さんは今日は授業に来ていない。よくわからないけれど、病気（　　　）。
  **Tanaka-san wa kyou wa jugyou ni kite inai. Yoku wakaranai keredo, byouki（　　　）.**

(2) 山下さんはいつもパーティーに来るから、今度のパーティーにもたぶん来る（　　　）。
  **Yamashita-san wa itsumo paatii ni kuru kara, kondo no paatii ni mo tabun kuru（　　　）.**

(3) 今晩一晩でこの仕事を終わらせるのは（　　　）。
  **Konban hitoban de kono shigoto o owaraseru no wa（　　　）.**

(4) まだ大学院に受かる（　　　）ので、あきらめないで、もう少し待ってみます。
  **Mada daigakuin ni ukaru（　　　）node, akiramenaide, mou sukoshi matte mimasu.**

(5) 消費税 (sales tax) がなくなるということは（　　　）。
  **Shouhizei (sales tax) ga naku naru to iu koto wa（　　　）.**

(6) 漢字をたくさん知らないと、日本語能力試験のN1にパスするのは（　　　）。
  **Kanji o takusan shiranai to, Nihongo nouryoku shiken no N1 ni pasu suru no wa（　　　）.**

⇨ 53.1, 53.2

# 54
# Certainty and uncertainty

**1** ★

Members of a baseball team are expressing their determination to win before the game. Choose the most appropriate phrase in each set.

A: 一生懸命練習して来たので、【① 絶対に・決して・おそらく】勝ちたいと思います。

B: このチームは【② 間違いなく・決して・やっと】最高のチームなので、【③ きっと・もしかすると・たぶん】勝てると信じています。

C: 今シーズンは絶好調なので、【④ 決して・まぎれもなく・もしかすると】負けません！

D: 今日の優勝は僕たちのチームに【⑤ 決めました・決まっています・します】。

A: **Isshoukenmei renshuu shite kita node, 【① zettai ni · kesshite · osoraku】 kachitai to omoimasu.**

B: **Kono chiimu wa 【② machigai naku · kesshite · yatto】 saikou no chiimu na node, 【③ kitto · moshika suru to · tabun】 kateru to shinjite imasu.**

C: **Kon-shiizun wa zekkouchou na node, 【④ kesshite · magiremo naku · moshika suru to】 makemasen!**

D: **Kyou no yuushou wa boku-tachi no chiimu ni 【⑤ kimemashita · kimatte imasu · shimasu】.**

⇨ 54.1

**2** ★

Fill in the blanks with expressions of doubt/uncertainty.

(1) A: 田中さんは会社をやめるそうですよ。
    **Tanaka-san wa kaisha o yameru sou desu yo.**
    B: あの人が会社をやめるなんて、＿＿＿＿＿＿＿＿＿＿＿＿。
    **Ano hito ga kaisha o yameru nante, ＿＿＿＿＿＿＿＿＿＿＿＿.**

(2) A: 今度のプロジェクトはどうですか。
    **Kondo no purojekuto wa dou desu ka.**
    B: うまくいくかどうか ＿＿＿＿＿＿＿＿＿＿＿＿。
    **Umaku iku ka dou ka ＿＿＿＿＿＿＿＿＿＿＿＿.**

(3) [契約 **keiyaku** 'contract'; 交渉 **koushou** 'negotiation'; 判 **han** 'stamp (of approval)']
    A: あの会社との契約の話はどうなってるの？
    **Ano kaisha to no keiyaku no hanashi wa dou natte ru no?**
    B: まだ交渉中ですが、来週までに契約書に判がもらえるかどうか
    ＿＿＿＿＿＿＿＿＿＿＿＿。
    **Mada koushou-chuu desu ga, raishuu made ni keiyakusho ni han ga moraeru ka dou ka ＿＿＿＿＿＿＿＿＿＿＿＿.**

⇨ 54.2

# 55

# Provisions, conditions, and hypotheses

1 ★ Change the phrases in parentheses using the appropriate conditional forms (i.e. **tara, to, ba,** or **nara**). There may be more than one correct answer.

Example: （日本に行く）日本語が上手になりますよ。
→ 日本に【行けば/行ったら/行くと】、日本語が上手になりますよ。
(Nihon ni iku) Nihongo ga jouzu ni narimasu yo.
→ Nihon ni 【ikeba / ittara / iku to】, Nihongo ga jouzu ni narimasu yo.

(1) A: あしたピクニックに行きませんか。
   B: （　天気がいい　）行きます。
   A: **Ashita pikunikku ni ikimasen ka.**
   B: （　**Tenki ga ii**　）**ikimasu.**
(2) A: （　お金がたくさんある　）どうしますか。
   B: 世界中を旅行します。
   A: （　**Okane ga takusan aru**　）**dou shimasu ka.**
   B: **Sekaijuu o ryokou shimasu.**
(3) A: この本を読もうと思っています。
   B: ああ、（　その本を読む　）辞書がいりますよ。
   A: **Kono hon o yomou to omotte imasu.**
   B: **Aa,** （　**sono hon o yomu**　）**jisho ga irimasu yo.**
(4) A: 最近は早く暗くなりますね。
   B: そうですね。午後（　五時になる　）もう暗いですよね。
   A: **Saikin wa hayaku kuraku narimasu ne.**
   B: **Sou desu ne. Gogo** （　**goji ni naru**　）**mou kurai desu yo ne.**
(5) A: ああ、もう遅い。クラスに間に合わない！
   B: （　急ぐ　）まだ間に合うよ。
   A: **Aa, mou osoi. Kurasu ni ma ni awanai!**
   B: （　**Isogu**　）**mada ma ni au yo.**
(6) A: B君、部長がちょっと来いって。
   B: ええ？困ったなあ。（　部長の前に出る　）いつも緊張してしまうんだ。
   A: **B-kun, buchou ga chotto koi tte.**
   B: **Ee? Komatta naa.** （　**Buchou no mae ni deru**　）**itsumo kinchou shite shimau n da.**
(7) A: 漢字が覚えられなくて困ってるんだけど。
   B: （　何度も書く　）覚えられるようになるよ。
   A: **Kanji ga oboerarenakute komatte ru n da kedo.**
   B: （　**Nando mo kaku**　）**oboerareru you ni naru yo.**

(8) A: 今年のお正月は日本に行くんです。
    B: いいですね。でも、（　日本に行く　）早く航空券を買った方がいいですね。
    A: **Kotoshi no o-shougatsu wa Nihon ni iku n desu.**
    B: **Ii desu ne. Demo, (　Nihon ni iku　) hayaku koukuuken o katta hou ga ii desu ne.**

⇨ 24, 55.1

**2** ★ Julie wants to improve her Japanese. Give her suggestions using **sae . . . sureba**.

Example: do a home-stay
→ ホームステイをしさえすれば、日本語が上手になりますよ。
**→ Hoomu sutei o shi sae sureba, Nihongo ga jouzu ni narimasu yo.**

(1) study abroad in Japan
(2) make Japanese friends
(3) speak Japanese every day
(4) watch Japanese TV dramas

⇨ 55.4.1

**3** ★ Express the following in Japanese.

(1) If I were to inherit a lot of money, I would give money to several charitable organizations.
(2) My friend does not use an air conditioner even if it's hot.
(3) If I was mistaken, please tell me so.
(4) No matter how difficult it is, if you try hard, you can do it.
(5) In Tokyo, wherever you go, it is crowded.
(6) Whenever he has free time, my younger brother is playing video games.
(7) If I had not eaten the leftovers, I would not have had a stomachache.

⇨ 55.2, 55.3.2, 55.4.2

# 56

# Understanding and knowing

1 ★ Choose the correct verb.

(1) おいしいコーヒーの入れ方を【知っています・わかります】。
   **Oishii koohii no ire-kata o 【shitteimasu・wakarimasu】.**
(2) コンピューターのことは、私には【知りません・わかりません】。
   **Konpyuutaa no koto wa, watashi ni wa 【shirimasen・wakarimasen】.**
(3) フランス語が【知っています・わかります】か。
   **Furansugo ga 【shitte imasu・wakarimasu】 ka.**
(4) 最近、妻のことがよく【知らなく・わからなく】なりました。
   **Saikin, tsuma no koto ga yoku 【shiranaku・wakaranaku】 narimashita.**
(5) よく話し合って、やっと娘の気持ちが【知る・わかる】ようになった。
   **Yoku hanashi-atte, yatto musume no kimochi ga 【shiru・wakaru】 you ni natta.**
(6) 東洋医学について【知る・わかる】ために、その分野の専門家に話をしてもらいました。
   **Touyou igaku ni tsuite 【shiru・wakaru】 tame ni, sono bun'ya no senmonka ni hanashi o shite moraimashita.**

⇨ 56.2, 56.4

2 ★ Answer each question by filling in the blanks.

(1) A: あの人、誰か知ってる？
   B: ううん、_____。
   A: **Ano hito, dare ka shitte ru?**
   B: **Uun, _____.**
(2) A: これ、わかる？
   B: ううん、_____。
   A: **Kore, wakaru?**
   B: **Uun, _____.**
(3) A: 田中さんの住所が知りたいんだけど …
   B: えー、ちょっと私には _____。
   A: **Tanaka-san no juusho ga shiritai n da kedo . . .**
   B: **Ee, chotto watashi ni wa _____.**
(4) A: 鈴木さんって、どんな人ですか。
   B: 鈴木さんですか。ちょっと変わっているというか、私にはあの人のことはよく _____。
   A: **Suzuki-san tte donna hito desu ka.**
   B: **Suzuki-san desu ka. Chotto kawatte iru to iu ka, watashi ni wa Ano hito no koto wa yoku _____.**

(5) A: 「第九」っていう喫茶店、知っていますか。(第九 '(Symphony) No. 9')

    B: ええ、＿＿＿＿＿＿＿＿＿＿＿＿＿＿ けど。

    A: どこにあるんですか。

    B: えっと、通りの名前は ＿＿＿＿＿＿＿＿＿＿＿＿ んですけど、フィットネスクラブのすぐ裏ですよ。

    A: 'Daiku' tte iu kissaten, shitte imasu ka. (daiku '(Symphony) No. 9')

    B: Ee, ＿＿＿＿＿＿＿＿＿＿＿＿ kedo.

    A: Doko ni aru n desu ka.

    B: Etto, toori no namae wa ＿＿＿＿＿＿＿＿＿＿＿＿ n desu kedo, **fittonesu kurabu no sugu ura desu yo.**

⇨ 56.2, 56.3

**3** ★ You are interviewing a person for an internship (インターンシップ **intaanshippu**) position in your accounting office. Ask the following questions in Japanese.

(1) Do you know how to use Excel? [エクセル **ekuseru**]
(2) How much do you know about accounting? [経理 **keiri**]
(3) Do you know (lit. 'understand') the internship requirements [資格要件 **shikaku youken**]?

⇨ 56.2, 56.4

# 57
# Remembering and forgetting

1 ⋆ Choose the correct verb.

(1) 明日テストをしますから、第4課の漢字を【覚えて・思い出して】きてください。
  **Ashita tesuto o shimasu kara, dai yonka no kanji o 【oboete・omoidashite】 kite kudasai.**
(2) 昨日の午後2時ごろ何をしていたか【覚えて・思い出して】ください。
  **Kinou no gogo niji goro nani o shite ita ka 【oboete・omoidashite】 kudasai.**
(3) この人のこと、【覚える・覚えてる】？
  **Kono hito no koto, 【oboeru・oboete ru】?**
(4) ずっと前のことを急に【覚えた・思い出した】。
  **Zutto mae no koto o kyuu ni 【oboeta・omoidashita】.**
(5) すみません、急用を【覚えました・思い出しました】ので、失礼します。
  **Sumimasen, kyuuyou o 【oboemashita・omoidashimashita】 node, shitsurei shimasu.**
(6) 子供のころの記憶が【あります・覚えています】か。
  **Kodomo no koro no kioku ga 【arimasu・oboeteimasu】 ka.**
(7) [つぶれる tsubureru 'go bankrupt']
  その店は2年前につぶれたと記憶【します・しています】。
  **Sono mise wa ninen mae ni tsubureta to kioku 【shimasu・shite imasu】.**
(8) いつか仕返ししてやるから、【おぼえろ・おぼえていろ】。
  **Itsuka shikaeshi shite yaru kara, 【oboero・oboete iro】.**

⇨ 19.2.1, 57.2, 57.3, 75.1

2 ⋆ Translate the English expressions below into Japanese.

(1)
A teacher is talking to a student who didn't submit the homework.

| | |
|---|---|
| 教師： | 宿題はどうしたんですか。 |
| 学生： | すみません。 (a) I forgot. |
| 教師： | うちに忘れてきたんですか。 |
| 学生： | (b) No, I forgot to do it. |
| 教師： | 仕方がありませんね。 (c) Don't forget it tomorrow. |
| 学生： | はい、すみません。 |

| | |
|---|---|
| **Kyoushi:** | **Shukudai wa dou shita n desu ka.** |
| **Gakusei:** | **Sumimasen.** (a) I forgot. |
| **Kyoushi:** | **Uchi ni wasurete kita n desu ka.** |
| **Gakusei:** | (b) No, I forgot to do it. |
| **Kyoushi:** | **Shikata ga arimasen ne.** (c) Don't forget it tomorrow. |
| **Gakusei:** | **Hai, sumimasen.** |

(2)

Hitomi is asking her friend Kenji if he did what she had asked him to do.

仁美： 太郎君に土曜日のパーティーのこと、伝えてくれた？
健司： (a) Sorry, I forgot.
仁美： えー、また？
健司： (b) I remembered it until I saw Taro, though.
仁美： じゃ、洋子ちゃんには言ってくれた？
健司： (c) Yes, but I don't remember if she said she was coming or not.
仁美： え、それじゃ、意味ないでしょ。
健司： (d) Oh, I remember now. バイトがあるから遅くなるけど、来るって。
仁美： (e) Do you remember what kind of (part-time) job she has?
健司： (f) No, I don't remember.
仁美： 私も。聞いたことあるんだけど、(g) I can't recall.

Hitomi: **Tarou-kun ni doyoubi no paatii no koto, tsutaete kureta?**
Kenji: (a) Sorry, I forgot.
Hitomi: **Ee, mata?**
Kenji: (b) I remembered it until I saw Taro, though.
Hitomi: **Ja, Youko-chan ni wa itte kureta?**
Kenji: (c) Yes, but I don't remember if she said she was coming or not.
Hitomi: **E, sore ja, imi nai desho.**
Kenji: (d) Oh, I remember now. **Baito ga aru kara osoku naru kedo, kuru tte.**
Hitomi: (e) Do you remember what kind of (part-time) job she has?
Kenji: (f) No, I don't remember.
Hitomi: **Watashi mo. Kiita koto aru n da kedo,** (g) I can't recall.

⇨ 15.3, 26.3, 57.2, 57.4

# 58
# General comments on the adjectives of emotions and sensations

⇨ See the exercises in chapters 59–71.

# 59
# Gratitude

1 ★

Today is Mother's Day. Members of your host family are saying thank you to **O-kaasan.** Fill in the blanks with appropriate phrases. The first and the last ones are given as examples.

[Xの面倒をみる **X no mendou o miru** 'take care of X']

みんな： 　　いつもおいしいご飯を <u>作ってくれて</u> ありがとう！
(1) 海： 　　いつもぼくの洗濯を ＿＿＿＿＿＿＿ ありがとう！
(2) まり： 　　いつもきれいで ＿＿＿＿＿＿＿ ありがとう！
(3) 夫： 　　いつもみんなの面倒を ＿＿＿＿＿＿＿ ありがとう！
(4) おばあちゃん： 　いつも歯医者に ＿＿＿＿＿＿＿ ありがとう！
(5) あなた： 　　＿＿＿＿＿＿＿ ありがとう！
みんな： 　　いつもいいお母さんで <u>いてくれて</u> ありがとう！

    **Minna:** 　　Itsumo oishii gohan o <u>tsukutte kurete</u> arigatou!
(1) **Kai:** 　　Itsumo boku no sentaku o ＿＿＿＿＿＿ arigatou!
(2) **Mari:** 　　Itsumo kirei de ＿＿＿＿＿＿ arigatou!
(3) **Otto:** 　　Itsumo minna no mendou o ＿＿＿＿＿＿ arigatou!
(4) **O-baachan:** 　Itsumo ha-isha ni ＿＿＿＿＿＿ arigatou!
(5) **Anata:** 　　＿＿＿＿＿＿ arigatou!
    **Minna:** 　　Itsumo ii o-kaasan de <u>ite kurete</u> arigatou!

⇨ 59.1

2 ★

How would you express your gratitude in the following situations?

(1) Your professor wrote a letter of recommendation for you.
(2) Your colleague helped you write a letter in Japanese.
(3) You are saying good-bye to your host family.
(4) Your host father praised your Japanese.
(5) Your younger brother's Aikido teacher has been very kind to him (lit. 'has always taken care of him').
(6) You want to thank your colleague for her/his hard work.
(7) You just finished eating, and want to thank the restaurant staff.
(8) You see an acquaintance who had you over for dinner last time you saw her/him.

⇨ 12.1, 30.1, 43, 59.1, 59.3

**3** Write appropriate responses to the following expressions of gratitude.

(1) 先生 ： 　　　　　　プロジェクターを運んでくれてどうもありがとう。
(2) 友人 ： 　　　　　　送ってもらっちゃって悪かったね。助かったぁ！
(3) 同僚の夫 ： 　　　　妻がいつもお世話になっております。
(4) 近所の人 ： 　　　　また荷物をあずかっていていただいたのね。いつもすみません。
(5) 課長 ： 　　　　　　あ、迎えに来てくれたの？あ〜、ありがたいなぁ。
(6) 部長 ： 　　　　　　例の報告書 ('report')、終わったの？ご苦労さん。
(7) （プロジェクトが終わって打ち上げ会 ('a gathering celebrating completion of a project') をしている時）
　　同僚 ： 　　　　　　お疲れさまでした！
(8) ホストファミリーの妹 （アイスクリームを買ってあげた時）：お兄ちゃん/お姉ちゃん、ありがとう！

(1) **Sensei:** 　　　　　　**Purojekutaa o hakonde kurete doumo arigatou.**
(2) **Yuujin:** 　　　　　　**Okutte moratchatte warukatta ne. Tasukattaa!**
(3) **Douryou no otto:** **Tsuma ga itsumo o-sewa ni natte orimasu.**
(4) **Kinjo no hito:** 　　**Mata nimotsu o azukatte ite itadaita no ne. Itsumo sumimasen.**
(5) **Kachou:** 　　　　　**A, mukae ni kite kureta no? Aa, arigatai naa.**
(6) **Buchou:** 　　　　　**Rei no houkokusho ('report'), owatta no? Go-kurou-san.**
(7) **(Purojekuto ga owatte uchiagekai o shiteiru toki)**
　　**Douryou:** 　　　　　**O-tsukare-sama deshita!**
(8) **Hosuto famirii no imouto (aisu kuriimu o katte ageta toki): O-niichan/ O-neechan, arigatou!**

⇨　12.1, 30.1, 43, 59.1, 59.3

# 60
# Apologies and forgiveness

**1** ★

Who are the likely addressees of the following **keitai meeru** ('cell phone mail')? Choose an appropriate one from the list. Use each addressee just once.

> a. client · b. colleague · c. roommate · d. husband/wife · e. professor
> f. subordinate at work · g. landlord/landlady · h. boyfriend/girlfriend

(1) ＿＿ ゴメン！今バイト先。デートすっかり忘れてた！
(2) ＿＿ 申し訳ございません。10分ぐらい遅れる見込みでございます。
またご連絡させていただきます。
(3) ＿＿ 3時に宅配が来るんですが、受け取っておいて下さいますか。
いつもすみません。
(4) ＿＿ ワルイ！今日も残業。夕食、先食べといて。帰りは23時っぽい。
(5) ＿＿ ゴメン！コンビニで何買って帰るんだっけ？

(1) ＿＿ Gomen! Ima baito-saki. Deeto sukkari wasurete ta!
(2) ＿＿ Moushiwake gozaimasen. Juppun gurai okureru mikomi de
gozaimasu. Mata go-renraku sasete itadakimasu.
(3) ＿＿ Sanji ni takuhai ga kuru n desu ga, uketotte oite kudasaimasu ka.
Itsumo sumimasen.
(4) ＿＿ Warui! Kyou mo zangyou. Yuushoku saki tabetoite. Kaeri wa
nijuusanji-ppoi.
(5) ＿＿ Gomen! Konbini de nani katte kaeru n da kke?

➪ 60.1, 60.2

**2** ★

Fill in the blanks with appropriate expressions. Choose the correct items where choices are given.

(1)
You are late for a Japan Club meeting due to traffic congestion. You are the president of the club, and the advisor and students had to wait for you to start.

あなた： ①＿＿＿＿＿＿＿＿＿＿＿＿＿＿＿＿＿。
先生： どうしたんですか。めずらしいですねぇ。
あなた： あのう、②＿＿＿＿＿＿＿＿＿＿＿＿＿ …。
先生： う～ん、今度からはもっと早く出るようにして下さいね。
あなた： はい、③＿＿＿＿＿＿＿＿＿＿＿＿＿＿＿。

Anata:   ① _____ .
Sensei:  Dou shita n desu ka. Mezurashii desu nee.
Anata:   Anou, ② _____ . . .
Sensei:  Uun, kondo kara wa motto hayaku deru you ni shite kudasai ne.
Anata:   Hai, ③ _____ .

(2)
You had homework due today, but couldn't submit it because you were sick
yesterday. Apologize to your professor and ask if you can submit it next
Monday.

あなた： あのう、① _____。② _____ なんですが … 。
先生：   はい。
あなた： ③ _____ が、月曜日に ④ _____ でしょうか。
　　　　昨日は【⑤ 病気で・具合が悪くて】ぜんぜん勉強ができなかった
　　　　【⑥ から・ん】です。
先生：   そうですか、それはいけませんねぇ。じゃ、いいですよ。もう良くなり
　　　　ました か。
あなた： はい、⑦ _____ ます。だいぶ良くなりました。

Anata:   Anou, ① _____ . ② _____ na n desu ga . . .
Sensei:  Hai.
Anata:   ③ _____ ga, getsuyoubi ni ④ _____ deshou
         ka. Kinou wa 【⑤ byouki de・guai ga warukute】zenzen benkyou
         ga dekinakatta 【⑥ kara・n】desu.
Sensei:  Sou desu ka. Sore wa ikemasen nee. Ja, ii desu yo. Mou yoku
         narimashita ka.
Anata:   Hai, ⑦ _____ masu. Daibu yoku narimashita.

(3)
You are a teacher in Japan. You took a day off several days ago because of
an emergency, and a colleague taught your class.

あなた： 先日は ① _____ て、② _____ でした。
同僚：   いえ、いえ、お互い様です。('I may have to ask you next time')
あなた： とても助かりました。本当に ③ _____ ございました。

Anata:   Senjitsu wa ① _____ te, ② _____ deshita.
Douryou: Ie, ie, o-tagaisama desu. ('I may have to ask you next time')
Anata:   Totemo tasukarimashita. Hontou ni ③ _____
         gozaimashita.

(4)
Reiko has lost a book she borrowed from a friend.

れい子： あのさぁ、先週借りた本のことなんだけど … 。いくらさがしても
　　　　① _____ 。② _____ 。
友人：   ええっ？あの本、明日使おうと思ってたんだけど … 。
れい子： ホント ③ _____ ね。ゆうべネットで注文したから、あさって
　　　　には届くと思うんだけど … 。④ _____ けど、明日はだれか
　　　　他の人のを借りてくれる？
友人：   うん、いいよ。かえって気をつかわせちゃったね。

Reiko:     Ano saa, senshuu karita hon no koto na n da kedo...Ikura
           sagashite mo ①_____. ②_____.
Yuujin:    Ee? Ano hon, ashita tsukaou to omotte ta n da kedo...
Reiko:     Honto, ③_____ ne. Yuube netto de chuumon shita
           kara, asatte ni wa todoku to omou n da kedo...④_____
           kedo, ashita wa dareka hoka no hito no o karite kureru?
Yuujin:    Un, ii yo. Kaette ki o tsukawasechatta ne.

(5)
Hiroshi accidentally breaks his roommate's lamp.

[ガッチャーン！**Gatchaan!** 'Crash!']

宏：              あ、まずっ！こわれちゃった … 。
ルームメイト：    ええっ！おい、おい …
宏：              ①_____。弁償する。('I'll pay for it')
ルームメイト：    いや、いいよ、気にしなくて。安物だから。
宏：              いや、本当に。明日同じの買って来る。ホント②_____。

Hiroshi:     A, mazu! Kowarechatta...
Ruumumeito:  Ee! Oi, oi...
Hiroshi:     ①_____. Benshou suru. ('I'll pay for it')
Ruumumeito:  Iya, ii yo, ki ni shinakute. Yasumono da kara.
Hiroshi:     Iya, hontou ni. Ashita onaji no katte kuru.
             Honto ②_____.

⇨ | 47, 60

**3** ✱✱✱  The following is a letter of apology written by Yamada Taro to his department
chief, Tsuruta Koji. Read the letter then mark the statements which follow,
true (○) or false (×).

鶴田光司営業部長殿、
　　このたびは多大なるご迷惑をおかけ致しまして、申し訳ございません
でした。
　　今回このようなことになった経緯ですが、部下達の間での連絡がほぼ全面
的に口頭でなされ、私の所まで正確に伝わって来ていなかった事項が若干あっ
たことが最大の原因と判明致しました。
　　今後このようなことが二度と起こらぬよう、連絡システムを改善し、逐
一、文書にて連絡を図り、それを規定の順に確認して行くという方法を徹底
させる所存でございます。営業部員一同、遺憾に思い、心より反省しており
ます。誠に申し訳ございませんでした。
　　今後ともご指導のほど、どうぞよろしくお願い申し上げます。
　　　　　　　　　　　　　　　　　　　　　　　　　　　山田太郎

Tsuruta Kouji Eigyou Buchou Dono
    Kono tabi wa tadai naru go-meiwaku o o-kake itashimashite, moushiwake gozaimasendeshita.
    Konkai kono you na koto ni natta keii desu ga, buka-tachi no aida de no renraku ga hobo zenmenteki ni koutou de nasare, watakushi no tokoro made seikaku ni tsutawatte kite inakatta jikou ga jakkan atta koto ga saidai no gen'in to hanmei itashimashita.
    Kongo kono you na koto ga nido to okoranu you, renraku shisutemu o kaizen shi, chikuichi, bunsho nite renraku o hakari, sore o kitei no jun ni kakunin shite iku to iu houhou o tettei saseru shozon de gozaimasu. Eigyoubu-in ichidou, ikan ni omoi, kokoro yori hansei shite orimasu. Makoto ni moushiwake gozaimasendeshita.
    Kongo tomo go-shidou no hodo, douzo yoroshiku o-negai moushi-agemasu.

                                                              Yamada Tarou

a.  (  ) The sales department staff are all remorseful.
b.  (  ) The main cause of the problem was an inadequate system of communication among the department staff, and not between Yamada and his staff.
c.  (  ) From now on all official communication will be documented.
d.  (  ) Mr Yamada will establish a chain of command for the staff to follow.

⇨  29.4, 48.2, 60.1

# 61
# Empathy

1 ★★

Express empathy, in one or two sentences, to someone who says the following.

(1) 数学のテストでAをもらっちゃった！
**Suugaku no tesuto de A o moratchatta!**

(2) あの課長、もうがまんできない！全く無責任なんだから！
**Ano kachou, mou gaman dekinai! Mattaku mu-sekinin na n da kara!**

(3) [ペットの犬の話　**Petto no inu no hanashi**]
うちのクイールくん、もう年で、手術してもだめだった … 。
**Uchi no Kuiiru-kun, mou toshi de, shujutsu shite mo dame datta ...**

(4) 最近、ズンバやり始めたんだけど、楽しいよぉ！
**Saikin Zumba yari-hajimeta n da kedo, tanoshii yoo!**

(5) この間アルバイト、首になっちゃって … 。今ちょっと経済的にきびしいんです。
**Kono aida arubaito, kubi ni natchatte ... Ima chotto keizaiteki ni kibishii n desu.**

(6) アレルギーがひどくて、仕事に集中できないんです。
**Arerugii ga hidokute, shigoto ni shuuchuu dekinai n desu.**

(7) いろんな会社を受けてみたんだけど、あんまり希望なさそう … 。
**Ironna kaisha o ukete mita n da kedo, anmari kibou nasa sou ...**

⇨ | 61.1, 61.2

# 62
# Likes and dislikes

**1** ⋆ The following table shows Yuri's likes and dislikes. The ratings range from 1 (dislike a lot) to 5 (like a lot). Complete the descriptions below based on the table.

| | ゆり **Yuri** | あなた **Anata** |
|---|---|---|
| 犬 **inu** | 5 | |
| ねこ **neko** | 3 | |
| すし **sushi** | 5 | |
| ステーキ **suteeki** | 1 | |
| 勉強 **benkyou** | 3 | |
| 読書 **dokusho** | 4 | |
| パーティーに行くこと **paatii ni iku koto** | 2 | |
| 買い物 **kaimono** | 5 | |

ゆりは、ペットは ① ＿＿＿＿＿＿＿ より ② ＿＿＿＿＿＿＿ の方が好きです。
③ ＿＿＿＿＿＿＿ 食べ物はすしです。ステーキは ④ ＿＿＿＿＿＿＿。勉強は
⑤ ＿＿＿＿＿＿＿ でも ⑥ ＿＿＿＿＿＿＿ でもありません。パーティーに
⑦ ＿＿＿＿＿＿＿ は、あまり ⑧ ＿＿＿＿＿＿＿ が、⑨ ＿＿＿＿＿＿＿ だり
⑩ ＿＿＿＿＿＿＿ たりするのが好きです。

**Yuri wa, petto wa** ① ＿＿＿＿＿＿ **yori** ② ＿＿＿＿＿＿ **no hou ga suki desu.** ③ ＿＿＿＿＿＿ **tabemono wa sushi desu. Suteeki wa** ④ ＿＿＿＿＿＿. **Benkyou wa** ⑤ ＿＿＿＿＿＿ **demo** ⑥ ＿＿＿＿＿＿ **demo arimasen. Paatii ni** ⑦ ＿＿＿＿＿＿ **wa, amari** ⑧ ＿＿＿＿＿＿ **ga,** ⑨ ＿＿＿＿＿＿ **dari** ⑩ ＿＿＿＿＿＿ **tari suru no ga suki desu.**

⇨ 38, 62.1

**2** ⋆ Rate each of the items in the table above in terms of your *own* likes and dislikes. Then, write a paragraph, like the one above, about yourself.

⇨ 38, 62.1

**Likes and dislikes**

**3** ⋆⋆ Ms. Yamada, whom you met just recently, wants to find out the following about you. First write the questions in Japanese, then answer them about yourself.

(1) what kind of food you like:
(2) what sports you like to play:
(3) whether there are any foods you don't like:
(4) what you enjoy doing when you have free time:
(5) which you like better – fish or meat:
(6) whether you like the computer you are using now (use **ki ni iru**):

⇨ 38.1, 62.1, 62.2

# 63
# Desires and preferences

**1** *   How would you express the following in Japanese? Use formal (**desu/masu**) style.

(1) You want a new car.
(2) You want to travel.
(3) Your younger sister wants a new computer.
(4) Your friend wants to study Japanese.
(5) You want your friend to visit (you).
(6) Your younger brother wants your mother to take him to the zoo.

⇨  63.1

**2** *   Mai and Yuri are good friends. Complete the following dialogue with expressions of desires and preferences.

ゆり：　来週の日曜日はまいさんの誕生日だけど、何か (1)＿＿＿＿＿＿＿＿＿
　　　　ものある？
まい：　そうだねえ、かっこいいネックレスが (2)＿＿＿＿＿＿＿＿＿　なぁ。
ゆり：　どこか (3)＿＿＿＿＿＿＿＿＿　レストランある？特に (4)＿＿＿＿＿＿＿＿＿
　　　　ものとか。
まい：　そうだねえ、やっぱり日本食が (5)＿＿＿＿＿＿＿＿＿　なあ。
ゆり：　じゃ、「むらさき」に行こうよ。それから、ボブも (6)＿＿＿＿＿＿＿＿＿
　　　　って言ってたから、誘ってもいい？
まい：　うん、もちろん！じゃ楽しみにしてる。

**Yuri:**　**Raishuu no nichiyoubi wa Mai-san no tanjoubi da kedo, nanika**
　　　(1)＿＿＿＿＿＿＿＿ **mono aru?**
**Mai:**　**Sou da nee, kakkoii nekkuresu ga** (2)＿＿＿＿＿＿＿＿ **naa.**
**Yuri:**　**Dokoka** (3)＿＿＿＿＿＿＿＿ **resutoran aru? Toku ni** (4)＿＿＿＿＿＿＿
　　　**mono toka.**
**Mai:**　**Sou da nee, yappari nihonshoku ga** (5)＿＿＿＿＿＿＿＿ **naa.**
**Yuri:**　**Ja, Murasaki ni ikou yo. Sorekara, Bobu mo** (6)＿＿＿＿＿＿＿＿ **tte**
　　　**itte ta kara, sasotte mo ii?**
**Mai:**　**Un, mochiron! Ja tanoshimi ni shite ru.**

⇨  63.1, 63.2, 63.3

**Desires and preferences**

**3**

Keiko and Ann work in the same office. Keiko is expecting a baby. Complete the following conversation with expressions of desires and preferences.

アン： 日本では子供を産むと仕事をやめる女性が多いって聞いたんですけど、恵子さんは、出産してからも仕事を続けるつもりですか。

恵子： (1)＿＿＿＿＿＿＿＿ けど、かなり難しいかもしれませんね。子供を預けるのが難しいし。

アン： ご主人は育児とか家事などを手伝ってくれないんですか。

恵子： 子供が産まれたら、主人に育児を (2)＿＿＿＿＿＿＿ と思うんですけど、主人も普通のサラリーマンなので、難しいかもしれません。でも、いったんやめてしまうと、また (3)＿＿＿＿＿＿＿ ても、いい仕事はみつけられないので、なるべく (4)＿＿＿＿＿＿ ですねえ。

アン： 会社が育児休暇などをちゃんと作るべきですよね。

恵子： ほんとうに。仕事と育児が両立できるような環境を会社に (5)＿＿＿＿＿＿＿ と思いますねえ。

アン： ところで、恵子さんはもう一人子供が (6)＿＿＿＿＿＿＿ と思いますか。

恵子： 二人が理想的だと思いますが、まだわかりません。

**An:** Nihon de wa kodomo o umu to shigoto o yameru josei ga ooi tte kiita n desu kedo, Keiko-san wa, shussan shite kara mo shigoto o tsuzukeru tsumori desu ka.

**Keiko:** (1)＿＿＿＿＿＿ kedo, kanari muzukashii kamo shiremasen ne. Kodomo o azukeru no ga muzukashii shi.

**An:** Go-shujin wa ikuji toka kaji nado o tetsudatte kurenai n desu ka.

**Keiko:** Kodomo ga umaretara, shujin ni ikuji o (2)＿＿＿＿＿＿ to omou n desu kedo, shujin mo futsuu no sarariiman na node, muzukashii kamo shiremasen. Demo, ittan yamete shimau to, mata (3)＿＿＿＿＿＿ te mo, ii shigoto wa mitsukerarenai node, narubeku (4)＿＿＿＿＿＿ desu nee.

**An:** Kaisha ga ikuji kyuuka nado o chanto tsukuru beki desu yo ne.

**Keiko:** Hontou ni. Shigoto to ikuji ga ryouritsu dekiru you na kankyou o kaisha ni (5)＿＿＿＿＿＿ to omoimasu nee.

**An:** Tokorode, Keiko-san wa mou hitori kodomo ga (6)＿＿＿＿＿＿ to omoimasu ka.

**Keiko:** Futari ga risouteki da to omoimasu ga, mada wakarimasen.

⇨ 63.1

**4**

Based on the previous two dialogues (2 and 3), report to a third party what Mai and Keiko want.

(1) まいは誕生日の贈り物に ＿＿＿＿＿＿＿。
(2) まいは誕生日に ＿＿＿＿＿＿＿。
(3) 恵子は子供が産まれてからも ＿＿＿＿＿＿＿。
(4) 恵子は育児休暇を ＿＿＿＿＿＿＿。
(5) 恵子はもう一人子供が ＿＿＿＿＿＿＿。

(1) Mai wa tanjoubi no okurimono ni ＿＿＿＿＿＿.
(2) Mai wa tanjoubi ni ＿＿＿＿＿＿.
(3) Keiko wa kodomo ga umarete kara mo ＿＿＿＿＿＿.
(4) Keiko wa ikuji kyuuka o ＿＿＿＿＿＿.
(5) Keiko wa mou hitori kodomo ga ＿＿＿＿＿＿.

⇨ 63.3

**157**

**5** ⭐

Answer the questions according to the cues. Begin your answers with a phrase like そうですねぇ **sou desu nee**, あのう **anou**, and うーん **uun**, and end with が **ga** or けど **kedo** ('but') to mitigate the impact.

(1) あしたでいいですか。
   **Ashita de ii desu ka.** (I prefer today.)
(2) 日本食でいいですか。
   **Nihonshoku de ii desu ka.** (I want to have steak.)
(3) みんなに見せてもいいですか。
   **Minna ni misete mo ii desu ka.** (I would prefer if you didn't show it to anyone.)
(4) だれか連れて行きましょうか。
   **Dareka tsurete ikimashou ka.** (I would like you to bring Susan with you.)
(5) ビールとワインとどっちにしましょうか。
   **Biiru to wain to dotchi ni shimashou ka.** (I prefer wine.)

⇨ 63.4

# 64
# Hopes and wishes

1 ★

Megumi tends to worry about things. The following are some of her worries. How would she express her hope that things won't turn out as she fears.

> Example: She hopes she won't oversleep tomorrow.
> → 明日寝坊しないといいんだけど。
> **Ashita nebou shinai to ii n da kedo.**

(1) She hopes it won't rain on Saturday as she's having a picnic.
(2) She hopes she can find a good job when she graduates from college.
(3) She hopes she'll pass the math test tomorrow.
(4) She hopes her cold will get better soon.
(5) She hopes she can graduate this year.
(6) She hopes her flight to New York won't be delayed.

⇨ | 64.1

2 ★

There are many things Ichiro wishes he had or had not done. How would he express his regrets about the following?

> Example 1: He regrets he got so drunk.
> → あんなに酔っぱらわなければよかった。
> **Anna ni yopparawanakereba yokatta.**

> Example 2: He regrets he didn't meet more people.
> → もっといろいろな人に会っておけば良かった。
> **Motto iroiro na hito ni atte okeba yokatta.**

(1) He regrets that he changed his job (change jobs = **tenshoku suru**).
(2) He regrets he bought an expensive car.
(3) He regrets he did not study hard in college.
(4) He regrets he got a divorce.
(5) He regrets he did not do what he likes to do.

⇨ | 64.1, Exercises in 67

# 65

# Joy and sorrow

1 * How would you express your feelings in the following situations?

(1) Your favorite team just won a championship. [to your friend]
(2) You are given a very prestigious award. [to someone who helped you]
(3) You spent hours making a dish from a new recipe, but it didn't taste good. [to your roommate]
(4) You broke up with your 'significant other'. [to your best friend]
(5) You won a round-the-world trip; you are so happy that you don't know what to do. [to an acquaintance in an e-mail]

⇨ 65.1

2 * Choose the appropriate expressions.

(1) 鈴木さんは昇格が決まって、とても【うれしいです・うれしいようです】。
[昇格 **shoukaku** 'promotion']
**Suzuki-san wa shoukaku ga kimatte, totemo 【ureshii desu・ureshii you desu】.**
(2) 私はみんなと一緒に旅行に行けなくて【残念です・残念らしいです】。
**Watashi wa minna to issho ni ryokou ni ikenakute 【zannen desu・zannen rashii desu】.**
(3) 洋子さんはご主人が単身赴任で【さびしいです・さびしがっています】。
**Youko-san wa go-shujin ga tanshin funin de 【sabishii desu・sabishi-gatte imasu】.** [単身赴任 **tanshin funin** 'to work and live away from family']
(4) 私はすばらしい友人に恵まれて本当に【幸せです・せつないです】。
**Watashi wa subarashii yuujin ni megumarete hontou ni 【shiawase desu・setsunai desu】.**
(5) 父は再就職が決まらなくてすごく【つらいです・つらそうです】。
**Chichi wa sai-shuushoku ga kimaranakute sugoku 【tsurai desu・tsura-sou desu】.**

⇨ 65.1, 65.2

3 * Sachi went to her friend Aya's, wedding. She is now telling her mother about the people she saw at the wedding. Choose the most appropriate alternative.

お母さん： 亜矢さんの結婚式、どうだった？
沙知： 亜矢、すごく幸せ【① a. だった　b. だ　c. そうだった】よ。
お母さん： そう、よかったわね。
沙知： ご両親もほっとしたんじゃないかな。お父さんはちょっと
【② a. さびしかった　b. さびしい　c. さびしそうだった】けど。
お母さん： やっぱりねえ。

沙知 ： 亜矢のお姉さんはニコニコしてたけど、本当は【③ a. 悔しがってるみ
たいだった b. 悔しかった c. 残念だった】よ。

お母さん ： まあ、そんなこと言うもんじゃないわよ。

Okaasan: Aya-san no kekkonshiki, dou datta?

Sachi: Aya, sugoku shiawase 【① a. datta b. da c. sou datta】 yo.

Okaasan: Sou, yokatta wa ne.

Sachi: Go-ryoushin mo hotto shita n ja nai ka na. O-tousan wa chotto
【② a. sabishikatta b. sabishii c. sabishi sou datta】 kedo.

Okaasan: Yappari nee.

Sachi: Aya no o-neesan wa nikoniko shite ta kedo, hontou wa
【③ a. kuyashigatte ru mitai datta b. kuyashikatta
c. zannen datta】 yo.

Okaasan: Maa, sonna koto iu mon ja nai wa yo.

⇨ 65.2

# 66
# Fear or worry

**1** ★ Junko has many fears and worries. She is talking to her school counselor about her feelings. Choose the correct one in each set.

私は地震が【① こわいです・こわがっています】。よく地震の夢を見ます。学校に行くのも【② 不安です・安心です】。友達に何か頼まれると、断れません。きらわれる【③ のが・のを】怖いんです。成績のことも【④ 悩んでいます・悩んでいるようです】。大学院に行きたいんですが、GPAが足りません。卒業までにGPAが上がるかどうかすごく【⑤ 心配で・心配して】夜眠れません。

**Watashi wa jishin ga 【① kowai desu・kowa-gatte imasu】. Yoku jishin no yume o mimasu. Gakkou ni iku no mo 【② fuan desu・anshin desu】. Tomodachi ni nanika tanomareru to, kotowaremasen. Kirawareru 【③ no ga・no o】 kowai n desu. Seiseki no koto mo 【④ nayande imasu・nayande iru you desu】. Daigakuin ni ikitai n desu ga, GPA ga tarimasen. Sotsugyou made ni GPA ga agaru ka douka sugoku 【⑤ shinpai de・shinpai shite】 yoru nemuremasen.**

⇨ 66.1, 66.3

**2** ★ Junko's counselor is talking to Junko's mother. Referring to the paragraph in #1 above, choose the most appropriate alternatives below.

先日潤子さんとお話したのですが、その時の様子をお話します。潤子さんはとても地震を【① おそれています・おそろしいです】。よく地震の夢を見るそうです。学校に行くことも【② 不安でした・不安がっていました】。友人関係では、友達に嫌われるのが【③ こわい・こわいらしい】と言っていました。大学の成績についても【④ 悩んでいそう・悩んでいるそう】です。GPAが上がるかどうかとても【⑤ 心配でした・心配していました】。

**Senjitsu Junko-san to o-hanashi shita no desu ga, sono toki no yousu o o-hanashi shimasu. Junko-san wa totemo jishin o 【① osorete imasu・osoroshii desu】. Yoku jishin no yume o miru sou desu. Gakkou ni iku koto mo 【② fuan deshita・fuangatte imashita】. Yuujin kankei de wa, tomodachi ni kirawareru no ga 【③ kowai・kowai rashii】 to itte imashita. Daigaku no seiseki ni tsuite mo 【④ nayande i sou・nayande iru sou】 desu. GPA ga agaru ka dou ka totemo 【⑤ shinpai deshita・shinpai shite imashita】.**

⇨ 66.2, 66.4

**3**

Express the following in Japanese.

(1) My roommate seems worried about whether he can win the tennis match next week.
(2) I am worried that my parents' restaurant will go out of business.
    [to go out of business: つぶれる **tsubureru**].
(3) I am uncertain (lit. 'insecure') whether what I decided was right.
(4) My friend Sue seems to be afraid of dogs.

⇨ | 66.2, 66.3, 66.4

# 67
# Distress and regret

1 ★ Choose the appropriate expressions below.

(1) You just came home and realized you don't have the key to get in.
ああ、【こまっている・こまったなあ】。
**Aa,【komatte iru・komatta naa】.**

(2) You just locked your car with your key inside.
ああ、【途方にくれている・どうしよう】。
**Aa,【tohou ni kurete iru・dou shiyou】.**

(3) You are telling your neighbors that you are troubled by their dog barking at night.
お宅の犬が毎晩吠えるので【困っている・困った】んですけど。
**Otaku no inu ga maiban hoeru node【komatte iru・komatta】 n desu kedo.**

(4) In an e-mail you tell your host brother that you've been out of work for 6 months even though you've been looking hard. You are feeling depressed.
もう6ヶ月も仕事が見つからなくて【落ち込んでいる・後悔している】。
**Mou rokkagetsu mo shigoto ga mitsukaranakute【ochikonde iru・koukai shite iru】.**

⇨ 67.1, 67.2

2 ★★★ A group of friends are telling each other what they regret in their lives. Combine the two sentences below into one. You will need to add some words and/or change the end of the first sentence.

Example 1: 大学の時にあまり授業に出なかった。後悔している。
→ 大学の時にあまり授業に出なかった<u>の</u>を後悔している。

Example 2: 勉強ばかりしていた。あまり旅行をしなかった。
→ 勉強ばかり<u>しないで</u>、もっと旅行を<u>すればよかった</u>。

Example 1: **Daigaku no toki ni amari jugyou ni denakatta. Koukai shite iru.**
→ **Daigaku no toki ni amari jugyou ni denakatta <u>no o</u> koukai shite iru.**

Example 2: **Benkyou bakari shite ita. Amari ryokou o shinakatta.**
→ **Benkyou bakari <u>shinai de</u>, motto ryokou o <u>sureba yokatta</u>.**

(1) 健： 大学の時にあまり勉強しなかった。後悔している。
(2) 優： 学生時代に留学しなかった。残念だなあ。
(3) 雪： 勉強ばかりしていた。いろいろな経験をしなかった。
(4) 沙知： 車の免許 ('license') をとらなかった。後悔している。
(5) 亮： 何もクラブに入らなかった。

(1) Ken:   Daigaku no toki ni amari benkyou shinakatta. Koukai shite iru.
(2) Yuu:    Gakusei jidai ni ryuugaku shinakatta. Zannen da naa.
(3) Yuki:   Benkyou bakari shite ita. Iroiro na keiken o shinakatta.
(4) Sachi:  Kuruma no menkyo ('license') o toranakatta. Koukai shite iru.
(5) Ryou:   Nani mo kurabu ni hairanakatta.

⇨  67.2

**3**  ⁑

Fill in the blanks with the appropriate forms of the words in the box. Use each word only once.

> うそをつく・練習しておく・電話してみる・つらい・落ち込む・残念
>
> **uso o tsuku · renshuu shite oku · denwa shite miru · tsurai · ochikomu · zannen**

(1)
[Talking to a colleague at work]

[散々 **sanzan** 'a disaster']

A:  ゴルフのコンペ、どうでしたか。
B:  いやあ、散々でした。もっと (a)＿＿＿＿＿＿＿＿ よかったんですが。
A:  そうですか。それは (b)＿＿＿＿＿＿＿ ね。

A:  **Gorufu no konpe, dou deshita ka.**
B:  **Iyaa, sanzan deshita. Motto** (a)＿＿＿＿＿＿＿ **yokatta n desu ga.**
A:  **Sou desu ka. Sore wa** (b)＿＿＿＿＿＿＿ **ne.**

(2)
[Talking to a friend in front of a restaurant (定休日 **teikyuubi** '(days) closed')]

C:  あれ、今日は定休日だって。
D:  あぁ、＿＿＿＿＿＿＿＿よかった！
C:  うん、でも、仕方ないね。

C:  **Are, kyou wa teikyuubi da tte.**
D:  **Aa,** ＿＿＿＿＿＿＿ **yokatta!**
C:  **Un, demo, shikata nai ne.**

(3)
[Talking to a colleague at a pub after work (それが **sorega** 'well, actually')]

E:  娘さん、お元気ですか。
F:  いや、それが、恋人にふられたらしく、一日中部屋で泣いてるんですよ。
E:  え？そんなに (a)＿＿＿＿＿＿＿＿ んですか。それは心配ですね。
F:  ええ、それなのに、何もしてあげられなくて、私も (b)＿＿＿＿＿＿＿＿。

E:  **Musume-san, o-genki desu ka.**
F:  **Iya, sorega, koibito ni furareta rashiku, ichinichi-juu heya de naite ru n desu yo.**
E:  **E? Sonna ni** (a)＿＿＿＿＿＿＿ **n desu ka. Sore wa shinpai desu ne.**
F:  **Ee, sore na noni, nanimo shite agerarenakute, watashi mo**
    (b)＿＿＿＿＿＿＿.

(4)
[Talking to a younger host brother at home]

I:   どうしたの？
J:   お母さんにうそがばれて、怒られた。
I:   だいじょうぶ？
J:   うん。＿＿＿＿＿＿＿＿＿＿ よかったなあ。

I:   **Dou shita no?**
J:   **O-kaasan ni uso ga barete, okorareta.**
I:   **Daijoubu?**
J:   **Un. ＿＿＿＿＿＿＿＿＿＿ yokatta naa.**

⇨   67.2, 67.3

# 68
# Surprise

1 ★

Akiko and Yoko are gossiping about their friends Ken and Sachi. Choose the most appropriate expression for (1)–(5) from the box. You may use each expression once.

> まさか！・信じられない！・え？・うそでしょ？・びっくりしたあ！
>
> **Masaka! · Shinjirarenai! · E? · Uso desho? · Bikkuri shitaa!**

明子 ：　健と沙知、別れたんだって。
洋子 ：　(1) Huh? (2) You are kidding, right?
明子 ：　ほんと。健が<u>浮気した</u> (had an affair) らしいよ。
洋子 ：　(3) I can't believe it!
明子 ：　うん、私も。沙知、大丈夫かな。変なこと考えないといいけど …
洋子 ：　(4) No way!
明子 ：　そうだよね。大丈夫だよね。

[Sachi sneaks up behind Akiko and Yoko.]

沙知 ：　大丈夫！
明子 ：　うわっ、(5) I'm surprised!

**Akiko:**　**Ken to Sachi, wakareta n da tte.**
**Youko:**　(1) Huh? (2) You are kidding, right?
**Akiko:**　**Honto. Ken ga <u>uwaki shita</u>** (had an affair) **rashii yo.**
**Youko:**　(3) I can't believe it!
**Akiko:**　**Un, watashi mo. Sachi, daijoubu ka na. Hen na koto kangaenai to ii kedo . . .**
**Youko:**　(4) No way!
**Akiko:**　**Sou da yo ne. Daijoubu da yo ne.**

[Sachi sneaks up behind Akiko and Yoko]

**Sachi:**　**Daijoubu!**
**Akiko:**　**Uwa,** (5) You surprised me! (Lit. I got surprised.)

⇨ 68.1

**2** *

A group of people are talking about what they found surprising during their recent trip. Choose the correct item in each pair.

[のら犬 **norainu** 'stray dog'; 運行 **unkou** 'service'; 正確 **seikaku** 'punctual']

A: 大都市な【のに・ので】緑が多くて驚きましたね。
B: 私はのら犬が多いの【に・を】びっくりしましたね。
C: 地下鉄の運行がとても正確【に・で】びっくりですよ。
D: 私は日曜日にレストランが閉まってしまうことにびっくり【します・しました】よ。
E: 私は美術館の質の高さに【驚いていました・驚きました】ね。

A: **Daitoshi na 【noni · node】 midori ga ookute odorokimashita ne.**
B: **Watashi wa norainu ga ooi no 【ni · o】 bikkuri shimashita ne.**
C: **Chikatetsu no unkou ga totemo seikaku 【ni · de】 bikkuri desu yo.**
D: **Watashi wa nichiyoubi ni resutoran ga shimatte shimau koto ni bikkuri 【shimasu · shimashita】 yo.**
E: **Watashi wa bijutsukan no shitsu no takasa ni 【odoroite imashita · odorokimashita】 ne.**

⇨ 68.2

# 69
# Hunger, thirst, and fatigue

1 * Express the following in Japanese, paying attention to each context.

(1) [Satoshi comes home hungry, and wants to eat something] 'I'm hungry!'
(2) [You have been playing tennis and need to drink something] 'I'm thirsty!'
(3) [You just climbed up five flights of stairs] 'I'm tired!'

⇨ 69.1

2 * Fill in the blanks with appropriate questions.

(1)
[Father and child are talking at home]

子： ただいま！
父： おかえり！(a)＿＿＿＿＿＿＿＿＿＿＿＿＿＿＿＿＿＿。
子： うん、ちょっと、すいた。何か食べるものある？
父： うん、あるよ。のど、(b)＿＿＿＿＿＿＿＿＿＿＿＿＿＿＿。
子： うん。お水ちょうだい。

**Child:** Tadaima!
**Father:** O-kaeri! (a) ＿＿＿＿＿＿＿＿＿＿＿＿＿＿＿＿.
**Child:** Un, chotto, suita. Nanika taberu mono aru?
**Father:** Un, aru yo. Nodo, (b) ＿＿＿＿＿＿＿＿＿＿＿＿＿.
**Child:** Un. O-mizu choudai.

(2)
[Two neighbors are talking on the street]

山本： マラソンはどうでしたか。＿＿＿＿＿＿＿＿＿＿＿＿＿＿＿
小林： はい、くたくたです。今日はおふろに入って早く寝ます。

**Yamamoto:** Marason wa dou deshita ka. ＿＿＿＿＿＿＿＿＿＿＿＿＿＿
**Kobayashi:** Hai, kutakuta desu. Kyou wa o-furo ni haitte hayaku nemasu.

(3)
[Two friends are talking in a coffee shop looking out the window]

春子： あれ、夏子さんの妹じゃない？
夏子： あ、ほんとだ。
春子： なんか、すごく＿＿＿＿＿＿＿＿＿＿＿＿＿＿＿＿？
夏子： うん、疲れきってる感じ。ちょっと様子、見て来る。

Haruko:    Are, Natsuko-san no imouto ja nai?
Natsuko:   A, honto da.
Haruko:    Nanka, sugoku _____?
Natsuko:   Un, tsukare-kitte ru kanji. Chotto yousu, mite kuru.

⇨  69.2, 69.3

**3** *  Three of your colleagues just got back to the office after staffing a street sale. Describe to another colleague how they are, based on your observations.

(1) Mr Okamoto is hungry.
(2) Ms Inoue is thirsty.
(3) Ms Kuno is tired.

⇨  69.3

# 70
# Pain or discomfort

1 ★

You are sick today. Explain to your friend Keiko that you have a headache, feel a chill, and also have a bad cough. Your friend suggests that you go home, take some medicine, and sleep.

恵子 ： 　ちょっと顔色が ①＿＿＿＿＿＿＿ ね。
あなた ： 　うん、今日は朝から ②＿＿＿＿＿＿＿ て、ちょっと
　　　　　③＿＿＿＿＿＿＿ し、④＿＿＿＿＿＿＿ し。
恵子 ： 　それはよくないね。早く ⑤＿＿＿＿＿＿＿ たらどう？
あなた ： 　うん、そうする。

**Keiko:** 　**Chotto kaoiro ga** ①＿＿＿＿＿＿＿ **ne.**
**Anata:** 　**Un, kyou wa asa kara** ②＿＿＿＿＿＿＿ **te, chotto**
　　　　　③＿＿＿＿＿＿＿ **shi,** ④＿＿＿＿＿＿＿ **shi.**
**Keiko:** 　**Sore wa yokunai ne. Hayaku** ⑤＿＿＿＿＿＿＿ **tara dou?**
**Anata:** 　**Un, sou suru.**

➪ 70.1, 72.2

2 ★

You are at a doctor's office. You have been experiencing a dull stomachache for about a week. It usually occurs after you eat. Explain your symptoms to the doctor.

医者 ： 　どうしましたか。
あなた ： 　(1)＿＿＿＿＿＿＿＿＿＿＿＿＿＿＿＿。
医者 ： 　いつごろからですか。
あなた ： 　(2)＿＿＿＿＿＿＿＿＿＿＿＿＿＿＿＿。
医者 ： 　どんな具合に痛みますか。「きりきり」痛いんですか。
あなた ： 　うーん、(3)＿＿＿＿＿＿＿＿＿＿＿＿＿＿＿。
医者 ： 　ずっと痛いんですか。それとも、食事の前？　後？
あなた ： 　そうですね、(4)＿＿＿＿＿＿＿＿＿＿＿＿＿＿。
医者 ： 　そうですか。じゃ、薬を出しますから、飲んでちょっと様子をみてください。
あなた ： 　はい、わかりました。ありがとうございました。

**Isha:** 　**Dou shimashita ka.**
**Anata:** 　(1)＿＿＿＿＿＿＿＿＿＿＿＿＿＿＿＿.
**Isha:** 　**Itsugoro kara desu ka.**
**Anata:** 　(2)＿＿＿＿＿＿＿＿＿＿＿＿＿＿＿＿.
**Isha:** 　**Donna guai ni itamimasu ka. 'kirikiri' itai n desu ka.**
**Anata:** 　**Uun,** (3)＿＿＿＿＿＿＿＿＿＿＿＿＿＿＿.
**Isha:** 　**Zutto itai n desu ka. Soretomo, shokuji no mae? Ato?**
**Anata:** 　**Sou desu ne,** (4)＿＿＿＿＿＿＿＿＿＿＿＿＿＿.

Isha: Sou desu ka. Ja, kusuri o dashimasu kara, nonde chotto yousu o mite kudasai.

Anata: Hai, wakarimashita. Arigatou gozaimashita.

⇨ 70.1, 70.2

**3** ★ This morning when you woke up you felt sick. You think you have caught a cold. You feel listless, nauseated and have a fever. Write a short e-mail message to your teacher for Japanese 345 and ask to be absent from class today. The whole message should be about 7–8 lines including the salutation and the closing phrase.

⇨ 70.1

# 71
# Satisfaction and dissatisfaction

**1** ☆ The following are online reviews, or **kuchi komi hyouka** (lit. 'mouth communication evaluation'), filled out by **handoru neemu** ('handle(s)') **Ken-bou** and **O-kayo**. They stayed at the same inn in Hakone, but had quite different opinions. Their ratings are shown below, in which 5 is the highest score. Based on these, complete their respective reviews using the Japanese equivalents of the English words in the box. The words are listed randomly, and you may use them more than once.

|  |  |  | ケン **Ken** | かよ **Kayo** |
|---|---|---|---|---|
| (a) | 価格 | **kakaku** | 4 | 3 |
| (b) | 立地 | **ritchi** | 5 | 4 |
| (c) | 寝心地 | **ne-gokochi** | 5 | 1 |
| (d) | 客室 | **kyakushitsu** | 3 | 2 |
| (e) | 清潔感 | **seiketsukan** | 5 | 4 |
| (f) | 接客・サービス | **sekkyaku, saabisu** | 5 | 2 |

[NOTE: a = 料金 **ryoukin**; b = 場所 **basho**; c = 寝やすいか **ne-yasui ka**;
d = 部屋 **heya**; e = きれいか **kirei ka**; f = 客への対応 **kyaku e no taiou**]

(A)
ケン坊さん **Ken-bou-san** [30代/男性 **sanjuu dai / dansei**]

> clean, kind, convenient, satisfied

[手頃 **tegoro** 'reasonable']

大学時代の仲間と初めて宿泊しました。価格は手頃、場所も ①＿＿＿＿＿＿ で、
②＿＿＿＿＿＿。部屋がちょっと狭いように感じましたが、気持ちよく眠れました。館内は ③＿＿＿＿＿＿ し、スタッフの方々も ④＿＿＿＿＿＿。また利用させてもらいたいと思います。

Daigaku jidai no nakama to hajimete shukuhaku shimashita. Kakaku wa tegoro, basho mo ① _____ de, ② _____ . Heya ga chotto semai you ni kanjimashita ga, kimochi yoku nemuremashita. Kannai wa ③ _____ shi, sutaffu no katagata mo ④ _____ . Mata riyou sasete moraitai to omoimasu.

(B)
おかよさん **O-kayo-san** [50代/女性 gojuu dai / josei]

terrible, could not sleep, clean, to drop

夫と一泊旅行に利用しました。今回二回目でしたが、ちょっと質が
① _____ ように思います。館内は ② _____ ことは ③ _____
が、サービスが ④ _____ 。また、隣の部屋がやかましくて、夜
⑤ _____ 。コストもまあまあだし、立地の良いお宿なので、残念です。

Otto to ippaku ryokou ni riyou shimashita. Konkai nikaime deshita ga, chotto shitsu ga ① _____ you ni omoimasu. Kannai wa ② _____ koto wa ③ _____ ga, saabisu ga ④ _____ . Mata, tonari no heya ga yakamashikute, yoru ⑤ _____ . Kosuto mo maamaa da shi, ritchi no yoi o-yado na node, zannen desu.

⇨ 71.1–3

**2** ★ Complete the descriptions below using one of the expressions in the box. Use each expression only once.

| | | |
|---|---|---|
| 1. まあまあです | 2. 最高でした | 3. だめです |
| 4. すてきです | 5. 最低でした | 6. 満足しています |
| 7. 物足りないと思います。 | 8. 気に入っています | |

| | | |
|---|---|---|
| 1. Maamaa desu. | 2. Saikou deshita. | 3. Dame desu. |
| 4. Suteki desu. | 5. Saitei deshita. | 6. Manzoku shite imasu. |
| 7. Monotarinai to omoimasu. | 8. Ki ni itte imasu. | |

(a) 前の仕事は給料も悪かったし、残業が多くて、(　　　　　　　)
   **Mae no shigoto wa kyuuryou mo warukatta shi, zangyou ga ookute,**
   (　　　　　　)

(b) 今の職場は、自分のやりたい仕事ができるし、同僚もいい人たちばかりなので、
   (　　　　)
   **Ima no shokuba wa, jibun no yaritai shigoto ga dekiru shi, douryou mo ii hito-tachi bakari na node,** (　　　　　　)

(c) 最近新しい携帯を買ったのですが、使いやすくて、（　　　　　　　）
   **Saikin atarashii keitai o katta no desu ga, tsukai-yasukute, (　　　　　　)**

(d) あのレストランのお寿司は特にすばらしくはありませんが、まずくもありません。（　　　　　　）
   **Ano resutoran no osushi wa tokuni subarashiku wa arimasen ga, mazuku mo arimasen. (　　　　　　)**

(e) 休みは温泉に行って、体を休められたし、おいしい料理も食べられて、
   （　　　　　　　）
   **Yasumi wa onsen ni itte, karada o yasumerareta shi, oishii ryouri mo taberarete, (　　　　　　)**

(f) 今の仕事は事務の仕事が多く、自分の能力を生かせられないので、
   （　　　　　　）
   **Ima no shigoto wa jimu no shigoto ga ooku, jibun no nouryoku o ikaserarenai node, (　　　　　　)**

(g) 友達が結婚式に出るためにドレスを買ったので、見せてもらったが、そのドレスは色もスタイルもよく（　　　　　　）
   **Tomodachi ga kekkonshiki ni deru tame ni doresu o katta node, misete moratta ga, sono doresu wa iro mo sutairu mo yoku**
   （　　　　　　）

(h) 先日コーヒーメーカーを買ったけれどすぐこわれてしまった。
   安物は、やっぱり（　　　　　　）
   **Senjitsu koohii meekaa o katta keredo sugu kowarete shimatta.**
   **Yasumono wa, yappari (　　　　　　)**

⇨ 71.1, 71.2

# 72
# Advice and suggestions

1 * You are seeking advice. Choose one alternative from each set.

(1) 最近、娘の帰りが遅いんですが、注意【した方が・しては・しなければ】
いいでしょうか。
**Saikin, musume no kaeri ga osoi n desu ga, chuui 【shita hou ga ·
shite wa · shinakereba】 ii deshou ka.**

(2) 親友の誕生日プレゼントを買い忘れちゃったんだけど、【何をしたら・
どうしたら・何をすることが】いいと思う？
**Shinyuu no tanjoubi purezento o kai-wasurechatta n da kedo, 【nani o
shitara · dou shitara · nani o suru koto ga】 ii to omou?**

(3) 銀行がもうお金を貸してくれないようなんですが、何か【いい方法・すること・
いいとき】はないでしょうか。
**Ginkou ga mou o-kane o kashite kurenai you na n desu ga, nanika
【ii houhou · suru koto · ii toki】 wa nai deshou ka.**

(4) 大学院に進学したいんですが、先生、ちょっと相談に【聞いて・して・のって】
いただけないでしょうか。
**Daigakuin ni shingaku shitai n desu ga, sensei, chotto soudan ni
【kiite · shite · notte】 itadakenai deshou ka.**

⇨ 72.1

2 * Complete the advice or suggestions in the following conversation.

(1)
A: 最近どう？
B: 夜、あんまり眠れなくて、疲れもたまってる感じ。
A: そうなの？少し運動でも ＿＿＿＿＿＿＿＿＿＿＿＿。
B: うーん、なかなか時間がなくて。

A: **Saikin dou?**
B: **Yoru, anmari nemurenakute, tsukare mo tamatte ru kanji.**
A: **Sou na no? Sukoshi undou demo ＿＿＿＿＿＿＿＿＿＿.**
B: **Uun, nakanaka jikan ga nakute.**

(2)
C: 今晩は徹夜でレポートを書くぞ。
D: えー、無理 ＿＿＿＿＿＿＿＿＿＿＿＿。
C: 大丈夫。昼間いっぱい寝たから。

C: **Konban wa tetsuya de repooto o kaku zo.**
D: **Ee, muri ＿＿＿＿＿＿＿＿＿＿＿.**
C: **Daijoubu. Hiruma ippai neta kara.**

(3)

E: あの、これから飲みに行きませんか。
F: 昨日も飲みましたよね？今日は早く帰 _____
E: ううん、今日は誰もうちにいないから、大丈夫！

E: **Ano, korekara nomi ni ikimasen ka.**
F: **Kinou mo nomimashita yo ne? Kyou wa hayaku kae** _____ **.**
E: **Uun, kyou wa daremo uchi ni inai kara, daijoubu!**

(4)

G: ああ、また課長におこられちゃったよ。
H: 今日は課長の機嫌 (mood) が悪かっただけだから、気に _____ 。
G: そうだけどさ、落ち込むなあ。

G: **Aa, mata kachou ni okorarechatta yo.**
H: **Kyou wa kachou no <u>kigen</u> (mood) ga warukatta dake da kara,**
   **ki ni** _____ **.**
G: **Sou da kedo sa, ochikomu naa.**

⇨ 72.2, 72.3

**3** ★★★  How would you ask for advice in the following situations? Start with a sentence explaining the background.

(1) You are invited to a wedding reception next week but you don't have anything decent to wear. You just bought a new computer and do not have money to buy new clothes. Ask your best friend for advice.
(2) You applied for graduate schools, and two of your top choices have accepted you. You now have to decide which one to go to. Ask your academic adviser for advice.
(3) You want to ask a colleague out on a date, but you are not sure if s/he is in a relationship with someone else. Ask your best friend for suggestions.
(4) You want your children to take music lessons but they are not interested. Ask other parents what you should do.

⇨ 72.1

# 73

# Requests

How would you make requests in the following situations?

(1) You want a passerby to take a picture of you and your friend.
(2) Your neighbor who lives in the apartment next door is having a party late at night, and it's very noisy.
(3) You finished preparing the documents (**shorui**) and you would like your boss to look them over (**me o toosu**).
(4) You would like your teacher to repeat what s/he said one more time.
(5) You want to ask your teacher to teach you how to say 'I love you' in Japanese.

⇨ 73.1

How would you ask your close friend to do the following?

(1) to help (you) with your homework
(2) to lend (you) money
(3) to introduce Ms Saito (to you)
(4) to show you the class notes
(5) to wake (you) up at 6 a.m.

⇨ 73.2

Complete the following dialogues.

(A)
A student wants to apply for a scholarship and wants to ask the professor to write a recommendation letter. Include an appropriate parting phrase.

学生： 先生、今二、三分よろしいでしょうか。
先生： いいですよ。何でしょう。
学生： 実は (1)＿＿＿＿＿＿＿＿ んですが、(2)＿＿＿＿＿＿＿＿。
先生： ああ、いいですよ。
学生： ありがとうございます。大学の宛先など、詳しいことはまたあとでメールで連絡 (3)＿＿＿＿＿＿＿＿ ます。では、(4)＿＿＿＿＿＿＿＿。

Gakusei:  Sensei, ima ni-sanpun yoroshii deshou ka.
Sensei:   Ii desu yo. Nan deshou.
Gakusei:  Jitsu wa (1)＿＿＿＿＿ n desu ga, (2)＿＿＿＿＿＿.
Sensei:   Aa, ii desu yo.
Gakusei:  Arigatou gozaimasu. Daigaku no atesaki nado, kuwashii koto wa mata ato de meeru de renraku (3)＿＿＿＿＿ masu. De wa (4)＿＿＿＿＿.

(B)

Satoshi and Takeshi, both males in their 20s, work part-time at a convenience store. Satoshi has a conflict with his schedule tomorrow, and wants Takeshi to take his shift. Takeshi, however, has already made other plans.

敏： あのさぁ、ちょっと (1)＿＿＿＿＿＿＿＿＿＿ んだ。

武： 何だよ、頼みって。

敏： 明日のシフトのことなんだけどー、オレ、ちょっと都合、悪くなったんで、
(2)＿＿＿＿＿＿＿＿＿＿ ？

武： 何時？

敏： 夜、五時から九時。

武： うーん、いやぁ、明日は (3)＿＿＿＿＿＿＿＿＿。 もう (4)＿＿＿＿＿＿＿＿＿。

敏： そうかぁ。だよねー。

武： うん、悪いな。

Satoshi:   Ano saa, chotto (1)＿＿＿＿＿＿＿＿＿ n da.
Takeshi:   Nan dayo, tanomi tte.
Satoshi:   Ashita no shifuto no koto na n da kedoo, ore, chotto tsugou, waruku natta n de, (2)＿＿＿＿＿＿＿＿＿？
Takeshi:   Nanji?
Satoshi:   Yoru, goji kara kuji.
Takeshi:   Uun, iyaa, ashita wa (3)＿＿＿＿＿＿＿＿. Mou (4)＿＿＿＿＿＿＿＿.
Satoshi:   Sou kaa. Da yo nee.
Takeshi:   Un, warui na.


(C)

Yuri bought a mid-year gift for her husband's boss at a department store. She wants it to be delivered to the boss' house.

ゆり： じゃ、これ (1)＿＿＿＿＿＿＿＿＿＿。

店員： はい、ありがとうございます。ご贈答品 ('gift') でしょうか。

ゆり： はい。

店員： のし紙はおつけしましょうか。[のし紙: a special paper for a formal gift]

ゆり： はい、(2)＿＿＿＿＿＿＿＿。それから先方宅まで (3)＿＿＿＿＿＿＿＿。

店員： はい、かしこまりました。それでは、こちらに先方様のお名前とご住所を
(4)＿＿＿＿＿＿＿＿＿。

Yuri:      Ja, kore (1)＿＿＿＿＿＿＿＿.
Ten'in:    Hai, arigatou gozaimasu. Go-zoutouhin ('gift') deshou ka.
Yuri:      Hai.
Ten'in:    Noshi-gami wa o-tsuke shimashou ka.
           (Noshi-gami = a special paper for a formal gift)
Yuri:      Hai, (2)＿＿＿＿＿＿＿＿. Sorekara senpou-taku made (3)＿＿＿＿＿＿＿＿.
Ten'in:    Hai, kashikomarimashita. Sore dewa, kochira ni senpou-sama no
           o-namae to go-juusho o (4)＿＿＿＿＿＿＿＿.

⇨  73.1, 73.2

**4** ⋮ How would you make a request in the following situations? Use . . . **te itadaku wake ni wa ikanai deshou ka**.

(1) You want to change the time of your appointment.
(2) You want to ask your teacher to correct your composition.
(3) You want to ask the addressee to participate in the survey.
(4) The deadline is today, but you want the addressee (= your boss) to wait until tomorrow.
(5) You could not read an email attachment, so you would like the addressee to send it again.

⇨ 73.1.1

**5** ⋮ How would you make requests in the following situations? Use either V(causative)-**te itadakenai deshou ka** 'could I be allowed to do . . .' or V-**te itadakenai deshou ka** 'could I ask you to do . . . ,' whichever is appropriate.

(1) You don't feel good today, so you want to go home early.
(2) You want the addressee (= your superior at work) to draw a map for you.
(3) You want to take a picture of your friend's mother.
(4) You want to borrow your teacher's book.
(5) You want your customer to wait a few minutes.
(6) You want to take a vacation next week. (take a vacation = **kyuuka o toru**)
(7) You want to rest in the room you are currently in.

⇨ 73.1.1, 78.1.2.1

# 74

# Offers and invitations

1 ★★ What would you say in the following situations?

(1) You offer to help your close friend with his/her homework.
(2) You offer to carry a bag for your friend's grandmother.
(3) You offer to make coffee for your department chief.
(4) You offer to meet your colleague (of equal status) at the airport.
(5) You offer to make a reservation for your company president.

⇨ 74.1

2 ★★ Make appropriate invitations.

(1) You have a ticket for a concert, so you invite your good friend.
(2) A new **izakaya** ('pub') has opened, and you (a section chief) want to invite your subordinates for a drink.
(3) Your class is going to a restaurant, so you invite your teacher.
(4) You invite your neighbor for golf on Sunday.
(5) You invite an acquaintance to have tea together.

⇨ 74.1, 74.3

3 ★★ For the invitations listed in #2, give both affirmative and negative responses. The reasons for declining invitations are given below.

(1) not very convenient today
(2) have a previous engagement
(3) have a child's birthday party
(4) have other commitments
(5) have a meeting soon

⇨ 74.4

4 ★★ You want to invite your section chief (**kachou**) to a farewell party for one of the colleagues in your section. Complete the dialogues.

あなた： 課長、今度の土曜日はもうご予定がおありですか。
課長： いや、別にないけど。
あなた： ○○さんが今度やめるので、お別れパーティーを家でしたいと思っているんですが、 (1)_____。
課長： そういうことだったら、喜んで (2)_____。何か
(3)_____。
あなた： いいえ、食べ物はこちらで用意いたしますので、どうぞご心配なく。
課長： じゃ土曜日 (4)_____。(= looking forward to it)

Anata: Kachou, kondo no doyoubi wa mou go-yotei ga o-ari desu ka.
Kachou: Iya, betsu ni nai kedo.
Anata: ○○san ga kondo yameru node, o-wakare paatii o uchi de shitai to omotte iru n desu ga, (1)_____.
Kachou: Sou iu koto dattara, yorokonde (2)_____.
Nanika (3)_____.
Anata: Iie, tabemono wa kochira de youi itashimasu node, douzo go-shinpai naku.
Kachou: Ja doyoubi (4)_____. (= looking forward to it)

⇨ 74.3, 74.4.1

**5** ⁎ You are invited to go to a karaoke bar after work, but you have some work you have to finish by the next day. Complete the following dialogue.

同僚： 今日仕事の後でみんなでカラオケバーに行こうと思ってるんだけど、
(1)_____？
あなた： ふーん、今晩？
同僚： うん、課長も来るって。カラオケ好きじゃなかったっけ？
あなた： 大好き。行きたいんだけど、(2)_____。
同僚： じゃあ、(3)_____。
あなた： うん、また今度 (4)_____。

Douryoo: Kyou shigoto no ato de minna de karaoke baa ni ikou to omotte ru n da kedo, (1)_____?
Anata: Fuun, konban?
Douryoo: Un, kachou mo kuru tte. Karaoke suki ja nakatta kke?
Anata: Daisuki. Ikitai n da kedo, (2)_____.
Douryou: Jaa, (3)_____.
Anata: Un, mata kondo (4)_____.

⇨ 74.3, 74.4.2

**6** ⁎ The following is an e-mail invitation from a former student to her/his professor.

川上先生、
　ご無沙汰しておりますが、お元気でいらっしゃいますか。私は忙しいですが、充実した毎日を過ごしております。
　さて、先生もご存知の○○さんが来月一日から一週間、遊びに来てくれる予定です。それでよろしかったら、お食事でもご一緒できないかと思っておりますが、ご都合はいかがでしょうか。こちらは月曜日か火曜日なら何時でもだいじょうぶです。
　では、ご連絡をお待ちしております。
　先生とゆっくりお話できるのを楽しみにしております。

吉田恵子

---

Kawakami sensei,

   Go-busata shite orimasu ga, o-genki de irasshaimasu ka. Watashi wa isogashii desu ga, juujitsu shita mainichi o sugoshite orimasu.

   Sate, sensei mo go-zonji no ○○-san ga raigetsu tsuitachi kara isshuukan, asobi ni kite kureru yotei desu. Sorede yoroshikattara, o-shokuji demo go-issho dekinai ka to omotte orimasu ga, go-tsugou wa ikaga deshou ka. Kochira wa getsuyoubi ka kayoubi nara nanji demo daijoubu desu.

   Dewa, go-renraku o o-machi shite orimasu.

   Sensei to yukkuri o-hanashi dekiru no o tanoshimi ni shite orimasu.

Yoshida Keiko

---

Write a message like this one inviting your teacher to a farewell party for one of your friends who will be studying in a graduate school abroad. The party is going to be at your house next Sunday at 5 p.m. There will be lots of food and drink.

⇨ 74.3

# 75
# Orders (commands)

1 ★ Choose the correct command form according to the English equivalent.

(1) 勉強【すなさい・すりなさい・しなさい】。'Study!'
   Benkyou 【sunasai · surinasai · shinasai】.
(2) 早く【食べるなさい・食べるな・食べな】よ。'Eat quickly.'
   Hayaku 【taberunasai · taberu na · tabena】 yo.
(3) もう【しゃべるな・しゃべる・しゃべりな】。'Don't talk any more!'
   Mou 【shaberu na · shaberu · shaberina】.
(4) あっちに【行け・行くな・行こう】。'Go away!'
   Atchi ni 【ike · iku na · ikou】.
(5) こっちに【くる・くるな・こい】。'Don't come this way!'
   Kotchini 【kuru · kuru na · koi】.
(6) お前が運転【すろ・しろ・すれ】。'You drive!'
   Omae ga unten 【suro · shiro · sure】.
(7) 文句【言わない・言えば・言いな】！'Don't complain!'
   Monku 【iwanai · ieba · iina】!
(8) もう【泣きな・泣かないの・泣け】！'Don't cry any more!'
   Mou 【naki na · nakanai no · nake】!

⇨ 75.1, 75.2

2 ★ You are babysitting a couple of Japanese children. Tell them to do the following. (Use forms other than rude commands like **tabero** 'eat!' and **mate** 'wait!')

(1) Clean your room.
(2) Brush your teeth.
(3) Put on your clothes immediately.
(4) Don't draw on the wall.
(5) Don't touch the computer.
(6) Stop fighting.

⇨ 75.1, 75.2

3 ★ Taro, a young male with a rough speech style, is bossy to his younger brother. How would he express the following commands?

(1) Don't tell anyone!
(2) Be quiet!
(3) Don't enter my room!
(4) Go get something to drink!
(5) Don't use my games!

⇨ 75.1, 75.2

# 76

# Directions and instructions

1 *
A police officer is giving directions to various places for different people. Choose the most appropriate phrase according to the English equivalents.

(1) 森さんのうちですね。だったら、この道を【① まっすぐ行って・まがって・わたって】、二つ目の【② かく・かど・まど】を右に【③ まげて・わたって・まがって】ください。それから5分位【④ 歩いたら・歩いて・歩いても】右手にパン屋があります。森さんの家はパン屋から【⑤ 3軒・3軒目・3軒まで】です。

**Mori-san no uchi desu ne. Dattara, kono michi o【① massugu itte・magatte・watatte】, futatsume no【② kaku・kado・mado】o migi ni【③ magete・watatte・magatte】kudasai. Sore kara gofun gurai 【④ aruitara・aruite・aruitemo】migite ni panya ga arimasu. Mori-san no ie wa panya kara【⑤ sangen・sangen me・sangen made】desu.**

*Mr Mori's house? Well then, go straight on this street and turn right on the second corner. If you walk another 5 minutes or so, there will be a bakery on your right. His house is the third one from the bakery.*

(2) ここから一番近い本屋ですか。じゃあ、ABCデパートの中ですね。線路にそって2-3分【① 歩いて・歩くと・歩けば】左に【② すぎて・まがって・わたって】ください。そして踏切を【③ まがります・行きます・わたります】。少し行って、喫茶店を【④ すぎても・すぎたら・すぎる】、十字路に出ます。デパートは左手に見えるはずです。本屋は【⑤ 5階・5台・5足】にあります。

**Koko kara ichiban chikai honya desu ka. Jaa, ABC depaato no naka desu ne. Senro ni sotte 2-3-pun【① aruite・arukuto・arukeba】hidari ni【② sugite・magatte・watatte】kudasai. Soshite fumikiri o 【③ magarimasu・ikimasu・watarimasu】. Sukoshi itte, kissaten o 【④ sugite mo・sugitara・sugiru】, juujiro ni demasu. Depaato wa hidarite ni mieru hazu desu. Honya wa【⑤ gokai・godai・gosoku】ni arimasu.**

*The closest bookstore from here? That'll be in the ABC department store. Walk along the train track for 2 to 3 minutes, and turn left. Then cross the railroad crossing. You go a bit further, pass a coffee shop, and you'll be at the crossroads. The department store will be on your left. The bookstore is on the fifth floor.*

⇨ 76.1

**2** ★

How would you ask for directions in the following situations? Use an appropriate level of formality depending on the person you are talking to.

(1) You are at a restaurant and your child needs to go to the bathroom. Ask the waiter where the bathroom is.
(2) You are looking for a cake shop called Sweet. Ask a sales clerk standing in front of a bookstore if s/he knows where it is.
(3) Your friend just told you about a coffee shop that serves the best and cheapest coffee. Ask her/him how to get there.
(4) You work for a gardening company. Your boss has told you about a new housing development in the neighboring city. Ask her/him to tell you how to get there.

[new housing development: 新興住宅地 **shinkou juutakuchi**]

⇨ 76.1

**3** ★

Change the phrases below into 'how to' phrases following the example.

Example: 魚を食べる　　→　魚の食べ方
**sakana o taberu** → **sakana no tabekata**

(1) 新しい携帯電話を使う　　**atarashii keitai denwa o tsukau** →
(2) 縦列駐車する　　**juuretsu chuusha** (parallel parking) **suru** →
(3) 着物を着る　　**kimono o kiru** →
(4) 同僚とつきあう　　**douryou to tsukiau** →
(5) 駅に行く　　**eki ni iku** →
(6) 自転車に乗る　　**jitensha ni noru** →
(7) 外国人を案内する　　**gaikokujin o annai suru** →
(8) 人前で話す　　**hitomae de hanasu** →

⇨ 76.2

**4** ★

How would you ask for instructions in the following situations?

(1) Your friend's mother made a wonderful omelet. You want to know how to make it.
(2) You are about to take a train for the first time in Japan. You can't figure out how to get the ticket from the machine. Ask a high school girl behind you to show you how to buy the ticket.
(3) You have recently started to play golf. You see one of your colleagues, a few years senior to you, practicing his swing during the lunch break. He seems really good. Ask him to show you how to improve your swing.

⇨ 76.2

# 77
# Confirmation

1

Put **ne** where appropriate in the following dialogues.

(A)
You are looking for an ATM and ask a passerby about its location.

| あなた： | すみません。このへんにATMがあるでしょうか。 |
| 通行人： | あのう、あそこに交差点があります。交差点を渡って右に少し行くと、コンビニがあります。その中にATMがあると思いますよ。 |
| あなた： | あそこを右です。ありがとうございます。 |

| Anata: | **Sumimasen. Kono hen ni ATM ga aru deshou ka.** |
| Tsuukounin: | **Anou, asoko ni kousaten ga arimasu. Kousaten o watatte migi ni sukoshi iku to, konbini ga arimasu. Sono naka ni ATM ga aru to omoimasu yo.** |
| Anata: | **Asoko o migi desu. Arigatou gozaimasu.** |

(B)
Mami shows Eri an article.

| 真美： | ねえ、ちょっとこれ見てください。 |
| えり： | 何ですか。ふうん、同じ仕事でも女性の給料の方が男性の給料より低いんです。 |
| 真美： | 仕事が同じなのに、給料が違うのは不公平ですよ。 |
| えり： | 本当にそうです。 |

| Mami: | **Nee, chotto kore mite kudasai.** |
| Eri: | **Nan desu ka. Fuun, onaji shigoto demo josei no kyuuryou no hou ga dansei no kyuuryou yori hikui n desu.** |
| Mami: | **Shigoto ga onaji na noni, kyuuryou ga chigau no wa fukouhei desu yo.** |
| Eri: | **Hontou ni sou desu.** |

⇨ 10.4.2, 77

**2** ★★ Fill in the blanks with one of the expressions of confirmation, **ne**, **desho**, or **yo ne**.

(1)
A: 今日の会議は11時からです（①　　　　）。
B: ええ。忘れないでください（②　　　　）。
A: はい。11時からです（③　　　　）。了解しました。

A: **Kyou no kaigi wa juuichiji kara desu** (①　　　　).
B: **Ee. Wasurenaide kudasai** (②　　　　).
A: **Hai. juuichiji kara desu** (③　　　　). **Ryoukai shimashita.**

(2)
A: レポートの最後のページがないんだけど、持ってる？
B: さっきあげた（　　　　）。

A: **Repooto no saigo no peeji ga nai n da kedo, motte ru?**
B: **Sakki ageta** (　　　　).

(3)
A: はっきり覚えてないんだけど、この間借りた本、もう返した（　　　　）。
B: うん。

A: **Hakkiri oboete nai n da kedo, kono aida karita hon, mou kaeshita**
(　　　　).
B: **Un.**

(4)
A: この間オフィスに来た人がいた（　　　　）。あの人、○○さんのフィアンセなんだって。
B: ふうん、知らなかった。

A: **Kono aida ofisu ni kita hito ga ita** (　　　　). **Ano hito, ○○-san no
fianse na n da tte.**
B: **Fuun, shiranakatta.**

(5)
先生：　　宿題は締め切りの日にちゃんと出してください（①　　　　）。
　　　　いいです（②　　　　）。
学生：　　はい、わかりました。すみません。

**Sensei:** **Shukudai wa shimekiri no hi ni chanto dashite kudasai**
(①　　　　). **Ii desu** (②　　　　).
**Gakusei:** **Hai, wakarimashita. Sumimasen.**

⇨ | 10.4.2, 10.4.4, 77

# 78
# Permission

1 ★

You are staying with a host family in Japan. How would you get permission from your host mother when you want to do the following. Use **-te mo ii desu ka**.

(1) You want to watch TV.
(2) You want to bring your friend to the house.
(3) You want to come home late.
(4) You want to do laundry.
(5) You want to drink juice in the refrigerator.

⇨  78.1.1

2 ★

Kenji is living in Japan. How would he get permission to use a computer from the following people respectively.

(1) His hostbrother.
(2) His close friend.
(3) His neighbor whom he does not know too well.
(4) His supervisor at work.

⇨  78.1.1, 78.1.2

3 ★

Complete the following dialogues using 'V(causative)-**te itadakenai deshou ka**,' 'V(causative)-**te moraenai?**' or 'V(causative)-**te kurenai?**,' whichever is appropriate.

(1) [学生は先生の写真がとりたい]
　　学生：　　_____。
　　先生：　　もちろん、いいですよ。
　　**[Gakusei wa sensei no shashin ga toritai]**
　　**Gakusei:**　_____.
　　**Sensei:**　　Mochiron, ii desu yo.

(2) [よし子は会社員で、一週間休みをとりたい。]
　　よし子：　大変申し訳ありませんが、来週_____。
　　上司：　　ああ、いいですよ。
　　**[Yoshiko wa kaishain de, isshuukan yasumi o toritai.]**
　　**Yoshiko:**　Taihen moushiwake arimasen ga, raishuu _____.
　　**Joushi:**　　Aa, ii desu yo.

(3) [よし子は今日気分が悪い]
　　よし子：　すみませんが、今日は気分が悪いので、_____。
　　上司：　　ああ、かまいませんよ。お大事に。
　　**[Yoshiko wa kyou kibun ga warui]**
　　**Yoshiko:**　Sumimasen ga, kyou wa kibun ga warui node, _____.
　　**Joushi:**　　Aa, kamaimasen yo. Odaiji ni.

(4) [あなたはコンピューターが使いたい]

あなた： 　コンピューター _____。

友達： 　うん、いいよ。

**[Anata wa konpyuutaa ga tsukaitai]**

**Anata:** 　Konpyuutaa _____.

**Tomodachi:** 　Un, ii yo.

(5) [あなたは友達の本をコピーしたい]

あなた： 　その本 _____。

友達： 　うん、いいよ。どうぞ。

**[Anata wa tomodachi no hon o kopii shitai]**

**Anata:** 　Sono hon _____.

**Tomodachi:** 　Un, ii yo. Douzo.

⇨ 78.1.2.1

**4** ⁕

Decline the following requests giving the reasons appearing in brackets. Begin your answers with an expression likeうーん、わるいけど **uun warui kedo**, あ、すみませんが **a, sumimasen ga**, or あのう、申し訳ありませんが **anou, moushiwake arimasen ga** ('um, I'm sorry, but . . .'), and end with one like ので **node** ('because') or んですが/けど **n desu ga/kedo** ('but') to mitigate the impact.

(1) [Requester: your friend. Reason: you are using it now]

その辞書借りてもいい？ **Sono jisho karite mo ii?**

(2) [Requester: a stranger at a theater. Reason: you are saving it for someone]

ここに座ってもいいですか。 **Koko ni suwatte mo ii desu ka.**

(3) [Requester: an acquaintance. Reason: you are busy right now.]

ちょっと聞きたいことがあるんですけど、今いいですか。

**Chotto kikitai koto ga aru n desu kedo, ima ii desu ka.**

(4) [Requester: a student. Reason: it is not very convenient.]

先生、あしたの午後オフィスに伺ってもよろしいでしょうか。

**Sensei, ashita no gogo ofisu ni ukagatte mo yoroshii deshou ka.**

⇨ 78.3

**5** ⁕

The following are situations where you are asking a big favor. Ask permission using the phrase with **wake ni wa ikanai**.

Example: You want your addressee to wait for one more day.

→ すみませんが、もう一日待っていただくわけにはいかないでしょうか。

**Sumimasen ga, mou ichinichi matte itadaku wake ni wa ikanai deshou ka.**

(1) You want to take the final exam early.
(2) You want to submit the paper after its due date.
(3) You want to ask your friend to let you use her/his car.
(4) You call your doctor and you want to be seen on the same day.
(5) You were asked to take on additional duties, but you want to think about it a little.

⇨ 78.1.2.5

# 79
# Prohibition

1 ★

Rephrase each of the following warnings using V-**te wa ikemasen** 'you may not do . . . , you must not do . . .'

| | | |
|---|---|---|
| (1) | | 携帯電話のご使用はご遠慮下さい。<br>**Keitai denwa no go-shiyou wa go-enryo kudasai.**<br>→ |
| (2) | | 出入り口につき駐車禁止<br>**De-iriguchi ni tsuki chuusha kinshi**<br>→ |
| (3) | | 立ち入り禁止<br>**Tachiiri kinshi**<br>→ |
| (4) | | ポイ捨て禁止（周辺にゴミを捨てないでください）<br>**Poi sute kinshi (shuuhen ni gomi o sutenai de kudasai.)**<br>→ |
| (5) | | 禁煙<br>**Kin'en**<br>→ |

⇨ 79.1.1

2 ★ ★

The following are some rules in Japan. How would you say them in Japanese?

> Example: You are not supposed to enter the house with shoes on.
> → くつをはいたまま家に【あがってはいけない/あがらない】
>   ことになっています。
> **Kutsu o haita mama ie ni 【agatte wa ikenai / agaranai】**
> **koto ni natte imasu.**

(1) You are not supposed to talk on a cell phone on trains.
(2) You are not supposed to address your social superiors by '**anata**'.
(3) You are not supposed to praise your own family to others.
(4) You are not supposed to step into a tatami room with slippers on.

⇨ 79.1.2

**3** ✱✱ Complete the following dialogues with prohibition expressions such as **-te wa ikemasen** or **-cha dame** or the like.

(A)
[You are at the doctor's office]

医者 ： 流感 ('the flu') ですから、二、三日学校に (1)_____ 。
それから消化の悪い食べ物も (2)_____ よ。
あなた ： わかりました。ありがとうございました。

**Isha:** **Ryuukan ('the flu') desu kara, ni-sannichi gakkou ni**
(1)_____.
**Sorekara shouka no warui tabemono mo** (2)_____ **yo.**
**Anata:** **Wakarimashita. Arigatou gozaimashita.**

(B)
息子 ： ああ、もうこんな時間。遅れる。朝ご飯食べる時間ないよ。
母 ： 朝ご飯食べないで (1)_____ よ。
息子 ： 今日部活の飲み会があるんだけど行ってもいい？
母 ： いいけど、あまり (2)_____ よ。
息子 ： わかった。

**Musuko:** **Aa, mou konna jikan. Okureru. Asagohan taberu jikan nai yo.**
**Haha:** **Asagohan tabenaide** (1)_____.
**Musuko:** **Kyou bukatsu no nomikai ga aru n da kedo itte mo ii?**
**Haha:** **Ii kedo, amari** (2)_____ **yo.**
**Musuko:** **Wakatta.**

(C)
[Yamada is often absent from class; he takes naps in class; he talks with his friends in class.]

先生 ： 山田さんは、このごろ欠席が多いですね。授業を
(1)_____ よ。それから授業中 (2)_____ 。
それに、友達と (3)_____ よ。
山田 ： はい、すみません。これから気をつけます。

**Sensei:** **Yamada-san wa konogoro kesseki ga ooi desu ne. Jugyou o**
(1)_____ **yo. Sorekara jugyou-chuu** (2)_____.
**Sore ni, tomodachi to** (3)_____ **yo.**
**Yamada:** **Hai, sumimasen. Korekara ki o tsukemasu.**

➪ 79.1.1

# 80
# Obligation and duty

**1** ★

You are hosting a party. List what you have to do in four or five sentences, using **-nakereba ikenai** or **-nakute wa ikenai** ('must') and one or more of the words given below. Supply verbs, where necessary.

> 飲み物、-ておく、招待状、料理、そうじ、買い物、ひやす
>
> **nomimono, -te oku, shoutaijou, ryouri, souji, kaimono, hiyasu**

⇨ 80.1.2

**2** ★★

The following are some rules and customs. Complete the sentences with **-nakereba naranai** or **-nakereba ikenai**.

(1) 外国に旅行したい人は、パスポートを＿＿＿＿＿＿＿＿。
   **Gaikoku ni ryokou shitai hito wa, pasupooto o ＿＿＿＿＿＿＿＿.**
(2) 日本では家にあがる時に ＿＿＿＿＿＿＿＿。
   **Nihon de wa ie ni agaru toki ni ＿＿＿＿＿＿＿＿.**
(3) 日本では大学に入りたい人は入学試験を ＿＿＿＿＿＿＿＿。
   **Nihon de wa daigaku ni hairitai hito wa nyuugaku shiken o**
   ＿＿＿＿＿＿＿＿.
(4) 能力試験のN1にパスしたければ、漢字を ＿＿＿＿＿＿＿＿。
   **Nouryoku shiken no N1 ni pasu shitakereba, kanji o**
   ＿＿＿＿＿＿＿＿.
(5) 銀行からお金を借りたら、利子を ＿＿＿＿＿＿＿＿。
   **Ginkou kara o-kane o karitara, rishi o ＿＿＿＿＿＿＿＿.**

⇨ 80.1.1

**3** ★★

The following is a conversation between two friends. Fill in the blanks with appropriate phrases using 'have to' forms.

キム： 友達の結婚披露宴 (reception) に招待されたんだけど、何か（①　　　　）よね。日本では現金が普通だって聞いたんだけど、現金を（②　　　　）の？

恵子： いや、物でもいいと思うよ。

キム： じゃ、プレゼントにしようかな。披露宴の前にデパートから（③　　　　）よね。

恵子： うん、一週間前ぐらいには届いていた方がいいと思うよ。

Kimu: Tomodachi no kekkon hirouen (reception) ni shoutai sareta n da kedo, nanika (①     ) yo ne. Nihon de wa genkin ga futsuu da tte kiita n da kedo, genkin o (②     ) no?

Keiko: Iya, mono demo ii to omou yo.

Kimu: Ja, purezento ni shiyou kana. Hirouen no mae ni depaato kara (③     ) yo ne.

Keiko: Un, isshuukan mae gurai ni wa todoite ita hou ga ii to omou yo.

⇨ 80.1

**4** ⁑ Complete the following conversations using V(negative) **wake ni wa ikanai** '(you) cannot not do . . . , (you) have no choice but to V.'

(1)
A: 教科書、高いよね。
B: うん、でも （           ） でしょ。

A: **Kyoukasho, takai yo ne.**
B: **Un, demo** （         ） **desho.**

(2)
A: アメリカに行くと、チップの習慣があって面倒ですね。
B: ほんとうに。でも （        ） し。

A: **Amerika ni iku to, chippu no shuukan ga atte mendou desu ne.**
B: **Hontou ni. Demo** （       ） **shi.**

(3)
A: 今度のピクニック、行く？
B: あんまり行きたくないけど、部長も来るって言うから、 （           ） と思うんだよね。

A: **Kondo no pikunikku, iku?**
B: **Anmari ikitakunai kedo, buchou mo kuru tte iu kara,** （           ） **to omou n da yo ne.**

(4)
A: だんだん漢字が難しくなって、覚えられなくてこまっているんです。
B: でも、 （          ） でしょ。

A: **Dandan kanji ga muzukashiku natte, oboerarenakute komatte iru n desu.**
B: **Demo,** （        ） **desho.**

(5)
A: パーティーの席でお酒を勧められると、あまり好きじゃなくても （          ） し、困ります。
B: 本当にそうですよね。

A: **Paatii no seki de o-sake o susumerareru to, amari suki ja nakutemo** （         ） **shi, komarimasu.**
B: **Hontou ni sou desu yo ne.**

⇨ 80.2.4

**5** *   Complete the sentences using verbs in the 'V-**zaru o enai**' form.

(1) 年取った親の世話をするために（　quit job　）女性もいます。
**Toshi totta oya no sewa o suru tame ni** (　quit job　) **josei mo imasu.**

(2) 私はクレジットカードをあまり使いたくないが、（　use　）状況もあります。
**Watashi wa kurejitto kaado o amari tsukaitakunai ga,** (　use　) **joukyou mo arimasu.**

(3) あの人はいつも自分が正しいと思っているようだが、今度は（　acknowledge one's mistakes　）でしょう。
**Ano hito wa itsumo jibun ga tadashii to omotte iru you da ga, kondo wa** (　acknowledge her/his own mistakes　) **deshou.**

(4) 普通は自分で何でもやるのだが、この仕事は複雑なので、（　ask someone else to do　）でしょう。
**Futsuu wa jibun de nan demo yaru no da ga, kono shigoto wa fukuzatsu na node,** (　ask someone else to do　) **deshou.**

(5) あしたまでに終わらせなければいけない仕事があるので、今晩は（　stay up all night　）かもしれません。
**Ashita made ni owarasenakereba ikenai shigoto ga aru node, konban wa** (　stay up all night　) **kamo shiremasen.**

⇨ 80.2.5

**6** *   Michiko has strong opinions about what one should do and should not do. Complete her opinions below using the words given in parentheses and **beki**.

(1) ＿＿＿＿＿＿＿＿＿＿＿＿＿＿＿＿＿＿。（約束、守る）
＿＿＿＿＿＿＿＿＿＿＿＿＿＿＿. (**yakusoku, mamoru**)

(2) 日本語専攻の学生は＿＿＿＿＿＿＿＿＿＿＿＿＿。（留学）
**Nihongo senkou no gakusei wa** ＿＿＿＿＿＿＿＿＿＿＿＿＿. (**ryuugaku**)

(3) 男性も＿＿＿＿＿＿＿＿＿＿＿＿＿＿。（育児）
**Dansei mo** ＿＿＿＿＿＿＿＿＿＿＿＿＿. (**ikuji**)

(4) 目上の人と話す時には＿＿＿＿＿＿＿＿＿＿＿＿＿。（敬語）
**Meue no hito to hanasu toki ni wa** ＿＿＿＿＿＿＿＿＿＿＿＿＿. (**keigo**)

⇨ 80.2.3

# 81
## Complaints

1 ★

Select the phrases from the list below that can be used to mitigate complaints.

> a. ところで・b. 本当のことをいうと・c. たいへん言いにくいのですが
> d. すみませんが・e. 恐縮ですが・f. はっきり言って
> g. あまり言いたくないけど・h. 悪いんだけど・i. つまり
>
> a. tokoro de・b. hontou no koto o iu to・c. taihen ii-nikui no desu ga
> d. sumimasen ga・e. kyoushuku desu ga・f. hakkiri itte
> g. amari iitaku nai kedo・h. warui n da kedo・i. tsumari

⇨ 81.1

2 ★★

Choose an appropriate way to express your complaint in each situation.

(1) You are trying to study for tomorrow's exam, but your roommate is playing music too loudly and you cannot concentrate. You and your roommate are close friends and have been on good terms.

　　a. すみません、ちょっと音がうるさいんですけど、もう少し小さくしてくれませんか。
　　b. ごめん、明日試験があるから、勉強しなくちゃならないんだ。悪いけど、もうちょっと、音を小さくしてもらってもいい？
　　c. 申し訳ないんですが、ちょっと静かにしていただけないでしょうか。

　　a. **Sumimasen, chotto oto ga urusai n desu kedo, mou sukoshi chiisaku shite kuremasen ka.**
　　b. **Gomen, ashita shiken ga aru kara, benkyou shinakucha naranai n da. Warui kedo, mou chotto, oto o chiisaku shite moratte mo ii?**
　　c. **Moushiwakenai n desu ga, chotto shizuka ni shite itadakenai deshou ka.**

(2) You reserved a room with an ocean view and paid extra for it. After you check into your room, you realize it faces the parking lot and you cannot see the ocean.

　　a. あの、海が見える部屋を予約したはずなんですが、どうなっているんでしょうか。
　　b. 言いにくいんですが、部屋から駐車場がみえるんですけど …
　　c. あまり言いたくないのですが、海が見えないんです。

    a.  Ano, umi ga mieru heya o yoyaku shita hazu na n desu ga, dou natte iru n deshou ka.
    b.  Ii-nikui n desu ga, heya kara chuushajou ga mieru n desu kedo . . .
    c.  Amari iitakunai no desu ga, umi ga mienai n desu.

(3)  You have been sitting at a table in a restaurant. It has been over half an hour since you ordered your food. You don't want to be rude, but you want to make sure that they are aware of the situation.

    a.  ちょっと、お腹空いてるんだから、早くできないの？
    b.  すみません、まだ注文したものが来てないんですけど …
    c.  申し訳ありませんが、私の食べ物を早く持ってきていただけませんでしょうか。

    a.  Chotto, onaka suite ru n da kara, hayaku dekinai no?
    b.  Sumimasen, mada chuumon shita mono ga kite nai n desu kedo . . .
    c.  Moushiwake arimasen ga, watashi no tabemono o hayaku motte-kite itadakemasen deshou ka.

⇨  81.1, 81.3

**3** ★  A wife is complaining to her husband about their son's grades and how her husband is not doing his part as a father. Choose the most appropriate alternatives.

[V っぱなし **-ppanashi** 'keep V-ing'; 接待 **settai** 'attend to guests'; つきあう **tsukiau** 'to go (with someone), to participate'; 言い訳 **iiwake** 'excuse']

妻：  あなた、武たら、ゲーム【① だけ・しか・ばっかり】していて、ぜんぜん勉強しないのよ。成績だって下がりっぱなしよ。
夫：  困ったやつだな。
妻：  本当よ。あなたは何も言って【② くれない・あげない・もらわない】し。
夫：  俺が言ったって、同じだよ。
妻：  そんなこと言って、学校に呼び出されて、注意【③ する・される・したい】のは、私なんだから。
夫：  俺は会社がある【④ んだから・ので・のに】、仕方ないだろう？
妻：  でも、少しは一緒に子供の教育のことを考えてくれてもいいでしょ？
夫：  俺だって、遅くまで接待【⑤ されたり・させられたり・させたり】部長のゴルフに【⑥ つきあわれたり・つきあわされたり・つきあわせたり】、大変なんだよ。
妻：  そうやって、父親【⑦ だけど・なのに・ですが】父親らしいことはぜんぜんしないで、言い訳ばっかり。
夫：  わかったよ。今度俺から話してみるよ。

Tsuma:  Anata, Takeshi ttara, geemu【① dake・shika・bakkari】shite ite, zenzen benkyou shinai no yo. Seiseki datte sagarippanashi yo.
Otto:  Komatta yatsu da na.
Tsuma:  Hontou yo. Anata wa nanimo itte【② kurenai・agenai・morawanai】shi.
Otto:  Ore ga itta tte, onaji da yo.
Tsuma:  Sonna koto itte, gakkou ni yobidasarete, chuui【③ suru・sareru・shitai】no wa, watashi na n da kara.
Otto:  Ore wa kaisha ga aru【④ n da kara・node・noni】, shikata nai darou?
Tsuma:  Demo, sukoshi wa issho ni kodomo no kyouiku no koto o kangaete kuretemo ii desho?

Otto: Ore datte, osoku made settai【⑤ saretari・saseraretari・sasetari】buchou no gorufu ni【⑥ tsukiawaretari・tsukiawasaretari・tsuki awasetari】, taihen na n da yo.

Tsuma: Sou yatte, chichioya【⑦ da kedo・na noni・desu ga】chichioya rashii koto wa zenzen shinaide, iiwake bakkari.

Otto: Wakatta yo. Kondo ore kara hanashite miru yo.

⇨ 81.1, 81.2

**4**

You are a member of the college tennis club. You have many complaints about how the club is run, as listed below. Write a letter to the faculty adviser. The beginning of the letter is written out for you.

- Only senior members (4年生 **yonensei**) can use the tennis courts.
- Freshmen must do all the laundry and cleaning for senior members.
- Senior members become violent (暴力をふるう **bouryoku o furuu**) when others do not obey their orders.
- Member fees, which are 5000 yen per month, are used to pay for senior members' drinking parties (飲み会 **nomikai**).
- Most new members quit within the first two weeks.

小出先生、
　突然手紙を出してすみません。テニス部のことで、どうしても聞いていただきたいことがあるのです。
　　実は、_____ …
_____
　このままでは、テニス部はだめになってしまうと思います。
　先生、テニス部の顧問として、なんとかしていただけないでしょうか。
　　　　　　　　　　　　　　　　　　　　　　　　　　　　　長井　孝

Koide Sensei,
　Totsuzen tegami o dashite sumimasen. Tenisu bu no koto de, doushite mo kiite itadakitai koto ga aru no desu.
　Jitsu wa _____ . . .
_____
　Kono mama de wa, tenisu bu wa dame ni natte shimau to omoimasu.
　Sensei, tenisu bu no komon toshite, nan toka shite itadakenai deshou ka.

　　　　　　　　　　　　　　　　　　　　　　　　　　　Nagai Takashi

⇨ 81.2

# 82
# Compliments

1 ⋆⋆ Choose the most appropriate way to a give a compliment in each of the following situations.

(1) You attended a wonderful lecture and you want to compliment the speaker who is much older than you.

   a. おめでとうございます。あなたの講義はとてもよかったです。
   b. とても勉強になりました。ありがとうございました。
   c. とてもいい講義でした。ご苦労様でした。

   **a. O-medetou gozaimasu. Anata no kougi wa totemo yokatta desu.**
   **b. Totemo benkyou ni narimashita. Arigatou gozaimashita.**
   **c. Totemo ii kougi deshita. Go-kurou-sama deshita.**

(2) Your friend Ken invited you to eat at his home. His mother prepared a feast for you and everything tasted very good. You want to compliment his mother.

   a. こんなにおいしいご飯を食べるのは本当に久しぶりです。感激です。
   b. この食べ物は全部すごくいいです。ありがとうございます。
   c. もうお腹いっぱいです。ごちそうさまでした。

   **a. Konna ni oishii gohan o taberu no wa hontou ni hisashiburi desu. Kangeki desu.**
   **b. Kono tabemono wa zenbu sugoku ii desu. Arigatou gozaimasu.**
   **c. Mou onaka ippai desu. Go-chisou-sama deshita.**

(3) You are a store manager. One of your employees worked especially hard this month and contributed to high overall sales. You want to compliment him/her.

   a. 今月はよくお働きになりましたね。売り上げもあがって、うれしいです。おめでとう。
   b. 今月の売り上げがこんなに上がったのは○○君のお陰だよ。本当によく頑張ってくれたね。これからもよろしく。
   c. 今月はよく働いてくれましたね。店の売り上げを上げてくれて、ありがとう。来月もよく働いてくださいね。

   **a. Kongetsu wa yoku o-hataraki ni narimashita ne. Uriage mo agatte, ureshii desu. O-medetou.**
   **b. Kongetsu no uriage ga konna ni agatta no wa ○○ kun no o-kage da yo. Hontou ni yoku ganbatte kureta ne. Kore kara mo yoroshiku.**
   **c. Kongetsu wa yoku hataraite kuremashita ne. Mise no uriage o agete kurete, arigatou. Raigetsu mo yoku hataraite kudasai ne.**

(4) You went to a concert by a seasoned singer. You had a chance to shake hands with her afterward. You wanted to compliment her on her singing skill.

    a.  すばらしいコンサートでした。あなたの歌唱力はすごいですよ。
    b.  歌うのがとても上手ですよ。すばらしい歌手だと思います。
    c.  とてもすばらしくて感動しました！本当にありがとうございました。

    **a.  Subarashii konsaato deshita. Anata no kashouryoku wa sugoi desu yo.**
    **b.  Utau no ga totemo jouzu desu yo. Subarashii kashu da to omoimasu.**
    **c.  Totemo subarashikute kandou shimashita! Hontou ni arigatou gozaimashita.**

(5) Your teacher is wearing a nice jacket. You want to compliment him/her on it.

    a.  すてきなジャケットですね。
    b.  先生のジャケットはいいですよ。
    c.  私はあなたのジャケットが好きです。

    **a.  Suteki na jaketto desu ne.**
    **b.  Sensei no jaketto wa ii desu yo.**
    **c.  Watashi wa anata no jaketto ga suki desu.**

⇨ 82.2

**2** ★ How would you respond to the following compliments? Choose the most appropriate responses.

(1) [Your younger colleague says そのスーツ、すごく似合ってますね。 **Sono suutsu, sugoku niatte masu ne.**]

    a.  いや、ぜんぜん似合わないよ。
    b.  【そう？ (F)/そうか。(M)】ありがとう。
    c.  信じられないよ。
    d.  そんなこと【言わないでよ (F)/言うなよ (M)】。

    **a.  Iya, zenzen niawanai yo.**
    **b.  【Sou? (F) / Sou ka. (M)】 Arigatou.**
    **c.  Shinjirarenai yo.**
    **d.  Sonna koto 〔iwanaide yo (F) / iu na yo (M)〕.**

(2) [Your boss says すごく気がきくね。 **Sugoku ki ga kiku** ('attentive') **ne.**]

    a.  いいえ、気がつかないことのほうが多くてすみません。
    b.  はい、いつも気をつかっているんです。
    c.  ありがとうございます。いつも気をつけて見ているんです。
    d.  いいえ、ぜんぜん気がきかないんです。

    **a.  Iie, ki ga tsukanai koto no hou ga ookute sumimasen.**
    **b.  Hai, itsumo ki o tsukatte iru n desu.**
    **c.  Arigatou gozaimasu. Itsumo ki o tsukete mite iru n desu.**
    **d.  Iie, zenzen ki ga kikanai n desu.**

(3) [Your supervisor says この報告書、よく書けてるよ。 **Kono houkokusho, yoku kakete ru yo.**]

    a.   もちろん、がんばりましたから。
    b.   そうですね。
    c.   ありがとうございます。先輩方がいろいろ教えて下さったおかげです。
    d.   やったあ！

    a.   **Mochiron, ganbarimashita kara.**
    b.   **Sou desu ne.**
    c.   **Arigatou gozaimasu. Senpai-gata ga iroiro oshiete kudasatta o-kage desu.**
    d.   **Yattaa!**

(4) [Referring to your new shirt, your friend says かっこいい！ **Kakko ii!**]

    a.   ほんとう？けっこう安かったんだけどね。
    b.   そうだよね。
    c.   たいしたことないでしょ？
    d.   もっといいの持ってるよ。

    a.   **Hontou? Kekkou yasukatta n da kedo ne.**
    b.   **Sou da yo ne.**
    c.   **Taishita koto nai desho?**
    d.   **Motto ii no motte ru yo.**

⇨ 82.3

# 83
# Promises and warnings

1 *

In the following conversations, various people are making a promise. Choose the most appropriate phrase to complete each sentence.

(1)
父 ： この成績はなんだ！
子 ： ごめんなさい。この次は【絶対・たぶん】勉強するって約束する。

**Chichi:** Kono seiseki wa nan da!
**Ko:** Gomen nasai. Kono tsugi wa【zettai · tabun】benkyou suru tte, yakusoku suru.

(2)
[うめあわせ **umeawase** 'to make up for . . .']

男 ： ごめん、仕事が入っちゃって、今夜は会えない。
女 ： えー、最悪。
男 ： 今度必ずうめあわせ【する・しよう】から。
女 ： しょうがないなあ。約束だからね。

**Otoko:** Gomen, shigoto ga haitchatte, konya wa aenai.
**Onna:** Ee, saiaku.
**Otoko:** Kondo kanarazu umeawase【suru · shiyou】kara.
**Onna:** Shouganai naa. Yakusoku da kara ne.

(3)
上司 ： 例の報告書、まだなの？締切は今日の5時だよ。
部下 ： はい、すみません。5時までには必ず書き上げる【ことに・ように】
いたします。ご迷惑をおかけして本当に申し訳ありません。

**Joushi:** Rei no houkokusho, mada na no? Shimekiri wa kyou no goji da yo.
**Buka:** Hai, sumimasen. Goji made ni wa kanarazu kaki-ageru【koto ni · you ni】itashimasu. Go-meiwaku o o-kake shite hontou ni moushiwake arimasen.

⇨ 83.1

2 * *

Choose an appropriate alternative in the following warnings.

(1) 早く【食べましょう・食べなさい】。遅刻しちゃうよ。
**Hayaku【tabemashou · tabenasai】. Chikoku shichau yo.**
(2) 社長に逆らわない【はずです・ほうがいいですよ】。
**Shachou ni sakarawanai【hazu desu · hou ga ii desu yo】.**

(3) 勝手に中に【入ってはいけません・入りません】。
**Katte ni naka ni 【haitte wa ikemasen・ hairimasen】.**
(4) 目に入らないように気をつけて【ください・もいいです】。
**Me ni hairanai you ni ki o tsukete 【kudasai・mo ii desu】.**
(5) 急がない【と・ので】間に合わないよ。
**Isoganai 【to・node】 ma ni awanai yo.**
(6) 漢字は毎日練習【しない・した】と、忘れちゃうよ。
**Kanji wa mainichi renshuu 【shinai・shita】 to, wasurechau yo.**

⇨ 83.2

**3** ★ How would you express your promises in the following situations?

(1) Your friend just told you his/her secret. Reassure him/her that you will never tell anyone.
(2) Your host parents are worried about your bike tour. Tell them that you promise to e-mail them every day.
(3) Your friend is upset because you lied to him/her. Tell him/her you will never lie again (lit. 'any more').
(4) Your 'significant other' is worried about your health. Tell him/her that you promise to quit smoking this year.

⇨ 83.1

# 84
# Opinions

1 *

The following sentences express opinions in varying degrees of directness. Rank them 1 to 4: 1 is the most direct and 4 the least direct.

a. ( ) そんなことをするべきじゃないんじゃないでしょうか。
   **Sonna koto o suru beki ja nai n ja nai deshou ka.**
b. ( ) そんなことをするべきじゃない。
   **Sonna koto o suru beki ja nai.**
c. ( ) そんなことをする べきじゃないと思う。
   **Sonna koto o suru beki ja nai to omou.**
d. ( ) そんなことをするべきじゃないような気がする。
   **Sonna koto o suru beki ja nai you na ki ga suru.**

⇨ 84.1

2 *

Complete the following sentences using expressions of opinion. Multiple answers are possible.

(1) 日本の伝統的な食事は、とても健康的だ _____。
   **Nihon no dentouteki na shokuji wa, totemo kenkouteki da _____.**
(2) 政治は、政治家のためではなく、国民のためにある _____。
   **Seiji wa, seijika no tame de wa naku, kokumin no tame ni aru _____.**
(3) むだなお金はつかう _____。
   **Muda na o-kane wa tsukau _____.**
(4) もう三回も失敗したんだから、あきらめた _____。
   **Mou sankai mo shippai shita n da kara, akirameta _____.**
(5) いつも本当のことを言う _____。
   **Itsumo hontou no koto o iu _____.**
(6) 彼の考えは間違っているような _____。
   **Kare no kangae wa machigatte iru you na _____.**

⇨ 84.1

3 *

Complete the following sentences using んじゃないでしょうか **n ja nai deshou ka** 'Isn't it (the case) that . . .' so that the resulting sentences convey the same ideas as the English cues.

(1) Bullying is not just a school problem.
   いじめは学校だけの問題 _____。
   **Ijime wa gakkou dake no mondai _____.**
(2) There are other ways to do it.
   もっと別の方法が _____。
   **Motto betsu no houhou ga _____.**

(3) It's not that s/he didn't know anything.
何も知らなかったわけ _____。
**Nani mo shiranakatta wake _____.**

(4) Unless we talk it over in depth, we cannot <u>solve</u> (解決する **kaiketsu suru**) it.
みんなでよく話し合わないと、_____。
**Minna de yoku hanashiawanai to, _____.**

(5) Whatever we don't know, all we have to do is ask someone.
分からないことは、誰かにきけば _____。
**Wakaranai koto wa, dareka ni kikeba _____.**

⇨ 84.1.3

**4** ⋆⋆ Express your opinions about each topic below. Try to express them in a short paragraph rather than in a simple sentence.

(1) 子供が小学校で外国語を習うことについて、どう思いますか。
**Kodomo ga shougakkou de gaikokugo o narau koto ni tsuite, dou omoimasu ka.**

(2) 「お金さえあれば幸せになれる」という考え方についてどう思いますか。
**'O-kane sae areba shiawase ni nareru' to iu kangae-kata ni tsuite dou omoimasu ka.**

⇨ 55.4.1, 84.1

# 85

# Agreement, disagreement and indifference

**1** ★  Ken and Mai, good friends, are at a sushi shop talking about going to a movie. Mai does not have a particular preference. Fill in the blanks with expressions of agreement or indifference.

健：　今日のすし、おいしかったね。
舞：　①＿＿＿＿＿＿＿、久し振りにおいしいお寿司を食べたって感じ。
　　　でも、ちょっと高いと思わない？
健：　②＿＿＿＿＿＿＿。
舞：　さて、お腹がいっぱいになったところで、映画でも見に行かない？
健：　③＿＿＿＿＿＿＿。久しぶりだし。コメディーとアクションとどっ
　　　ちがいい？
舞：　④＿＿＿＿＿＿＿＿＿＿＿。
健：　じゃ、映画館に行ってどんなのやってるか見てから決めようか。
舞：　うん、⑤＿＿＿＿＿＿＿。('good idea')

Ken:  Kyou no sushi, oishikatta ne.
Mai:  ①＿＿＿＿＿＿＿, hisashiburi ni oishii o-sushi o tabeta tte kanji.
　　　Demo, chotto takai to omowanai?
Ken:  ②＿＿＿＿＿＿＿.
Mai:  Sate, onaka ga ippai ni natta tokoro de, eiga demo mini ikanai?
Ken:  ③＿＿＿＿＿＿＿. Hisashiburi dashi. Komedii to akushon to dotchi
　　　ga ii?
Mai:  ④＿＿＿＿＿＿＿＿＿＿＿.
Ken:  Ja, eigakan ni itte donna no yatte ru ka mite kara kimeyou ka.
Mai:  Un, ⑤＿＿＿＿＿＿＿. ('good idea')

⇨ 85.1, 85.2

**2** ★  Fill in the blanks with appropriate expressions from the list. Use each expression just once. In each dialogue, the speakers are equal in status.

| | | |
|---|---|---|
| (a) そうかな | (b) そうですか | (c) 私も賛成です |
| (d) いいんじゃない | (e) 私は反対です | (f) 私はそう思わない |
| (a) sou ka na | | (b) sou desu ka |
| (c) watashi mo sansei desu | | (d) ii n ja nai |
| (e) watashi wa hantai desu | | (f) watashi wa sou omowanai |

(1)
A: 田中さんって、困った人だね。無責任で。
B: (①            )? (②                ) けど。

A: **Tanaka-san tte, komatta hito da ne. Mu-sekinin de.**
B: **(①            )? (②                ) kedo.**

(2)
[年功序列 **nenkou joretsu** 'seniority system'; 制度 **seido** 'system']

C: 日本ではまだまだ年功序列の会社が多いですが、仕事ができる人はどんどん上に
上がれるような制度にするべきだと思うんですが。
D: ええ、(③            )。

C: **Nihon de wa madamada nenkou joretsu no kaisha ga ooi desu ga,
shigoto ga dekiru hito wa dondon ue ni agareru you na seido ni suru
beki da to omou n desu ga.**
D: **Ee, (③            ).**

(3)
E: この仕事、三宅さんに頼もうと思っているんだけど、どう思う？
F: うん、(④            )？

E: **Kono shigoto, Miyake-san ni tanomou to omotte iru n da kedo,
dou omou?**
F: **Un, (④            )?**

(4)
[原子力発電 **genshiryoku hatsuden** 'nuclear power generation'; 安全性 **anzensei**
'safety'; 保証 **hoshou** 'to guarantee']

G: 原子力発電を続けるべきだという意見もありますが、どう思われますか。
H: うーん、(⑤            ) ねぇ。やはり安全性が保証できないので。

G: **Genshiryoku hatsuden o tsuzukeru beki da to iu iken mo arimasu ga,
dou omowaremasu ka.**
H: **Uun, (⑤            ) nee. Yahari anzensei ga hoshou
dekinai node.**

(5)
I: 幼児の時から英語を習えば英語が上手になると思うんですけど。
J: (⑥            )。必ずしもそうは思いませんけど。

I: **Youji no toki kara Eigo o naraeba Eigo ga jouzu ni naru to omou n
desu kedo.**
J: **(⑥            ). Kanarazu shimo sou wa omoimasen kedo.**

⇨ 85.1, 85.2

FUNCTIONS

**3** ★

Mr Tanaka and Mr Machida, currently residing in Australia with their families, are discussing changes in the educational system in Japan.
Fill in the blanks with expressions of agreement and disagreement.

[導入 **dounyuu** 'introduction, adoption'; 講座 **kouza** 'course']

田中： 日本の大学では秋入学の導入が話題となっているようですね。
町田： ええ、秋入学にすると学生が海外の大学に留学しやすくなりますよね。
田中： まあ、(1) (that might be true) が、いろいろ問題もあるらしいですよ。
町田： え、どんな？
田中： 例えば、高校生は三月に卒業するので、それから九月まで空き時間ができてしまうとか。
町田： (2) (I see) 。
田中： それに日本の大学では普通、一講座が一年を通して開かれ、前期、後期と両方受けて単位になるので、そういうところも変えなければならないでしょう？
町田： (3) (That's true) 。それにやっぱり桜の花の咲くころに入学式がなくなるっていうのもさびしいですよね。
田中： (4) (I agree, I feel the same way.) 。

| | |
|---|---|
| Tanaka: | **Nihon no daigaku de wa aki nyuugaku no dounyuu ga wadai to natte iru you desu ne.** |
| Machida: | **Ee, aki nyuugaku ni suru to gakusei ga kaigai no daigaku ni ryuugaku shiyasuku narimasu yo ne.** |
| Tanaka: | **Maa, (1) (that might be true) ga, iroiro mondai mo aru rashii desu yo.** |
| Machida: | **E, donna?** |
| Tanaka: | **Tatoeba, koukousei wa sangatsu ni sotsugyou suru node, sorekara kugatsu made aki jikan ga dekite shimau toka.** |
| Machida: | (2) (I see) . |
| Tanaka: | **Sore ni Nihon no daigaku de wa futsuu, ichikouza ga ichinen o tooshite hirakare, zenki, kouki to ryouhou ukete tan'i ni naru node, sou iu tokoro mo kaenakereba naranai deshou?** |
| Machida: | (3) (That's true) . **Sore ni yappari sakura no hana no saku koro ni nyuugakushiki ga nakunaru tte iu no mo sabishii desu yo ne.** |
| Tanaka: | (4) (I agree, I feel the same way.) . |

⇨ 85.1, 85.2

208

# 86
# Choosing and deciding

**1** ★ Megumi and Shouta are having dinner at a restaurant. Complete the following dialogue with appropriate expressions.

ウェイター： お飲物は何 (1)＿＿＿＿＿＿＿＿＿＿＿＿＿＿＿＿＿＿＿。
恵： 私はワインを (2)＿＿＿＿＿＿＿＿＿＿＿＿＿＿＿＿＿。
翔太： あ、僕も。
ウェイター： はい、白と赤とございますが、(3)＿＿＿＿＿＿＿＿ がよろしいでしょうか。
翔太： 僕は赤。今日は肉だから。
恵： 私は白 (4)＿＿＿＿＿＿＿＿＿＿＿＿＿＿＿＿＿。

＊　＊　＊　＊　＊　＊　＊

ウェイター： お食事の方はお決まりですか。
翔太： 僕はステーキ。
恵： 何かお勧めのものありますか。
ウェイター： 今日のお勧めはシーフードパスタとなっておりますが。
恵 ： じゃ、私はそれ (5)＿＿＿＿＿＿＿＿＿＿＿＿＿＿＿＿＿。
ウェイター： ステーキおひとつとシーフードパスタおひとつですね。かしこまりました。

Weitaa: O-nomimono wa nani (1)＿＿＿＿＿＿＿＿＿＿＿＿＿＿＿＿.
Megumi: Watashi wa wain o (2)＿＿＿＿＿＿＿＿＿＿＿＿＿＿＿.
Shouta: A, boku mo.
Weitaa: Hai. Shiro to aka to gozaimasu ga, (3)＿＿＿＿＿＿＿＿ ga yoroshii deshou ka.
Shouta: Boku wa aka. Kyou wa niku da kara.
Megumi: Watashi wa shiro (4)＿＿＿＿＿＿＿＿＿＿＿＿＿＿＿.

＊　＊　＊　＊　＊　＊　＊

Weitaa: O-shokuji no hou wa o-kimari desu ka.
Shouta: Boku wa suteeki.
Megumi: Nani ka o-susume no mono arimasu ka.
Weitaa: Kyou no o-susume wa shiifuudo pasuta to natte orimasu ga.
Megumi: Ja, watashi wa sore (5)＿＿＿＿＿＿＿＿＿＿＿＿＿＿＿＿.
Weitaa: Suteeki o-hitotsu to shiifuudo pasuta o-hitotsu desu ne. Kashikomarimashita.

⇨ 86.1

**209**

**2** ★ Makoto is a 28-year-old employee of a company. The following is a list of things he has decided to do or not to do. Express them in Japanese, using V **koto ni suru** in appropriate forms.

(1) He has decided not to change jobs. [change jobs = 転職する **tenshoku suru**]
(2) He has decided to attend a graduate school abroad one year later.
(3) He has decided to study English in order to score high (lit. take a good score) on TOEFL.
(4) He has decided not to borrow money from his parents.
(5) He wants to get married, but has decided to wait for a year.

⇨ 86.2

**3** ★ Choose the more appropriate expressions of the two.

(A)
学生： 先生、このたび奨学金がもらえる【① ことにしました・② ことになりました】。先生に推薦状を書いていただいたおかげです。本当にありがとうございました。

Gakusei: **Sensei, kono tabi shougakukin ga moraeru【① koto ni shimashita.・② koto ni narimashita.】Sensei ni suisenjou o kaite itadaita o-kage desu. Hontou ni arigatou gozaimashita.**

(B)
翔太： ところでインターンシップ、やるの？
謙一： いろいろ考えたんだけど、やっぱりやらない【① ことにした・② ことになった】よ。

Shouta: **Tokorode intaanshippu, yaru no?**
Ken'ichi: **Iroiro kangaeta n da kedo, yappari yaranai【① koto ni shita・② koto ni natta】yo.**

(C)
部下： 部長、おかげさまで、このたび結婚する【① ことにしました・② ことになりました】。
部長： それはおめでとう。

Buka: **Buchou, o-kage-sama de, kono tabi kekkon suru【① koto ni shimashita.・② koto ni narimashita.】**
Buchou: **Sore wa o-medetou.**

(D)
今新しい車を買うのは無理かなと思ったのですが、思い切って買う【① ことにしました・② ことになりました】。

**Ima atarashii kuruma o kau no wa muri kana to omotta no desu ga, omoikitte kau【① koto ni shimashita.・② koto ni narimashita.】**

⇨ 86.2, 86.3

# 87
## Shopping

**1** ★★ Kim, a college student in Japan, is interested in buying a blue sweater. Complete the dialogue.

店員　：　いらっしゃいませ。
キム　：　すみません。①＿＿＿＿＿＿＿＿＿＿＿＿＿＿＿。
店員　：　はい、ございます。これはいかがですか。
キム　：　そうですねぇ。②＿＿＿＿＿＿＿＿＿＿＿＿＿＿。
店員　：　八千五百円です。
キム　：　これ、Lサイズですよね。③＿＿＿＿＿＿＿＿＿＿＿＿。
店員　：　はい、こちらはMサイズですが。
キム　：　あ、それ、よさそう … 。④＿＿＿＿＿＿＿＿＿＿＿＿。
店員　：　こちらは六千円です。今、セールでお安くなっております。
キム　：　じゃ、⑤＿＿＿＿＿＿＿＿＿＿＿＿＿＿＿＿。
店員　：　はい、ありがとうございます。

Ten'in:　Irasshaimase.
Kimu:　Sumimasen. ①＿＿＿＿＿＿＿＿＿＿＿＿＿＿.
Ten'in:　Hai, gozaimasu. Kore wa ikaga desu ka.
Kimu:　Sou desu nee. ②＿＿＿＿＿＿＿＿＿＿＿＿＿.
Ten'in:　Hassen-gohyaku en desu.
Kimu:　Kore, eru saizu desu yo ne. ③＿＿＿＿＿＿＿＿＿＿＿.
Ten'in:　Hai, kochira wa emu saizu desu ga.
Kimu:　A, sore, yosa soo . . . ④＿＿＿＿＿＿＿＿＿＿＿＿＿.
Ten'in:　Kochira wa rokusen en desu. Ima, seeru de o-yasuku natte orimasu.
Kimu:　Ja, ⑤＿＿＿＿＿＿＿＿＿＿＿＿＿＿.
Ten'in:　Hai, arigatou gozaimasu.

⇨　87.1, 87.2, 87.3, Exercises in 1.3, 9.2

**2** ★ Kim is calling the store because s/he found a hole in the sweater, and s/he wants to exchange it. Fill in the blanks with appropriate phrases.

店員　：　はい、KAMEYAでございます。いつもお世話になっております。
キム　：　もしもし、あのう、昨日そちらでセーターを買ったんですけど。
店員　：　はい、ありがとうございます。
キム　：　あのう、①＿＿＿＿＿＿＿＿＿＿＿＿＿＿んですけど。
店員　：　あ、それは申し訳ございません。
キム　：　それで、新しいのと ②＿＿＿＿＿＿＿＿＿＿＿＿＿んですけど。
店員　：　はい、承知致しました。
キム　：　③＿＿＿＿＿＿＿＿＿＿＿＿＿＿。

店員：　はい、あした開いております。

キム：　④＿＿＿＿＿＿＿＿＿＿＿＿＿＿。

店員：　あしたは11時から5時まででございます。では、ご来店をお待ちしております。('I'll be waiting for you')

Ten'in:  Hai, KAMEYA de gozaimasu. Itsumo o-sewa ni natte orimasu.

Kimu:  Moshimoshi, anou, kinou sochira de seetaa o katta n desu kedo.

Ten'in:  Hai, arigatou gozaimasu.

Kimu:  Anou, ①＿＿＿＿＿＿＿＿＿＿＿＿＿ n desu kedo.

Ten'in:  A, sore wa moushiwake gozaimasen.

Kimu:  Sorede, atarashii no to ②＿＿＿＿＿＿＿＿＿＿＿＿＿ n desu kedo.

Ten'in:  Hai, shouchi itashimashita.

Kimu:  ③＿＿＿＿＿＿＿＿＿＿＿＿.

Ten'in:  Hai, ashita, aite orimasu.

Kimu:  ④＿＿＿＿＿＿＿＿＿＿＿＿.

Ten'in:  Ashita wa juuichi-ji kara go-ji made de gozaimasu. Dewa, go-raiten o o-machi shite orimasu. ('I'll be waiting for you')

⇨ | 87.4, 87.5

# 88
# Ordering

1 *

You are calling a restaurant to order takeout. Ask how long it takes, and request that they deliver the order as quickly as possible. Complete the following with appropriate phrases.

[出前 **demae** 'delivery']

店の人： はい、「藤本」です。毎度お世話になっております。
あなた： もしもし、すみません。出前を ① ＿＿＿＿＿＿＿＿＿＿ けど。
店の人： はい、ご注文、どうぞ。
あなた： えー、② ＿＿＿＿＿＿＿＿ と、③ ＿＿＿＿＿＿＿＿ と、
④ ＿＿＿＿＿＿＿＿ お願いします。
店の人： はい、照り焼きチキンが一つ、ちらし寿司一つ、親子どんぶり
一つですね？
あなた： いえ、ちらしは ⑤ ＿＿＿＿＿＿＿＿ です。
店の人： あ、ちらしは二つですか。
あなた： はい、そうです。4丁目の寺山アパートの5号室なんですけど、
⑥ ＿＿＿＿＿＿＿＿。
店の人： そうですね … 今ちょっと込んでいるんで、45分から1時間くらい
だと思いますが …
あなた： あのう、すみませんが、⑦ ＿＿＿＿＿＿＿＿ か。
店の人： はい、わかりました。毎度ありがとうございます！

Mise no hito:   Hai, Fujimoto desu. Maido o-sewa ni natte orimasu.
Anata:          Moshi moshi, sumimasen. Demae o ① ＿＿＿＿＿＿ kedo.
Mise no hito:   Hai, go-chuumon, douzo.
Anata:          Ee, ② ＿＿＿＿＿＿ to, ③ ＿＿＿＿＿＿ to,
④ ＿＿＿＿＿＿ o-negai shimasu.
Mise no hito:   Hai, teriyaki-chikin ga hitotsu, chirashizushi hitotsu, oyako
donburi hitotsu desu ne?
Anata:          Ie, chirashi wa ⑤ ＿＿＿＿＿＿ desu.
Mise no hito:   A, chirashi wa futatsu desu ka.
Anata:          Hai, sou desu. Yon-choume no Terayama Apaato no
go-goushitsu na n desu kedo, ⑥ ＿＿＿＿＿＿.
Mise no hito:   Sou desu ne . . . Ima chotto konde iru n de, yonjuugo-fun
kara ichijikan kurai da to omoimasu ga . . .
Anata:          Anou, sumimasen ga, ⑦ ＿＿＿＿＿＿ ka.
Mise no hito:   Hai, wakarimashita. Maido arigatou gozaimasu!

⇨ | 88.2

**2** ★★★  You want to buy a mystery novel, and are visiting an online book store.

(A)
Below are **rebyuu** ('reviews') of the book you are interested in. Read the reviews and mark the summary statements which follow them, true (○) or false (×).

A さん **A-san**  [40代/女性 **yonjuu dai / josei**]

現実にあり得る出来事、そしてその恐怖 … 背中がゾクゾクし、どんどん読み進みました。この本すごくお勧めです。

**Genjitsu ni ari-uru dekigoto, soshite sono kyoufu . . . Senaka ga zokuzoku shi, dondon yomi-susumimashita. Kono hon sugoku o-susume desu.**

B さん **B-san**  [50代/男性 **gojuu dai / dansei**]

テレビのCMで気になり購入し、あっという間に読み終えました。情景の描写が素晴らしいです。とても面白く読ませてもらいました。

**Terebi no CM de ki ni nari kounyuu shi, a tto iu ma ni yomi-oemashita. Joukei no byousha ga subarashii desu. Totemo omoshiroku yomasete moraimashita.**

C さん **C-san**  [30代/女性 **sanjuu dai / josei**]

電車や新聞の広告で見かけ、電子書籍版で注文しました。すぐに一気読み。この作家、文章表現が特にうまく、物語のシーンが目に浮かんで来ます。こんなにおもしろい本、他にありません！

**Densha ya shinbun no koukoku de mikake, denshi shoseki-ban de chuumon shimashita. Sugu ni ikki yomi. Kono sakka, bunshou hyougen ga toku ni umaku, monogatari no shiin ga me ni ukande kimasu. Konna ni omoshiroi hon, hoka ni arimasen!**

a. (   ) Two people wrote positive reviews, and one negative.
b. (   ) The author's descriptions of the scenes seem particularly good.
c. (   ) This book is advertised in the newspaper and on the train, but not on TV.
d. (   ) An electronic version of the book is available.

(B)
Read the following ordering information, then choose the correct alternatives from the statements which follow.

| 『嘘』青木空代【著】 | 'Uso' Aoki Sorayo【cho】 |
|---|---|
| 価格　¥1560（税込）<br>○○書房（2013/08発売）<br>★★★★☆<br>12時間以内にご注文いただくと、24時間以内にお届けします。<br>5点在庫あり。<br>ご注文はお早めに。<br>送料無料（国内配送のみ）<br>こちらもご購入いただけます。<br>　　中古品・文庫本 | Kakaku ¥1560 (zeikomi)<br>○○Shobou (2013/08 hatsubai)<br>★★★★☆<br>**Juunijikan inai ni go-chuumon itadaku to, nijuuyojikan inai ni o-todoke shimasu.**<br>**Goten zaiko ari.**<br>**Go-chuumon wa o-hayame ni.**<br>**Souryou muryou (kokunai haisou nomi)**<br>**Kochira mo go-kounyuu itadakemasu.**<br>**Chuukohin・Bunkobon** |

① The purchaser of the book【(a) must　(b) need not】pay for shipping.
② The tax【(a) is　(b) is not】included in the price of the book.
③ A paperback version of the book is【(a) available　(b) unavailable】.
④ Used books are【(a) available　(b) unavailable】.
⑤ This book can be shipped【(a) only within Japan　(b) abroad】.
⑥ Shipping will take at most【(a) 12　(b) 24】hours from the time of purchase.

⇨ 88.3

# 89
# Reservation

1 *

You want to reserve a double room for 3 nights. Fill in the blanks with appropriate phrases.

ホテル： はい、ホテル「錦」でございます。
あなた： もしもし、あのう、3泊 ① ＿＿＿＿＿＿＿＿＿＿＿＿＿＿＿＿ が。
ホテル： ご予約でございますね。ありがとうございます。お名前とご住所をうかがってもよろしいでしょうか。
あなた： [省略 'omitted']
ホテル： お泊まりのご予定はいつになりますでしょうか。
あなた： ② ＿＿＿＿＿＿＿＿＿＿＿＿＿＿＿＿＿。
ホテル： はい、8月7日から8月10日でございますね。お部屋はシングルでよろしいでしょうか。
あなた： いえ、大人二人ですので、③ ＿＿＿＿＿＿＿＿＿＿＿＿＿＿＿。
ホテル： おタバコのほうは？
あなた： タバコは吸いませんので、ノースモーキングの部屋を
④ ＿＿＿＿＿＿＿＿＿＿＿＿＿ んですが。
ホテル： ノースモーキングのダブルでございますね。かしこまりました。

| | |
|---|---|
| Hoteru: | Hai, Hoteru Nishiki de gozaimasu. |
| Anata: | Moshi moshi, anou, sanpaku ① ＿＿＿＿＿＿＿＿＿＿＿ ga. |
| Hoteru: | Go-yoyaku de gozaimasu ne. Arigatou gozaimasu. O-namae to go-juusho o ukagatte mo yoroshii deshou ka. |
| Anata: | [Shouryaku 'omitted'] |
| Hoteru: | O-tomari no go-yotei wa itsu ni narimasu deshou ka. |
| Anata: | ② ＿＿＿＿＿＿＿＿＿＿＿. |
| Hoteru: | Hai, hachigatsu nanoka kara hachigatsu tooka de gozaimasu ne. O-heya wa shinguru de yoroshii deshou ka. |
| Anata: | Ie, Otona futari desu node, ③ ＿＿＿＿＿＿＿＿＿＿＿. |
| Hoteru: | O-tabako no hou wa? |
| Anata: | Tabako wa suimasen node, noo sumookingu no heya o ④ ＿＿＿＿＿＿＿＿＿＿＿ n desu ga. |
| Hoteru: | Noo sumookingu no daburu de gozaimasu ne. Kashikomarimashita. |

⇨ 89.2

2 *

You reserved a hotel room for August the 7th to the 10th, but now need to check out on the 9th. Call the hotel and change your reservation.

ホテル： はい、ホテル「錦」でございます。
あなた： もしもし、あのう、すみませんが、予約を
① ＿＿＿＿＿＿＿＿＿＿＿＿＿。

ホテル： お客様のお名前をうかがってもよろしいでしょうか。
あなた： ○○××です。
ホテル： ○○様、お泊まりは8月7日から3泊のご予定ですね。
あなた： その予定だったんですが、8月9日に
　　　　 ② ＿＿＿＿＿＿＿＿＿＿＿＿＿＿＿＿＿＿。
ホテル： そういたしますと、チェックアウトが8月9日ということでよろしいでしょうか。
あなた： はい、そうです。
ホテル： では、2泊ということで。承知いたしました。
あなた： よろしく ③ ＿＿＿＿＿＿＿＿＿＿＿＿＿＿＿＿＿＿。

Hoteru: Hai, Hoteru Nishiki de gozaimasu.
Anata: Moshimoshi, anou, sumimasen ga, yoyaku o
　　　　① ＿＿＿＿＿＿＿＿＿＿＿＿＿＿＿＿.
Hoteru: O-kyaku-sama no o-namae o ukagatte mo yoroshii deshou ka.
Anata: ○○×× desu.
Hoteru: ○○-sama, o-tomari wa hachigatsu nanoka kara san-paku no
　　　　go-yotei desu ne.
Anata: Sono yotei datta n desu ga, hachigatsu kokonoka ni
　　　　② ＿＿＿＿＿＿＿＿＿＿＿＿＿＿＿＿.
Hoteru: Sou itashimasu to, chekku auto ga hachigatsu kokonoka to iu
　　　　koto de yoroshii deshou ka.
Anata: Hai, sou desu.
Hoteru: Dewa, nihaku to iu koto de. Shouchi itashimashita.
Anata: Yoroshiku ③ ＿＿＿＿＿＿＿＿＿＿＿＿＿＿＿＿.

➡ 89.3

**3** ★

What would you have to do if you reserved the hotel online? Based on conversation 2 above, fill out the following form. Hotel Nishiki is in Nagoya. You want to use the Internet in the room, and want breakfast included.

(A)
地図から探す **Chizu kara sagasu**
一つ選んで下さい。 → ＿＿＿＿＿＿＿＿＿＿＿＿＿＿＿＿
**Hitotsu erande kudasai.**

> a. 北海道・b. 本州・c. 首都圏・d. 四国・e. 九州・f. 沖縄 …
>
> a. **Hokkaidou**・b. **Honshuu**・c. **Shutoken**・d. **Shikoku**・
> e. **Kyuushuu**・f. **Okinawa** . . .

(B)
宿名・ホテル名から探す **Yado-mei, hoteru-mei kara sagasu**
宿・ホテルの名前を書いて下さい。 → ＿＿＿＿＿＿＿＿＿＿＿＿＿＿＿＿
**Yado, hoteru no namae o kaite kudasai.**

(C)
日付から探す　**Hizuke kara sagasu**

① 宿泊日 ：　　　　 20XX 年 　　　 月 　　　 日から 　　　 泊
　**Shukuhaku-bi:**　　　 **nen**　 **gatsu**　 **nichi kara**　 **haku**

② 人数等 ：　　　 部屋　 大人 　 名　　 子供 　 名
　**Ninzuu nado:**　 **heya**　 **otona mei**　 **kodomo mei**

③ 部屋タイプ：一つ選んで下さい。　→ _____
　**Heya taipu: Hitotsu erande kudasai.**

> a. シングル・b. ツイン・c. ダブル・d. トリプル
>
> a. **Shinguru**・b. **Tsuin**・c. **Daburu**・d. **Toripuru**

④ 食事タイプ：一つ選んで下さい。　→ _____
　**Shokuji taipu: Hitotsu erande kudasai.**

> a. 指定しない・b. 食事なし・c. 朝のみ・d. 夕のみ・e. 朝/夕あり
>
> a. **Shitei shinai**・b. **Shokuji nashi**・c. **Asa nomi**・d. **Yuu nomi**・
> e. **Asa/yuu ari**

⑤ インターネット：一つ選んで下さい。　→ _____
　**Intaanetto: Hitotsu erande kudasai.**

> a. 部屋で使用・b. ロビーで使用・c. 使用しない
>
> a. **Heya de shiyou**・b. **Robii de shiyou**・c. **Shiyou shinai**

⇨ 89.2

# Answer key

## A Structures

## 1 Introduction: major features of Japanese grammar

**1** ②で 英語 を 教えています。 **de Eigo o oshiete imasu.** ③ は 横浜 に あります。 **wa Yokohama ni arimasu.** ④とても 忙しい です。 **totemo isogashii desu.**

**2** ② [簡単な] 漢字 ; [短い] 話 **[Kantan na] kanji; [mijikai] hanashi** ③ [村上春樹が書いた] 本 **[Murakami Haruki ga kaita] hon** ④ [速く] 読む ; [とても] 面白い **[hayaku] yomu; [totemo] omoshiroi**

**3** (A) ① が **ga** ② は **wa** ③ は **wa** ④ は **wa** ⑤ は **wa**

(B) ① は **wa** ② は **wa** ③ が **ga** ④ が **ga**

**4** ① d ② a ③ e ④ c ⑤ b

**5** (A) ① は **wa** ② 単三電池は **tansan denchi wa** ③ 私ども ('we (humble)') は **watashi-domo ('we (humble)') wa** ④ 私は **watashi wa**

(B) ① は **wa** ② を **o** ③ あいつは **aitsu wa** ④ が **ga** ⑤ 俺達 **ore-tachi** (or 僕達 **boku-tachi**, etc.) は **wa** ⑥ に **ni** ⑦ か **ka** ⑧ 俺は **ore wa**

## 2 Pronunciation

**1** 7 syllables (**Kok.kai.gi.ji.dô.an.nai**); 12 moras (**Ko.k.ka.i.gi.ji.do.o.a.n.na.i**) (こっかい ぎじどう あんない)

**2** (A) ① アクセサリー **akusesarii** 'accessory (e.g. necklace, earring)' ② エンターテインメント **entaateinmento** 'entertainment' ③ コラボレーション **koraboreeshon** 'collaboration' ④ カーナビゲーション **kaa nabigeeshon** 'car navigation (system)' ⑤ コンパチブル **konpachiburu** 'compatible' ⑥ アプリケーション **apurikeeshon** '(computer) application'

(B) ① 着メロ **chakumero** ② コピペ **kopipe** ③ マスコミ **masu komi** ④ モバゲー **mobagee** ⑤ 就活 **shuukatsu**

**3** ① あおぞら **ao-zora** ② きょうだいげんか **kyoudai-genka** ③ ひどけい **hi-dokei** ④みかづき **mika-zuki**

**4** ① HL, HLL　② LH, LHH　③ LHLL, LHLLL　④ LHHH, LHHHL

## 3　Writing system

**1** ① あし　② うめ　③ おんな　④ おばあちゃん　⑤ かがみ　⑥ けっこう
⑦ しゅうまつ

**2** ① ギター　② フットボール　③ コンピューター　④ ニャン　⑤ ソフト
⑥ キンコン

**3** *Kanji*: nouns and substantive parts of (almost all) the verbs and adjectives
*Katakana*: loan words
*Hiragana*: particles and inflected parts of verbs and adjectives

## 4　Words

**1** a. (J)　b. (F)　c. (C)　d. (J)　e. (M)　f. (C)　g. (J)

**2** a. ○　b. ×　c. ○　d. ×　e. ×

## 5　Sentences and sentence patterns

**(A)** ① d　② a　③ d　④ a　⑤ c　⑥ d
**(B)** ① b　② b　③ d　④ c　⑤ b　⑥ d

## 6　Register and style

**1** (a) W　(b) S　(c) S　(d) W　(e) S　(f) W　(g) S　(h) S

**2** (Possible conversation between two male students.)

| | |
|---|---|
| 山田健二： | あ、ジム、ひさしぶり。 |
| ジム・スミス： | あ、健二、ひさしぶりだね。 |
| 健二： | いつ帰って来たの？ |
| ジム： | きのう。 |
| 健二： | じゃ、時差ぼけで大変だろ？留学はどうだった？ |
| ジム： | すっごい楽しかったよ。いろんな日本文化が体験できてよかったよ。 |
| 健二： | そりゃあ、よかったね。また今度話を聞きたいな。 |
| ジム： | うん、そのうち一度会おうよ。 |
| 健二： | うん。じゃまたね。 |
| ジム： | うん。また。 |

| | |
|---|---|
| **Yamada Kenji:** | **A, Jimu, hisashiburi.** |
| **Jimu Sumisu:** | **A, Kenji, hisashiburi da ne.** |
| **Kenji:** | **Itsu kaette kita no?** |
| **Jimu:** | **Kinou.** |

Kenji:          Ja, jisaboke de taihen daro? Ryuugaku wa dou datta?
Jimu:           Suggoi tanoshikatta yo. Iron na Nihon bunka ga taiken dekite yokatta yo.
Kenji:          Soryaa, yokatta ne. Mata kondo hanashi o kikitai na.
Jimu:           Un, sono uchi ichido aou yo.
Kenji:          Un. Ja mata ne.
Jimu:           Un. Mata.

(Between two female students.)

山田花子：          あ、キャロル、ひさしぶり。
キャロル・スミス：      ほんとうにひさしぶり。
花子：             いつ帰って来たの？
キャロル：           きのう。
花子：             じゃ、時差ぼけで大変でしょう？留学はどうだった？
キャロル：           とっても楽しかった。いろんな日本文化が体験できてよかったよ。
花子：             そりゃあ、よかったね。また今度話を聞かせて？
キャロル：           うん、そのうち一度会わない？
花子：             うん。じゃまたね。
キャロル：           うん。また。

Yamada Hanako:      A, Kyaroru, hisashiburi.
Kyaroru Sumisu:     Hontou ni hisashiburi.
Hanako:             Itsu kaette kita no?
Kyaroru:            Kinou.
Hanako:             Ja, jisaboke de taihen deshou? Ryuugaku wa dou datta?
Kyaroru:            Tottemo tanoshikatta. Iron na Nihon bunka ga taiken dekite yokatta yo.
Hanako:             Soryaa, yokatta ne. Mata kondo hanashi o kikasete?
Kyaroru:            Un, sono uchi ichido awanai?
Hanako:             Un. Ja mata ne.
Kyaroru:            Un. Mata.

**3**  a. F  b. N  c. N  d. M  e. M  f. F  g. N  h. F  i. M  j. N

## 7  Nouns and noun phrases

**1**  (1) 彼女がよく行く「こまち」という喫茶店のウェイター kanojo ga yoku iku 'Komachi' to iu kissaten no weitaa   (2) あの子供の大きな犬 ano kodomo no ookina inu   (3) 中学生のむすめの先生の家 chuugakusei no musume no sensei no ie   (4) 山の中の「ゆず」という旅館の主人 yama no naka no 'Yuzu' to iu ryokan no shujin   (5) あるお寺にゆうれいが出るといううわさ aru o-tera ni yuurei ga deru to iu uwasa

**2**  (1) と to; を o   (2) や ya; や ya; を o   (3) の no; を o   (4) か ka   (5) なり nari; なり nari   (6) とか toka or や ya

## 8 Pronouns

**1** (A) あなた **anata**, わた（く）し **wata(ku)shi** (B) わたしたち **watashi-tachi** (C) おれ **ore**, おまえ **o-mae**

**2** ① you (singular) ② I ③ we ④ you (plural) ⑤ I ⑥ he

**3** a. 自分 **jibun** b. お互い **o-tagai** c. 自分 **jibun**, 自分 **jibun** d. お互い **o-tagai**

**4** a. 'you, my beloved' b. 'I, who am a parent' c. 'she, who is blessed with a good family and good health' d. 'you, who look forever young'

## 9 Demonstratives (*ko-so-a(-do)* words)

**1** ① 東京銀行の田中さんです。 **Toukyou Ginkou no Tanaka-san desu.** ② こちらへどうぞ。 **Kochira e douzo.** ③ どの人ですか。 **Dono hito desu ka.** ④ あの眼鏡をかけている **Ano megane o kakete iru**

**2** ① その **sono** ② これ **kore** (or この時計 **kono tokei**) ③ あの **ano** ④ あれ **are** (or あのカメラ **ano kamera**) ⑤ この **kono** ⑥ その **sono** ⑦ これ **kore**

## 10 Particles

**1** (A) I. ① に **ni** ② に **ni** (or へ **e**) ③ まで **made** ④ で **de** ⑤ に **ni** ⑥ を **o** ⑦ が **ga** II. ⑧ で **de** ⑨ を **o** ⑩ の **no** ⑪ が **ga** ⑫ の **no** ⑬ が **ga** ⑭ が **ga** ⑮ と **to** III. ⑯ まで **made** ⑰ に **ni** ⑱ に **ni** (or へ **e**) ⑲ の **no** ⑳ に **ni** ㉑ の **no** ㉒ が **ga** ㉓ から **kara** ㉔ が **ga** ㉕ に **ni** IV. ㉖ と **to** (or から **kara**) ㉗ の **no** ㉘ に **ni** ㉙ の **no** ㉚ の **no** ㉛ で **de** ㉜ に **ni**

(B) ① まで **made** ② まで **made** ③ が **ga** ④ を **o** ⑤ の **no** ⑥ を **o** (or で **de**) ⑦ に **ni** ⑧ に **ni** ⑨ が **ga** ⑩ で **de**

(C) ① で **de** ② を **o** ③ の **no** ④ に **ni** ⑤ を **o** ⑥ に **ni** ⑦ の **no** ⑧ に **ni** ⑨ の **no** ⑩ と **to**

**2** (1) しか **shika** (2) しか **shika** (3) だけ **dake** (4) だけ **dake**

**3** ① と **to** ② と **to** ③ の **no** ④ を **o** ⑤ に **ni** ⑥ が **ga** ⑦ を **o** ⑧ の **no** ⑨ と **to** ⑩ で **de** ⑪ に **ni** ⑫ に **ni** ⑬ が **ga** ⑭ の **no** ⑮ の **no** ⑯ の **no** ⑰ の **no** ⑱ を **o** ⑲ で **de** ⑳ に **ni** (or へ **e**) ㉑ が **ga** ㉒ を **o** ㉓ に **ni** ㉔ と **to**

## 11 Topic marker *wa*

**1** (2) 子供は外で遊んでいる。 **Kodomo wa soto de asonde iru.** (3) 田中さんには会ったことがありません。 **Tanaka-san ni wa atta koto ga arimasen.** (4) 先生とは電話で話しました。 **Sensei to wa denwa de hanashimashita.** (5) 日本では温泉に入った。 **Nihon de wa onsen ni haitta.** (6) イギリスからは代表が三人来た。 **Igirisu kara wa daihyou ga sannin kita.**

**2**

(1) ① が **ga**  ② が **ga**  ③ は **wa**  ④ が **ga**  ⑤ は **wa**  ⑥ が **ga**  (2) が **ga**
(3) は **wa**  (4) が **ga**  (5) ① が **ga**  ② は **wa**  ③ が **ga**  (6) ① は **wa**
② が **ga**  ③ は **wa**  ④ が **ga**  ⑤ が **ga**  ⑥ は **wa**  (7) ① は **wa**  ② が **ga**
③ は **wa**  (8) が **ga**

**3**

が₁→が (First mention of the fisherman.)

が₂→が (First mention of the children. It also describes a scene.)

が₃→は (Urashima has been mentioned before.)

が₄→は (Urashima has been mentioned before.)

が₅→が (Subject of a subordinate clause.)

が₆→が (First mention of the voice. It is also a description of a scene.)

が₇→が (Description of a scene.)

が₈→は (Kame has been mentioned before.)

が₉→は (The focus of the sentence is what follows **wa**.)

が₁₀→は (Urashima has been mentioned before.)

## 12  Verbs

**1**

① 書きます **kakimasu**  ② 書けば **kakeba**  ③ 会わない **awanai**  ④ 会えば **aeba**
⑤ 会おう **aou**  ⑥ 読まない **yomanai**  ⑦ 読みます **yomimasu**  ⑧ 読めば **yomeba**
⑨ 読もう **yomou**  ⑩ 待たない **matanai**  ⑪ 待ちます **machimasu**  ⑫ 待とう
**matou**  ⑬ とります **torimasu**  ⑭ とれば **toreba**  ⑮ 食べない **tabenai**
⑯ 食べれば **tabereba**  ⑰ こない **konai**  ⑱ きます **kimasu**  ⑲ くれば **kureba**
⑳ こよう **koyou**  ㉑ 見ない **minai**  ㉒ 見ます **mimasu**  ㉓ 見よう **miyou**
㉔ しない **shinai**  ㉕ します **shimasu**  ㉖ すれば **sureba**

**2**

① しまる **shimaru** 'X closes'  ② つく **tsuku** 'X comes on'  ③ でる **deru** 'X
goes out'  ④ なおる **naoru** 'X is repaired/heals'  ⑤ こわれる **kowareru** 'X
breaks'  ⑥ とめる **tomeru** 'stop X'  ⑦ かえる **kaeru** 'change X'  ⑧ あける
**akeru** 'open X'  ⑨ いれる **ireru** 'put X in'  ⑩ おこす **okosu** 'wake X up'

**3**

(1) vi  (2) vt  (3) vi  (4) vi  (5) vt  (6) vi  (7) vt  (8) vi  (9) vi  (10) vt, vi

**4**

(1) A: ついてる **tsuite ru**  B: 起きてる **okite ru**  (2) B: かわかしてる
**kawakashite ru**  (3) B: 売れて **urete**  (4) A: 折っちゃった **otchatta**
(5) 子: 見つからない **mitsukaranai**  母: 見つけよう **mitsukeyou**
(6) A: あけて **akete**  B: あけよう **akeyou**, あかなかった **akanakatta**
(7) A: わいてる **waite ru**  B: わかして **wakashite**  (8) A: けして **keshite**
B: けして **keshite**

**5**

(1) 見えます **miemasu**  (2) 聞こえない **kikoenai**  (3) できて **dekite**
(4) 聞ける **kikeru**  (5) 見られます **miraremasu**  (6) 思われる **omowareru**
(or 思われている **omowarete iru**)  (7) A: 見えない **mienai**  B: 聞こえる
**kikoeru**

**6** (1) もらって **moratte** (2) くれた **kureta** (3) さしあげ **sashiage** (4) やる **yaru** (5) あげた **ageta** (6) 下さった **kudasatta** (7) 母: もらった **moratta** (or いただいた **itadaita**) 子: くれた **kureta** 母: もらっちゃ **moratcha**

**7** (1) さとしさんは車の運転ができます。**Satoshi-san wa kuruma no unten ga dekimasu.** (2) 一日5時間働けません。**Ichinichi gojikan hatarakemasen.** (3) エクセルが使えます。**Ekuseru ga tsukaemasu.** (4) 朝早く会社に来られません。**Asa hayaku kaisha ni koraremasen.** (5) ビデオクリップの編集ができます。**Bideo kurippu no henshuu ga dekimasu.**

## 13 Adjectives

**1** ① 忙しかった **isogashikatta** ② 暑かった **atsukatta** ③ ねむかった **nemukatta** ④ 冷たい **tsumetai** ⑤ 新しい **atarashii** ⑥ おいしかった **oishikatta** ⑦ ちかい **chikai** ⑧ しずかだった **shizuka datta** ⑨ 大変な **taihen na** ⑩ 多く **ooku**

**2** ① つまらなかったです **tsumaranakatta desu** ② たかかった **takakatta** ③ ざんねんでした **zannen deshita** ④ たいへんでした **taihen deshita**

**3** (1) a. ひま **hima** b. ひまだ **hima da** c. いそがしく **isogashiku** d. あたらしい **atarashii** e. やすく **yasuku** f. おいしい **oishii**

(2) a. ちいさい **chiisai** b. おいしい **oishii** c. おもしろくない **omoshirokunai** d. つまらない **tsumaranai** e. しずかで **shizuka de** f. おいしい **oishii**

(3) a. たいへんだった **taihen datta** b. たのし **tanoshi** c. たのしい **tanoshii**

## 14 Adverbs

**1** ① 早めに **hayame ni** ② はやく **hayaku** ③ よく **yoku** ④ 適度に **tekido ni**

**2** ① なかなか **nakanaka** ② めったに **metta ni** ③ ぜんぜん **zenzen** ④ おそらく **osoraku** ⑤ ぜひ **zehi** ⑥ また **mata** ⑦ まんがいち **man ga ichi**

**3** ① b ② a ③ d ④ e ⑤ g ⑥ h ⑦ c ⑧ f

## 15 Negation

**1** (1) 日本人じゃありません **Nihonjin ja arimasen** (2) しずかじゃありません **shizuka ja arimasen** (3) たかくない（です）**takaku nai (desu)** (4) しませんでした **shimasen deshita** (5) ない **nai** (6) 会わない **awanai** (7) （勉強）しません **(benkyou) shimasen** (8) 食べなかった **tabenakatta** (9) おもしろくなかった **omoshiroku nakatta** (10) 大変じゃなかった **taihen ja nakatta**

**2** (A) ① 飲めなかった **nomenakatta** ② おいしくなかった **oishiku nakatta** ③ 親切じゃなかった **shinsetsu ja nakatta** ④ よくなかった **yoku nakatta** ⑤ 行かない **ikanai**

(B) ① 帰ってこない **kaette konai**　② 勉強しません **benkyou shimasen**
③ 食べない **tabenai**　④ 聞きません **kikimasen**　⑤ わかりません **wakarimasen**

(C) ① おもしろくなかった **omoshiroku nakatta**　② なかった **nakatta**
③ 行かなかった **ikanakatta**　④ 出られなかった **derarenakatta**
⑤ できなかった **dekinakatta**

**3**　(1) じゃなくて **ja nakute**　(2) 遠くなくて **tooku nakute**　(3) すわないで
**suwanaide**　(4) できなくて **dekinakute**　(5) 言わないで **iwanaide**
(6) 寝ないで **nenaide**　(7) わからなくて **wakaranakute**　(8) しないで **shinaide**

**4**　① ぜんぜん **zenzen**　② めったに**metta ni**　③ 何も **nani mo**　④ 決して **kesshite**
⑤ 別に **betsu ni**　⑥ まさか **masaka**

**5**　(1) いいえ、学生しか来ませんでした。**Iie, gakusei shika kimasen deshita.**
(2) いいえ、十人しか来ませんでした。**Iie, juunin shika kimasen deshita.**
(3) いいえ、すししか出ませんでした。**Iie, sushi shika demasen deshita.**
(4) いいえ、一度しか食べたことがありませんでした。**Iie, ichido shika tabeta
koto ga arimasendeshita.**　(5) いいえ、コーラしか飲みませんでした。**Iie,
koora shika nomimasen deshita.**　(6) いいえ、知っている人としか話しません
でした。**Iie, shitte iru hito to shika hanashimasen deshita.**

**6**　(1) 無 **mu**　(2) 不 **fu**　(3) 未 **mi**　(4) 不 **fu**　(5) 非 **hi**　(6) 未 **mi**　(7) 無 **mu**
(8) 不 **fu**　(9) 非 **hi**　(10) 無 **mu**

## 16   Numbers and classifiers

**1**　(1) じゅうに　たす　きゅうは　にじゅういち **juu ni tasu kyuu wa ni juu ichi**
(2) ひゃくにじゅうろく　わる　さんは　よんじゅうに **hyaku ni juu roku waru
san wa yon juu ni**　(3) ご　かける　ななは　さんじゅうご **go kakeru nana wa
san juu go**　(4) ひゃく　ひく　ごじゅうはちは　よんじゅうに **hyaku hiku go
juu hachi wa yon juu ni**

**2**　(A) (1) にいてんよん **nii ten yon**　(2) せんひゃく **sen hyaku**　(3) れいてんにい
ろく **rei ten nii roku**　(4) ひゃくはちじゅうさん **hyaku hachijuu san**
(5) せんろっぴゃくきゅう **sen ryoppyaku kyuu**　(6) さんびゃくろくじゅうご
**sanbyaku rokujuu go**　(7) さんぜんななひゃくななじゅうろく **sanzen
nanahyaku nanajuu roku**

(B) (1) 約一億二千六百六十五万人 **yaku ichioku nisen roppyaku rokujuu go
man nin**　(2) 約十二億千三百万人 **yaku juuni oku sen sanbyaku man nin**
(3) 約四百九万円 **yaku yonhyaku kyuu man en**　(4) 約三千八百八十一万円
**yaku sanzen happyaku hachijuu ichi man en**

**3**　(1) さんじ　じゅうごふん **sanji juugo fun**　(2) よじ　にじゅっぷん **yoji nijup
pun**　(3) じゅうにじ　さんじゅっぷん **juuniji sanjup pun** or じゅうにじ　はん
**juuniji han**　(4) ごぜん　はちじ　よんじゅっぷん **gozen hachiji yonjup pun**
(5) くじ　きゅうふん **kuji kyuu fun**　(6) ろくじ　さんじゅうろっぷん **rokuji
sanjuurop pun**　(7) ごぜん　しちじ　ごじゅうななふん **gozen shichiji gojuunana
fun**　(8) ごご　じゅういちじ　ごふん **gogo juuichiji go fun**

**4** (1) みっかと むいか **mikka to muika** (2) ようかと とおか **youka to tooka**
(3) ここのかと じゅうににち **kokonoka to juuni nichi** (4) じゅうしちにちと
はつか **juushichinichi to hatsuka** (5) にじゅうよっかと さんじゅうにち
**nijuuyokka to sanjuunichi**

**5** (1) はっぴゃく きゅうじゅう きゅうえん **happyaku kyuujuu kyuu en**
(2) よんせん ごひゃくえん **yonsen gohyaku en** (3) ろくせん ななひゃく ごじ
ゅうえん **rokusen nanahyaku gojuu en** (4) はっせん ろっぴゃくえん **hassen
roppyaku en** (5) にまん さんぜん さんびゃくえん **niman sanzen sanbyaku en**
(6) じゅういちまん ごせん にひゃくえん **juuichi man gosen nihyaku en**

**6** (1) 5本 **gohon** (2) 1つ **hitotsu** (3) 6冊 **rokusatsu** (4) 1本 **ippon**
(6) 10枚 **juumai**

**7** (A) a. 八人 **hachi-nin** b. 三人 **san-nin** c. 三匹 **san-biki** d. 五匹 **go-hiki**
e. 二匹 **ni-hiki** f. 四羽 **yon-wa** g. 十匹 **jup-piki** h. 二頭 **ni-tou**

(B) a. 一足 **is-soku** b. 二着 **ni-chaku** c. 一つ **hito-tsu** d. 一袋 **hito-fukuro**
e. 二本 **ni-hon**

**8** (A) a. じゅうまい **juumai** b. さんぼん **sanbon** c. ろっぽん **roppon** d. ひとつ
**hitotsu** or 一個 **ikko**

(B) a. さんまい **sanmai** b. ふたつ **futatsu** or にこ **niko** c. いっぽん **ippon**
d. さんばい **sanbai**

# 17 Compounds

**1** (1) c (2) b (3) c (4) a (5) e (6) d (7) b (8) d

**2** (1) 薄暗い **usu-gurai** (2) 根強い **ne-zuyoi** (3) 気持ちいい **kimochi-ii**
(4) 歯がゆい **ha-gayui** (5) 気らくな **ki-raku na** (6) 心細い **kokoro-bosoi**

**3** (1) c (2) g (3) h (4) f (5) e (6) a (7) d (8) b

# 18 Formal nouns

**1** (A) ① の **no** ② こと **koto** ③ の **no** ④ もの **mono** ⑤ こと **koto** ⑥ の **no**

(B) ① こと **koto** ② こと **koto** ③ こと **koto** ④ の **no** ⑤ もの **mono**
⑥ こと **koto**

**2** ① ところ **tokoro** ② よう **you** ③ よう **you** ④ つもり **tsumori** ⑤ ん **n**
⑥ こと **koto** ⑦ ため **tame** ⑧ こと **koto** ⑨ こと **koto** ⑩ もん **mon**
⑪ つもり **tsumori** ⑫ わけ **wake**

**3** (A) 一生懸命勉強している **isshoukenmei benkyou shite iru** (B) お金持ちな
**o-kanemochi na** (C) 【キャンセルされた/なくなった】【**kyanseru sareta /
nakunatta**】 歯がいたい **ha ga itai** (D) 一緒にテニスができない **issho ni
tenisu ga dekinai**

**4** ① もの **mono**  ② だけ **dake**  ③ ばかり **bakari**  ④ ところ **tokoro**
⑤ の **no**  ⑥ こと **koto**  ⑦ もの **mono**  ⑧ こと **koto**  ⑨ よう **you**
⑩ こと **koto**  ⑪ ため **tame**  ⑫ こと **koto**

## 19 Auxiliary verbs

**1** (1) ① あった **atta**  ② しめ **shime**  ③ 来る **kuru**  ④ あげる **ageru**

(2) ① 始めた **hajimeta**  ② すぎた **sugita**  ③ 太って **futotte**  ④ みませんか
**mimasenka**  ⑤ あげたら **agetara**

**2** (1) 航空券を買っておく **koukuuken o katte oku**  (2) ホテルを予約しておく
**hoteru o yoyaku shite oku**  (3) 観光地を調べておく **kankouchi o shirabete oku**

## 20 The causative construction

**1** (1) 書かせる **kakaseru**  (2) 読ませる **yomaseru**  (3) 歌わせる **utawaseru**
(4) 覚えさせる **oboesaseru**  (5) 走らせる **hashiraseru**  (6) ふかせる **fukaseru**
(7) 決めさせる **kimesaseru**  (8) もってこさせる **motte kosaseru**

**2** (1) 金魚を死なせてしまった。**Kingyo o shinasete shimatta.**
(2) 友人カップルを別れさせてしまった。**Yuujin kappuru o wakaresasete
shimatta.**  (3) 両親を苦しめた/苦しませた/苦しませてしまった。**Ryoushin o
kurushimeta / kurushimaseta / kurushimasete shimatta.**

**3** (1) b  (2) a  (3) b

## 21 The passive construction

**1** (1) 子供は母親にしかられました。**Kodomo wa hahaoya ni shikararemashita.**
(2) 学生達は教師に多くの課題を出されました。**Gakusei-tachi wa kyoushi ni
ooku no kadai o dasaremashita.**  (3) 私はルームメイトに「しずかにして！」と
言われました。**Watashi wa ruumumeito ni 'Shizuka ni shite!' to iwaremashita.**
(4) この本は遠藤周作によって書かれました。**Kono hon wa Endou Shuusaku ni
yotte kakaremashita.**  (5) いたずらを注意したら、子供に泣かれました。**Itazura
o chuui shitara, kodomo ni nakaremashita.**  (6) 私は雨に降られてぬれてしま
いました。**Watashi wa ame ni furarete nurete shimaimashita.**

**2** ① よばれ **yobare**  ② だまされた **damasareta**  ③ 払わせられた/払わされた
**harawaserareta/harawasareta**  ④ 食べさせられ **tabesaserare**

**3** ① ふられた **furareta**  ② ふまれた **fumareta**  ③ 呼ばれ **yobare**
④ しかられ **shikarare**  ⑤ 当てられた **aterareta**  ⑥ 走らされた/走らせられた
**hashirasareta/hashiraserareta**  ⑦ やらされた/やらせられた **yarasareta/
yaraserareta**  ⑧ 食べられた **taberareta**  ⑨ 汚された **yogosareta**

**4** Sample answers   (1) 子供の時、にんじんを食べさせられました。**Kodomo no toki, ninjin o tabesaseraremashita.**   (2) 家に帰った時は、まず手を洗わされます。**Ie ni kaetta toki wa, mazu te o arawasaremasu.**   (3) いつも銀行で長い時間待たされるので、いやになります。**Itsumo ginkou de nagai jikan matasareru node, iya ni narimasu.**

## 22   Conjunctions and connectives

**1** (1) で de   (2) が ga, から kara   (3) して shite, 行って itte   (4) し shi, し shi   (5) のに noni   (6) とか toka, とか toka   (7) あれば areba

**2** (1) な na   (2) な na   (3) だ da   (4) 暇だ hima da   (5) にぎやかだ nigiyaka da   (6) した shita   (7) したい shitai   (8) あった atta

**3** ① から kara   ② のに noni   ③ から kara   ④ けど kedo   ⑤ から kara   ⑥ それに soreni   ⑦ から kara

**4** (1) 大学生で、19歳です。**Daigakusei de, juukyuu sai desu.**   (2) 専攻は美術ですが／けど、日本語も勉強しています。**Senkou wa bijutsu desu ga/kedo, Nihongo mo benkyou shite imasu.**   (3) 日本語は難しいですが／けど、クラスは楽しいです。**Nihongo wa muzukashii desu ga/kedo, kurasu wa tanoshii desu.** (4) 九月に日本に行きますから/行くので、漢字もたくさん勉強しています。**Kugatsu ni Nihon ni ikimasu kara/iku node, kanji mo takusan benkyou shite imasu.**   (5) 僕はよく水泳をするし、料理もします。**Boku wa yoku suiei o suru shi, ryouri mo shimasu.**   (6) よく図書館に行って、本を借ります。**Yoku toshokan ni itte, hon o karimasu.**   (7) 外国の映画を見るのが大好きで、日本の映画もよく見ます。**Gaikoku no eiga o miru no ga daisuki de, Nihon no eiga mo yoku mimasu.**   (8) まだ日本語は上手に話せません【が/けれど】、みなさんに会うのを楽しみにしています。**Mada Nihongo wa jouzu ni hanasemasen【ga/keredo】minasan ni au no o tanoshimi ni shite imasu.**

## 23   Temporal clauses

**1** (1) 中学生の時 Chuugakusei no toki   (2) 忙しい時（は）Isogashii toki (wa)   (3) 暇な時（は）Hima na toki (wa)   (4) 日本にいる時（は）Nihon ni iru toki (wa) or 日本にいた時（は）Nihon ni ita toki (wa)   (5) 疲れた時（は）Tsukareta toki (wa)   (6) （これは）日本に行った時（銀座で買いました）。(Kore wa) Nihon ni itta toki (Ginza de kaimashita).   (7) ネットで買い物をする時 Netto de kaimono o suru toki   (8) お金があまりない時は O-kane ga amari nai toki wa

## 24   Conditional clauses

**1** (1) 食べるなら taberu nara   (2) 食べると taberu to   (3) 読んだら yondara   (4) 読めば yomeba   (5) 読むと yomu to   (6) したら shitara   (7) するなら suru nara   (8) すれば sureba   (9) 来るなら kuru nara   (10) 来れば kureba   (11) 来ると kuru to   (12) 見たら mitara   (13) 見れば mireba   (14) 見ると

**miru to** (15) 行ったら **ittara** (16) 行くなら **iku nara** (17) 行けば **ikeba** (18) 医者だったら **isha dattara** (19) 医者だと **isha da to** (20) 高かったら **takakattara** (21) 高いなら **takai nara** (22) 高いと **takai to** (23) 簡単だったら **kantan dattara** (24) 簡単なら **kantan nara**

**2**

(1) ① (2) ② (3) ② (4) ① (5) ② (6) ① (7) ① (8) ②

**3**

(1) 宿題が終わったらやる。**Shukudai ga owattara yaru.** (2) 暇があったらやる。**Hima ga attara yaru.** (3) お金をくれればやる。**O-kane o kurereba yaru.** (4) 洗濯ならやる。**Sentaku nara yaru.** (5) 三十分で終わる（ん）ならやる。/ 三十分で終わる仕事ならやる。**Sanjuppun de owaru (n) nara yaru. / Sanjuppun de owaru shigoto nara yaru.**

## 25 Relative (noun-modifying) clauses

**1**

(1) 私がするスポーツはゴルフです。**Watashi ga suru supootsu wa gorufu desu.** (2) きのう喫茶店で食べたケーキはおいしかったです。**Kinou kissaten de tabeta keeki wa oishikatta desu.** (3) きのう会った人は出版社に勤めています。**Kinou atta hito wa shuppan-sha ni tsutomete imasu.** (4) 部長と話している人はだれですか。**Buchou to hanashite iru hito wa dare desu ka.** (5) 日本で人気【が/の】あるスポーツの一つは野球です。**Nihon de ninki 【ga/no】 aru supootsu no hitotsu wa yakyuu desu.** (6) 駅の前にある喫茶店で友達に会いました。**Eki no mae ni aru kissaten de tomodachi ni aimashita.** (7) 田中さんが京都でとった写真を見せてもらいました。**Tanaka-san ga Kyouto de totta shashin o misete moraimashita.** (8) 先生がお書きになった本を授業で使っています。**Sensei ga o-kaki ni natta hon o jugyou de tsukatte imasu.** (9) ベストセラーを書いた作家の講演を聞きに行きました。**Besutoseraa o kaita sakka no kouen o kiki ni ikimashita.** (10) 大学時代にお世話になった先生にお礼を言いたいです。**Daigaku-jidai ni o-sewa ni natta sensei ni o-rei o ii tai desu.**

**2**

(A) ① [アメリカで私が面倒だと思う] 習慣 [**Amerika de watashi ga mendou da to omou**] **shuukan** ② [部屋に荷物を運んでくれる] ベルボーイ [**heya ni nimotsu o hakonde kureru**] **berubooi** ③ [髪を切ってくれる] 美容師さん [**kami o kitte kureru**] **biyoushi-san** ④ [ピザを家まで届けてくれる] 人 [**piza o ie made todokete kureru**] **hito**

(B) ① [そのころ行っていた] 塾 [**sono koro itte ita**] **juku** ② [イギリスから来た] 先生 [**Igirisu kara kita**] **sensei** ③ [それまで好きではなかった] 英語 [**sore made suki de wa nakatta**] **eigo** ④ [母語話者の先生が英語だけで教える] 授業 [**bogo-washa no sensei ga eigo dake de oshieru**] **jugyou**

**3**

(1) 生まれた日 **umareta hi** (2) 目上の人と話す時に使う丁寧な言葉 **meue no hito to hanasu toki ni tsukau teinei na kotoba** (3) 学校に入るために受ける試験 **gakkou ni hairu tame ni ukeru shiken** (4) お正月に子供にあげるお金 **o-shougatsu ni kodomo ni ageru o-kane** (5) 年末に、お世話になっている人にあげる贈り物 **nenmatsu ni, o-sewa ni natte iru hito ni ageru okurimono** (6) 普通の就職をしないでアルバイトなどをして生活している人 **futsuu no shuushoku o shinaide arubaito nado o shite seikatsu shite iru hito**

**4**

(1) 編集の経験のある人を探しています。 **Henshuu no keiken no aru hito o sagashite imasu.** (2) 一年間日本に滞在したい人はビザをもらわなければならない。 **Ichinen kan Nihon ni taizai shitai hito wa biza o morawanakereba naranai.** (3) 出張で日本に来ている友達を一泊でどこかに連れて行ってあげたいんですが、東京の近くでどこかいい所をご存知ですか。 **Shutchou de Nihon ni kite iru tomodachi o ippaku de doko ka ni tsurete itte agetai n desu ga, Toukyou no chikaku de doko ka ii tokoro o go-zonji desu ka.** (4) 引っ越しを手伝っていただいたお礼です。 **Hikkoshi o tetsudatte itadaita o-rei desu.** (5) だれかがドアを開ける音が聞こえた。 **Dare ka ga doa o akeru oto ga kikoeta.** (6) メールに添付してくださった書類は、文字化けしていて読めません。 **Meeru ni tenpu shite kudasatta shorui wa, mojibake shite ite yomemasen.**

## 26   Complement clauses

**1**

(1) 乗っ取られる **nottorareru** (2) 入れる **ireru** (3) しない **shinai** (4) 難しい **muzukashii**

**2**

(1) は **wa**, が **ga**, こと **koto** (2) と **to** (3) が **ga**, の **no** (4) が **ga**, の **no** (5) は **wa**, が **ga**, こと **koto** (6) と **to** (7) が **ga**, の **no** (8) の **no** (9) と **to**, の **no** (10) こと **koto**

**3**

(1) 首相がどこに住んでいるか知りません。 **Shushou ga doko ni sunde iru ka shirimasen.** (2) 漢字がどうやってできたか習いたいです。 **Kanji ga douyatte dekita ka naraitai desu.** (3) 今日、早く帰れるかどうか分かりません。 **Kyou, hayaku kaereru ka douka wakarimasen.** (4) どうして嘘をついたかたずねました。 **Doushite uso o tsuita ka tazunemashita.**

**4**

(1) とれるかどうか **toreru ka dou ka** (2) とれるかどうか **toreru ka dou ka** (3) 行きたいか **ikitai ka**

## 27   Tense and aspect

**1**

(1) ① 来ました **kimashita** ② 遅れる **okureru** ③ 来ました **kimashita**

(2) ① 食べた **tabeta** ② 食べた **tabeta** ③ できた **dekita** ④ 思った **omotta** ⑤ ある **aru** ⑥ 食べた **tabeta**

(3) ① 出る **deru** ② 書いてる **kaite ru** ③ 終わる **owaru** ④ する **suru**

**2**

① する **suru** ② 悪かった **warukatta** ③ しなかった **shinakatta** ④ なった **natta** ⑤ できる **dekiru** ⑥ 出す **dasu** ⑦ する **suru** ⑧ 終わった **owatta** ⑨ 書いていない **kaite inai**

**3**

(1) 作った **tsukutta** (2) いる **iru** (3) 来た **kita** (4) 訪ねる **tazuneru** (5) 書いた **kaita**, 会った **atta** (6) 来た **kita** (7) 食べる **taberu** (8) おりる **oriru** (9) 読んだ **yonda** (10) 行く **iku**

## 28　Evidential markers

**1**

(1) だれもいない **daremo inai**　(2) こわれている **kowarete iru**　(3) 入っていない **haitte inai**　(4) かみなりだ **kaminari da**　(5) そう **sou**　(6) ふりだし **furi dashi**

**2**

(1) おいしそうだ **oishi sou da**, あま **ama**　(2) やめるらしい **yameru rashii**
(3) 留守のようだ **rusu no you da**

**3**

(1) 重そうですね。てつだいましょうか。**Omosou desu ne. Tetsudai mashou ka.**　(2) コーヒー豆を自分で煎るのは、けっこう難しいらしいですよ。**Koohii mame o jibun de iru no wa, kekkou muzukashii rashii desu yo.**
(3) 陽子さんはずいぶん落ち込んでいるようですね。**Youko-san wa zuibun ochikonde iru you desu ne.**　(4) 谷口さんの家にはペットがたくさんいるらしいです。**Taniguchi-san no ie ni wa petto ga takusan iru rashii desu.**
(5) となりの家にはペットがたくさんいるようです。**Tonari no ie ni wa petto ga takusan iru you desu.**

## 29　Honorifics (*keigo*)

**1**

a. ○　b. ×　c. ×　d. ○　e. ○　f. ×　g. ○

**2**

(A) ① はなされる **hanasareru**　② こられる **korareru**　③ される **sareru**
④ またれる **matareru**　⑤ でられる **derareru**　⑥ はらわれる **harawareru**
⑦ けんきゅうされる **kenkyuu sareru**

(B) ① おはなしになる **o-hanashi ni naru**　② おききになる **o-kiki ni naru**
③ おかりになる **o-kari ni naru**　④ おまちになる **o-machi ni naru**　⑤ おとりになる **o-tori ni naru**　⑥ おうけになる **o-uke ni naru**　⑦ ごしゅっせきになる **go-shusseki ni naru**

(C) ① おっしゃる **ossharu**　② おやすみになる **o-yasumi ni naru**
③ なさる **nasaru**　④ いらっしゃる **irassharu** or【おいで/おこし】になる【**o-ide/ o-koshi**】**ni naru**　⑤ いらっしゃる **irassharu**　⑥ くださる **kudasaru**
⑦ ごぞんじ **go-zonji**

**3**

① お元気 **o-genki**　② なられた **narareta**　③ ご安心 **go-anshin**　④ やすまれ **yasumare** or おやすみになり **o-yasumi ni nari**　⑤ 歩かれたり **arukaretari**
⑥ 読まれたり **yomaretari**　⑦ おられました **oraremashita** or いらっしゃいました **irasshaimashita**　⑧ おっしゃって **osshatte** (言われて **iwarete** sounds odd here.)

**4**

(A) ① おもちする **o-mochi suru**　② おかえしする **o-kaeshi suru**
③ おかりする **o-kari suru**　④ おみせする **o-mise suru**　⑤ おあけする **o-ake suru**
⑥ おききする **o-kiki suru**　⑦ ごそうだんする **go-soudan suru**

(B) ① うたわせていただく **utawasete itadaku**　② させていただく **sasete itadaku**　③ やめさせていただく **yamesasete itadaku**　④ こさせていただく **kosasete itadaku**　⑤ かえらせていただく **kaerasete itadaku**　⑥ しめさせていただく **shimesasete itadaku**　⑦ ひかせていただく **hikasete itadaku**　⑧ ごせつめいさせていただく **go-setsumei sasete itadaku**

(C) ① もうす **mousu** or もうしあげる **moushi-ageru**  ② まいる **mairu** or うかがう **ukagau**  ③ いたす **itasu**  ④ おる **oru**  ⑤ うかがう **ukagau**  ⑥ いただく **itadaku**

**5**

① どう **dou** (or どのように **dono you ni**)  ② 過ごしていますか **sugoshite imasu ka**  ③ いて **ite**  ④ すみません **sumimasen**  ⑤ 連絡しています **renraku shite imasu**  ⑥ 頼んでもいいですか **tanondemo ii desu ka**  ⑦ 引き受けてもらえる **hikiukete moraeru**  ⑧ 送ります **okurimasu**  ⑨ 待っています **matte imasu**  ⑩ します **shimasu**

# B Functions

## 30 Social interaction

**1**

(A) Sample answers.

① (1)（カナダは）すっごい良かった **(Kanada wa) suggoi yokatta**
   (2) あ、カロリーの多いものよく食べてたんで（大きくなった）。**A, karorii no ooi mono yoku tabeteta n de (ookiku natta)**
② (1) 大ちゃん（は）**Dai-chan (wa)**  (2) またそんなこと（を）言っちゃって **mata sonna koto (o) itchatte**
③ (1) 1年ぶりだよ<u>ね</u>。**Ichinen-buri da <u>yo ne</u>.**  (2) あの<u>さー</u> **ano <u>saa</u>**
④ (1)（由利：<u>うん</u> Yuri: <u>Un</u>）  (2) <u>ふーん</u>、良かったねー。<u>**Fuun**</u>, **yokatta nee.**
⑤ (1) <u>あ</u>、由利。<u>**A**</u>, **Yuri.**  (2) <u>まぁ</u>、そのおかげでー <u>**Maa**</u>, **sono o-kage dee**
⑥ (1) <u>ちょっと</u>つまんない、<u>みたいな…</u>。<u>**Chotto**</u> **tsumannai,** <u>**mitai na . . .**</u>
   (2)自分の意見<u>とか</u> **Jibun no iken <u>toka</u>**
⑦ (1) すっごい ← すごい **suggoi ← sugoi**  (2) ほーんとー ← ほんとう **hoontoo ← hontou**
⑧ (1) Ø どっか留学したいなー、<u>あたしも</u>。Ø **dokka ryuugaku shitai naa,** <u>**atashi mo**</u>.  (2) Ø けっこう大変だったんだけどー、<u>特に最初ね</u>？Ø **kekkou taihen datta n da kedoo,** <u>**toku ni saisho ne**</u>?

(B) ① とてもよかった **totemo yokatta**  ② 一回り大きくなった **hito-mawari ookiku natta**  ③ 上手になった **jouzu ni natta**  ④ 同じことの繰り返し **onaji koto no kurikaeshi**  ⑤ 留学したい **ryuugaku shitai**

**2**

(1) B: おはようございます。**Ohayou gozaimasu.**  A: そうですね。**Sou desu ne.**  (2) B: ええ、おかげさまで。**Ee, o-kagesama de.**  (3) B: ご無沙汰しておりまして **go-busata shite orimashite**  (4) B: お疲れさま。**O-tsukare sama.** or ご苦労さま。**Go-kurou-sama.**  (5) A: 行ってきます。**Itte kimasu.** or 行ってまいります。**Itte mairimasu.**  (6) B: おかえり（なさい）。**O-kaeri (nasai).**  (7) A: ご結婚、おめでとうございます。**Go-kekkon, o-medetou gozaimasu.**

**3**

Sample

はじめまして。○○と申します。シカゴにあるシアーズ大学の学生です。専攻は教育です。趣味は音楽を聞くことと絵を描くことです。どうぞよろしくお願いします。**Hajimemashite. ○○ to moushimasu. Shikago ni aru Shiaazu Daigaku no gakusei desu. Senkou wa kyouiku desu. Shumi wa ongaku o kiku koto to e o kaku koto desu. Douzo yoroshiku onegai shimasu.**

**4** ① はじめまして　② アニメワークスの宮崎かおると申します　③ どうぞよろしく
お願いいたします　④ です　⑤ どうぞよろしく

① Hajimemashite　② Anime Waakusu no Miyazaki Kaoru to moushimasu
③ Douzo yoroshiku onegai itashimasu　④ desu　⑤ Douzo yoroshiku

**5** (A) ① g　② c　③ a　④ e　⑤ h　⑥ j　⑦ i　⑧ d　⑨ b　⑩ f

(B) ① e　② d　③ g　④ c　⑤ j　⑥ h　⑦ f　⑧ b　⑨ a　⑩ i

**6** ① 申します **moushimasu**　② おられます **oraremasu**　③ 大城 **Ooshiro**
④ もどられ **modorare**　⑤ 下さる **kudasaru**　⑥ お伝え **o-tsutae**
⑦ までに **made ni**　⑧ お聞きしても **o-kiki shitemo**

## 31 Basic communication strategies

**1** (A) (1) ねえ、あや。（ちょっといい？）**Nee, Aya. (Chotto ii?)** (2) ん、なに？
**N, nani?** (3) あやべって、漢字でどう【書くの？／書くんだっけ？】**Ayabe tte,
kanji de dou kaku no? / kaku n dakke?** (4) えっとねえ **Etto nee** (5) 実は
大学院のこととか聞きたいんだよね。**Jitsu wa daigakuin no koto toka kikitai
n da yo ne.** (6) えー？／へえ！**Ee? / Hee!** (7) うーん、東大とか慶応とかだけど
**Uun, Toudai toka Keiou toka dakedo** (8) え？**E?** (9) ところで、来週なんだ
けど、バイトのシフト、代わってもらえないかな。**Tokorode, raishuu na n da
kedo, baito no shifuto, kawatte moraenai kana.** (10) えー、来週はちょっと。
**Ee, raishuu wa chotto.** (11) うーん、しょうがないなあ。**Uun, shouganai naa.**

(B) (1) あの、すみません、ちょっとお聞きしたいんですけど。**Ano, sumimasen,
chotto o-kiki shitai n desu kedo** (2) はい、何でしょう。**Hai, nan deshou**
(3) あのぉ **Anoo** (4) すみません。歯医者さんの名前をもう一度言っていただけま
せんか。**Sumimasen. Haisha-san no namae o mou ichido itte itadakemasen
ka.** (5) ここをまっすぐ行ってください、5分位。**Koko o massugu itte kudasai,
go-fun gurai.**

**2** (A) (1) b　(2) d　(3) a　(4) c　(B) (5) f　(6) e　(7) g　(8) h　(C) (9) l
(10) i　(11) n　(12) j　(13) k　(14) m　(D) (15) q　(16) o　(17) p
(E) (18) s　(19) t　(20) r

## 32 Questions

**1** (1) 行きますか/行く？ **ikimasu ka. / iku?** (2) あったんですか。/あったの？
**atta n desu ka. / atta no?** (3) 勉強しているんですか。/勉強してるの？
**benkyou shite iru n desu ka. / benkyou shite ru no?** (4) おもしろかったで
すか。/おもしろかった？ **omoshirokatta desu ka. / omoshirokatta?** (5) おい
しいですか。/おいしい？ **Oishii desu ka. / Oishii?** (6) 買ったんですか。/買っ
たの？ **katta n desu ka. / katta no?** (7) しましたか。**shimashita ka.**

**2** (1) はい **hai** (2) ううん **uun** (3) ううん **uun** (4) うん **un** (5) はい/ええ
**hai/ee** (6) ええ/はい **ee/hai** (7) うん **un**

**3**

(1) 対象は【大人/大学生】【でしょうか。/ですか。】Taishou wa 【otona / daigakusei】【deshou ka / desu ka】. (2) 教えた経験がなくては【いけませんか。/だめですか。】Oshieta keiken ga nakute wa 【ikemasen ka. / dame desu ka.】 (3) 一週間に何時間ぐらい教えますか。Isshuukan ni nanjikan gurai oshiemasu ka. (4) 時給はいくら【でしょうか。/ですか。】Jikyuu wa ikura 【deshou ka / desu ka】. (5) いつ始めたらいい【でしょうか。/ですか。】Itsu hajimetara ii 【deshou ka / desu ka】.

**4**

(a) 春休みどうだった？ Haru-yasumi dou datta? (b) どこかに行った（の）？ Doko ka ni itta (no)? (c) 一人で行ったの？だれかと一緒に行ったの？ Hitori de itta no? Dare ka to issho ni itta no? (d) 新幹線で行ったの？ Shinkansen de itta no? (e) 切符はいくらだった？ Kippu wa ikura datta? (f) 旅行は何日ぐらい？ Ryokou wa nannichi gurai? (g) 旅館に泊まった？ Ryokan ni tomotta? (h) 一泊いくらだった？ Ippaku ikura datta?

## 33 Reporting

**1**

① 大阪に出張に行く Oosaka ni shutchou ni iku ② 次の日までに書類を見ておいてくれ tsugi no hi made ni shorui o mite oite kure ③ 英語を教えてくれる Eigo o oshiete kureru ④ 首相は中国を訪問する shushou wa Chuugoku o houmon suru ⑤ どんな食べ物が好きか donna tabemono ga suki ka ⑥ 京都に行ったことがあるか Kyouto ni itta koto ga aru ka ⑦ 勉強しろ benkyou shiro ⑧ 静かにする shizuka ni suru ⑨ 授業中は携帯電話を使わない Jugyou-chuu wa keitai denwa o tsukawanai

**2**

きのう近所で強盗事件があったそうだ。それで、刑事が聞き込みに来た。家にいたかとか何か音を聞かなかったかとか変な人をみかけたかとか聞かれた。私は、別に変わったことはなかったと答えた。刑事によると犯人はまだみつかっていないそうだ。十分に注意するように言われた。

**Kinoo kinjo de goutou jiken ga atta sou da. Sorede, keiji ga kikikomi ni kita. Uchi ni ita ka toka nani ka oto o kikanakatta ka toka hen na hito o mikaketa ka toka kikareta. Watashi wa betsu ni kawatta koto wa nakatta to kotaeta. Keiji ni yoru to hannin wa mada mitsukatte inai sou da. Juubun ni chuui suru you ni iwareta.**

**3**

① 犬を毎日散歩【させてくれと/させるように】頼まれた。Inu o mainichi sanpo 【sasete kure to / saseru you ni】tanomareta. ② 一郎の部屋には入らないように言われた。Ichirou no heya ni wa hairanai you ni iwareta. ③ 何かあったら携帯に電話【してくれと/するように】言われた。Nani ka attara keitai ni denwa 【shite kure to / suru you ni】iwareta. ④ まどを閉めて出かけるように言われた。Mado o shimete dekakeru you ni iwareta. ⑤ 指定日にごみを【出すように/出してくれと】頼まれた。Shiteibi ni gomi o 【dasu you ni / dashite kure to】tanomareta.

## 34 Asking and giving personal information

**1**

(1) 初めまして。**Hajimemashite** (2) と【申します/言います】。**to moushimasu/iimasu.** (3) 初めまして。**Hajimemashite** (4) と申します **to moushimasu** (5) ご出身はどちらですか。**Go-shusshin wa dochira desu ka.** (6) 大学生ですか **Daigakusei desu ka.** (7) 専攻していらっしゃるんですか。**senkou shite irassharu n desu ka.** (8) 専攻 **senkou** (9) どんなお仕事ですか **Donna o-shigoto desu ka.** (10) お子さんがいらっしゃいますか **O-ko-san ga irasshaimasu ka.** (11) おいくつですか **O-ikutsu desu ka.** (12) ご兄弟がいらっしゃいますか **Go-kyoudai ga irasshaimasu ka.** (13) 趣味は何ですか **Shumi wa nan desu ka.** (14) 是非お願いします **Zehi o-negai shimasu.**

**2**

Sample answer

初めまして。キャロル・ブラウンと申します。今大学二年生で、電気工学を専攻しています。私はカナダ人で、今トロントに住んでいます。生まれたのはバンクーバーです。家族は五人家族で、兄が一人と妹が一人います。趣味は絵をかくことです。どうぞ宜しくお願いします。

**Hajimemashite. Kyaroru・Buraun to moushimasu. Ima daigaku ninensei de, denki-kougaku o senkou shite imasu. Watashi wa Kanadajin de, ima Toronto ni sunde imasu. Umareta no wa Bankuubaa desu. Kazoku wa gonin kazoku de, ani ga hitori to imouto ga hitori imasu. Shumi wa e o kaku koto desu. Douzo yoroshiku o-negai shimasu.**

**3**

(1) 昭和62年1月15日に生まれました。**Shouwa 62nen 1gatsu 15nichi ni umaremashita.** (2) 神奈川県藤沢市に住んでいます。**Kanagawa-ken Fujisawa-shi ni sunde imasu.** (3) 平成21年です。**Heisei 21nen desu.** (4) 経済を専攻しました。**Keizai o senkou shimashita.** (5) 銀行に勤めています。**Ginkou ni tsutomete imasu.** (6) 料理をするのが好きです。**Ryouri o suru no ga suki desu.** (7) 日本舞踊が上手です。**Nihon buyou ga jouzu desu.**

## 35 Identifying

**1**

① こちら **kochira** ② 言います **iimasu**・申します **moushimasu** ③ の **no** ④ だ **da** ⑤ ここ **koko** (これ **kore** would be appropriate for a place only when one is pointing to it or referring to it on a map, etc., not when one is actually there.) ⑥ な **na** ⑦ 人 **hito**・かた **kata** ⑧ です **desu**

## 36 Telling the time, dates, etc.

**1**

① 今度30歳になるんだ **Kondo sanjussai ni naru n da** ② 六月三日 **rokugatsu mikka** ③ 誕生会をする (or やる) **tanjoukai o suru (or yaru)** ④ 六月一日 **rokugatsu tsuitachi** ⑤ 土曜日 **doyoubi**

**2**

①【おかあさん (F)/おふくろ (M)】が来るんだ【**O-kaasan (F) / O-fukuro (M)**】**ga kuru n da.** ② (アル) バイト (がある) **(Aru)baito (ga aru)** ③ 3時から10時まで **Sanji kara juuji made** ④ 来週の土曜日も (アル) バイトがあるんだ **Raishuu no doyoubi mo (aru)baito ga aru n da** ⑤ 12時から5時まで **Juuniji kara goji made** ⑥ うん、いいよ **Un, ii yo** ⑦ 映画は何時から **Eiga wa nanji kara** ⑧ 何時に会おうか **Nanji ni aou ka**

## 37 Describing people, places, states and conditions

**1**

(A) ① これはリンさんの本ですか Kore wa Rin-san no hon desu ka
② りんさんの（本）は どれですか Rin-san no (hon) wa dore desu ka

(B) ① 新宿ホテルはどこでしょうか Shinjuku Hoteru wa doko deshou ka
② あの建物/あれは何ですか Ano tatemono / Are wa nan desu ka

(C) ① 川崎さんのご出身はどちらですか Kawasaki-san no go-shusshin wa dochira desu ka　② 青森ってどんなところですか Aomori tte donna tokoro desu ka　③ 時々帰られるんですか Tokidoki kaerareru n desu ka
④ 帰りました Kaerimashita

(D) ① 大きいんですか Ookii n desu ka　② 色は？/何色ですか Iro wa? / Nani iro desu ka　③ 形は？/どんな形ですか Katachi wa? / Donna katachi desu ka　④ 革製ですか Kawa-sei desu ka

(E) ① 何をしていましたか Nani o shite imashita ka　②（どこにも）出かけなかった (doko ni mo) dekakenakatta　③ 何を見ていた nani o mite ita.
④ どの (or どこの) チームが勝ちましたか dono (or doko no) chiimu ga kachimashita ka　⑤ 覚えていない Oboete inai　⑥ どこに止めてありましたか doko ni tomete arimashita ka　⑦ だれかに貸した dare ka ni kashita

**2**

① 着物を着ている kimono o kite iru　② をかぶっている o kabutte iru
③ の (or が) 長い no/ga nagai　④ どの dono　⑤ 話している hanashite iru
⑥ を持っている o motte iru　⑦ をしめ o shime　⑧ をかけている o kakete iru ⑨ がついてい ga tsuite i

**3**

a. ◯　b. ×　c. ◯　d. ◯　e. ×　f. ◯　g. ◯　h. ×

## 38 Comparisons

**1**

(A) ① 1月はもっと寒いです ichigatsu wa motto samui desu　② が ga
③ が ga　④ ほど hodo　④ より yori

(B) ① さえ sae　② に ni　③ も mo　④ が ga　⑤ も mo

(C) ① に ni　② と to　③ と to

**2**

(1) Distance from the station

- しろがね荘からJRの駅までは歩いて10分ですが、メゾンマツカワから地下鉄の駅までは車で15分かかります。
- しろがね荘の方がメゾンマツカワより駅に近いです。

- Shirogane-sou kara JR no eki made wa aruite juppun desu ga, Mezon Matsukawa kara chikatetsu no eki made wa kuruma de juugofun kakarimasu.
- Shirogane-sou no hou ga Mezon Matsukawa yori eki ni chikai desu.

(2) Apartment size

- しろがね荘は1LDKですが、メゾンマツカワは3LDKです。
- メゾンマツカワのほうがしろがね荘より広いです。

- **Shirogane-sou wa 1LDK desu ga, Mezon Matsukawa wa 3LDK desu.**
- **Mezon Matsukawa no hou ga Shirogane-sou yori hiroi desu.**

(3) Years since construction

- しろがね荘は建てられてから10年ですが、メゾンマツカワは新築です。
- メゾンマツカワのほうがしろがね荘より新しいです。

- **Shirogane-sou wa taterarete kara juunen desu ga, Mezon Matsukawa wa shinchiku desu.**
- **Mezon Matsukawa no hou ga Shirogane-sou yori atarashii desu.**

(4) Rental fee

- しろがね荘は家賃が一ヶ月43,000円ですが、メゾンマツカワは一ヶ月148,000円です。
- メゾンマツカワのほうがしろがね荘より高いです。

- **Shirogane-sou wa yachin ga ikkagetsu yonman sanzen en desu ga, Mezon Matsukawa wa ikkagetsu juuyon man hassen en desu.**
- **Mezon Matsukawa no hou ga Shirogane-sou yori takai desu.**

## 39 Contrast

**1**

① でも **demo**　② いっぽう **ippou**　③ けど **kedo**　④ だけど **dakedo**
⑤ しかし **shikashi**　⑥ ぎゃくに **gyakuni**　⑦ それに **soreni**

**2**

[Where けど **kedo** is possible, so are けれど **keredo** and けれども **keredomo**.]

(1) けど **kedo**/が **ga**　(2) でも **demo**/しかし **shikashi**/それに対して **sore ni taishite**　(3) けど **kedo**/が **ga**　(4) でも **demo**/しかし **shikashi**　(5) けど **kedo**/が **ga**　(6) でも **demo**/しかし **shikashi**　(7) でも **demo**/しかし **shikashi**/それに対して **sore ni taishite**　(8) けど **kedo**/が **ga**

## 40 Location and distance

**1**

A: 市立病院 **Shiritsu Byouin**　B: 喫茶店 **kissaten**　C: 公園 **kouen**　D: 花咲大学 **Hanasaka Daigaku**　E: 駐車場 **chuushajou**　F: コンビニ **konbini**　G: コンビニ **konbini**

**2**

① 僚太は部屋にいる（or … 部屋だ）**Ryouta wa heya ni iru** (or . . . **heya da**)
② ポチ（は）いない **Pochi (wa) inai**　③ ソファの下にいない **Sofa no shita ni inai**　④ 冷蔵庫の上にいる（or … 上だ）**Reizouko no ue ni iru** (or . . . **ue da**)
⑤ どこにあった **doko ni atta** (NOT どこだった **doko datta**)　⑥ あの箱の中 **ano hako no naka**

**3**

(a) ① の所にあります **no tokoro ni arimasu** ② かかります **kakarimasu**

(b) ① 5–6キロあります **Go-rok-kiro arimasu.** ② ちょっとかかります **chotto kakarimasu** ③ どのぐらいかかりますか（or どのぐらいですか）**dono gurai kakarimasu ka (or dono gurai desu ka)** ④ 10分もかかりません **juppun mo kakarimasen**

## 41　Possession

**1**

① が **ga** ② を **o** ③ に **ni** ④ ある **aru**

**2**

① いる **iru** ② かって **katte**

**3**

(a) 父は髪が短い。**Chichi wa kami ga mijikai.** (b) 母は手がきれいだ。**Haha wa te ga kirei da.** (c) 姉は足が長い。**Ane wa ashi ga nagai.** (d) 弟は鼻が高い。**Otouto wa hana ga takai.** (e) 私は顔が丸い。**Watashi wa kao ga marui.** (f) 猫は目が大きくて青い。**Neko wa me ga ookikute aoi.**

## 42　Gifts

**1**

① もらっちゃった **moratchatta** ② いただいた **itadaita** ③ くれた **kureta** ④ くださった **kudasatta** ⑤ くださった **kudasatta** ⑥ いただいた **itadaita** ⑦ さしあげなきゃ **sashiagenakya**

**2**

女１：父に靴下をあげました。**Onna 1: Chichi ni kutsushita o agemashita.** 女２：義父にネクタイを送りました。**Onna 2: Gifu ni nekutai o okurimashita.** 男１：僕は何もしなかったんですが、妹は父に手作りのケーキをあげていました。**Otoko 1: Boku wa nanimo shinakatta n desu ga, imouto wa chichi ni tezukuri no keeki o agete imashita.** 男２：両親に温泉旅館の宿泊券をあげました。**Otoko 2: Ryoushin ni onsen ryokan no shukuhaku-ken o agemashita.** 男３：息子からゴルフのクラブをもらいました。**Otoko 3: Musuko kara gorufu no kurabu o moraimashita.**

## 43　Kind acts

**1**

(1) c　(2) b　(3) c　(4) a　(5) b

**2**

① いただき **itadaki** ② くださった **kudasatta** ③ くださった **kudasatta** ④ くださった **kudasatta** ⑤ くださり **kudasari** ⑥ ください **kudasai** ⑦ いただいた **itadaita** ⑧ いただいた **itadaita** ⑨ さしあげられる **sashiagerareru** ⑩ さしあげる **sashiageru**

## 44　Experience

**1**

(1) 何回もすしを作ったことがあるよ。**Nankai mo sushi o tsukutta koto ga aru yo.** (2) 一度日本に行ったことがあるよ。**Ichido Nihon ni itta koto ga aru yo.** (3) 日本の映画は何本も見たことがあるんだ。**Nihon no eiga wa nanbon**

mo mita koto ga aru n da.　(4)【一年間日本で/日本で一年間】日本語を
勉強したことがあるんだ。【Ichinenkan Nihon de / Nihon de ichinenkan】
Nihongo o benkyou shita koto ga aru n da.　(5) 何度か夏のキャンプで日本語
を教えたことがあるよ。**Nando ka natsu no kyanpu de Nihongo o oshieta
koto ga aru yo.**

**2**　(1) 日本の会社で二ヵ月(間)インターンとして働いた【こと/経験】がありま
す。**Nihon no kaisha de nikagetsu(kan) intaan toshite hataraita【koto /
keiken】ga arimasu.**　(2) ボランティアで日本語の通訳をした【こと/経験】があ
ります。**Borantia de Nihongo no tsuuyaku o shita【koto / keiken】ga
arimasu.**　(3) コンビニでアルバイトをした【こと/経験】があります。**Konbini
de arubaito o shita【koto / keiken】ga arimasu.**　(4) 仕事に遅刻したことはあ
りません。**Shigoto ni chikoku shita koto wa arimasen.**　(5) 四年間日本語を勉
強しています。**Yonen kan Nihongo o benkyou shite imasu.**　(6) 日米学生会議
に参加したことがあります。**Nichibei gakusei kaigi ni sanka shita koto ga
arimasu.**

## 45　Intentions and plans

**1**　(1) 一週間に三度運動を【しようと思います/するつもりです】。**Isshuukan ni
sando undou o【shiyou to omoimasu / suru tsumori desu】.**　(2) もっといい
仕事を【探すつもりです/探そうと思っています】。**Motto ii shigoto o【sagasu
tsumori desu / sagasou to omotte imasu】.**　(3) たばこを【やめるつもりです/
やめようと思っています】。**Tabako o【yameru tsumori desu / yameyou to
omotte imasu】.**　(4) 無駄づかいをしないように【するつもりです/しようと思っ
ています】。**Mudazukai o shinai you ni【suru tsumori desu / shiyou to
omotte imasu】.**

**2**　(A) (1) しようと思っていたんです/するつもりだったんです **shiyou to omotte
ita n desu / suru tsumori datta n desu**　(2) 取ろうと思っています/取るつも
りです。**torou to omotte imasu/toru tsumori desu.**　(3) するつもりです。
**suru tsumori desu.**　(4) 留学する予定な **ryuugaku suru yotei na**

(B) (1) 出る予定だけど **deru yotei da kedo**　(2) 選んでもらおうと思っている
**erande moraou to omotte iru**

(C) (1)【商社/貿易会社】に勤める予定だ **Shousha / boueki-gaisha ni
tsutomeru yotei da**　(2) 働くつもりはない **hataraku tsumori wa nai**
(3) 行くつもりだ **iku tsumori da**

## 46　Temporal relations

**1**　(2) 洗濯をしてからテレビを見ながら昼ご飯を食べた。**Sentaku o shite kara
terebi o mi-nagara hirugohan o tabeta.**　(3) 昼ご飯を食べた後で映画を見に行
った。**Hirugohan o tabeta ato de eiga o mi ni itta.**　(4) 五時に映画が終わっ
た。そしてすし屋に行った。**Goji ni eiga ga owatta. Soshite sushiya ni itta.**
(5) 居酒屋に行って、酒を飲みながら話をした。**Izakaya ni itte, sake o nomi-
nagara hanashi o shita.**　(6) 遅くならないうちに寝た。**Osoku naranai uchi
ni neta.**

**2**

(1) 間　aida　(2) 間は　aida wa　(3) ないうちに　nai uchi ni　(4) 間に　aida ni
(5) 出たら　detara　(6) 間に　aida ni　(7) ないうちに　nai uchi ni
(8) する前に　suru mae ni

**3**

(A) ① 着いてから　tsuite kara　② 来た　kita　③ 来る　kuru　④ 来る　kuru
⑤ 来て　kite　⑥ ならないうちに　naranai uchi ni

(B) (1) ○　(2) ○　(3) ×　(4) ○　(5) ×

## 47　Explanation, reason and purpose

**1**

(1) ので　node・から　kara　(2) なので　na node・だから　da kara　(3) ので　node・んです　n desu　(4) から　kara

**2**

(1) e　(2) d　(3) c　(4) b　(1) a

**3**

(1) 見られるように/見たいから　mirareru you ni / mitai kara　(2) 使うため/使いたいから　tsukau tame / tsukaitai kara　(3) ため　tame　(4) とるため　toru tame　(5) なるため/なりたいから　naru tame / naritai kara

**4**

① ように　you ni　② ように　you ni　③ ために　tame ni　④ ために　tame ni
⑤ ために　tame ni

## 48　Cause and effect

**1**

(1) d　(2) e　(3) f　(4) a　(5) b　(6) c

**2**

(1) 原因　(2) せい　(3) 原因　(4) どうして

**3**

(1) 足が【痛くて/痛いので/痛いから】、歩けない。ashi ga【itakute / itai node / itai kara】, arukenai.　(2) みんなから【愛されて/愛されているので/愛されているから】、幸せです。minna kara【aisarete / aisarete iru node / aisarete iru kara】, shiawase desu.　(3) 事故【で/のせいで】、足を折った。jiko【de / no sei de】, ashi o otta.　(4) 雨が【降らなくて/降らないので/降らないから】水不足になった。Ame ga【furanakute / furanai node / furanai kara】mizu-busoku ni natta.　(5) うそを【ついて/ついたから/ついたので】、信用を失った。Uso o【tsuite / tsuita kara / tsuita node】, shinyou o ushinatta.

## 49　Describing procedures

**1**

まず最初にATMにカードを入れます。次に画面で引き落としを選びます。そして暗証番号を入力します。最後に必要金額を入力すると、お金が出てきます。

**Mazu saisho ni ATM ni kaado o iremasu. Tsugi ni gamen de hikiotoshi o erabimasu. Soshite anshou bangou o nyuuryoku shimasu. Saigo ni hitsuyou kingaku o nyuuryoku suru to, o-kane ga dete kimasu.**

**2**

(C)-(A)-(D)-(B)

## 50 Changes

**1**

健二は大学に入ってから **Kenji wa daigaku ni haitte kara** (1) 勉強するように なりました。**benkyou suru you ni narimashita.** (2) 日本語が読めるようになり ました。**Nihongo ga yomeru you ni narimashita.** (3) すしが食べられるよう になりました。**sushi ga taberareru you ni narimashita.** (4) 料理が上手になり ました。**ryouri ga jouzu ni narimashita.** (5) たいへん忙しくなりました。 **taihen isogashiku narimashita.** (6) 貯金がなくなりました。**chokin ga naku narimashita.**

**2**

(1) 暖かくなってきました **atatakaku natte kimashita** (2) おもしろくなってきま した **omoshiroku natte kimashita** (3) 難しくなってきました **muzukashiku natte kimashita** (4) 書けなくなってきました **kakenaku natte kimashita**

**3**

(1) ① 西洋化 **seiyouka** ② 食事 **shokuji** ③ 若い **wakai** ④ 味覚 **mikaku** ⑤ 変化 **henka**

(2) ① 社会進出 **shakai shinshutsu** ② 晩婚化 **bankonka** ③ 低下 **teika**

(3) ① 戦後 **sengo** ② 女性 **josei** ③ 家事 **kaji** ④ 育児 **ikuji** ⑤ 家事 **kaji** ⑥ 育児 **ikuji** ⑦ 男性 **dansei** ⑧ 変身 **henshin**

## 51 Expressing abilities

**1**

(1) 何語が話せますか。**Nanigo ga hanasemasu ka.** (2) 英語でビジネスレターが 書けますか。**Eigo de bijinesu retaa ga kakemasu ka.** (3) エクセルを使ってレ ポートが作れますか。**Ekuseru o tsukatte repooto ga tsukuremasu ka.** (4) 夜遅くまで働けますか。**Yoru osoku made hatarakemasu ka.** (5) 同僚とう まくやっていけますか。**Douryou to umaku yatte ikemasu ka.**

**2**

(1) 買えます **kaemasu** (2) 見渡せます **miwatasemasu** (3) 入れる、食べ られます **haireru, taberaremasu** (4) 話ができます/話せます **hanashi ga dekimasu / hanasemasu** (5) 行けます **ikemasu** (6) 乗れます **noremasu** (7) 見られます **miraremasu** (8) とれます **toremasu**

**3**

(1) JRパスで「のぞみ」に乗れますか。**JR pasu de 'Nozomi' ni noremasu ka.** (2) JRパスは東京都内でも使えますか。**JR pasu wa Toukyou tonai de mo tsukaemasu ka.** (3) 指定席にすわれますか。**Shiteiseki ni suwaremasu ka.** (4) 観光バスに乗ると、どんな所が見られますか。**Kankou basu ni noru to, donna tokoro ga miraremasu ka.** (5) ツアーの途中で観光バスを降りることが できますか。**Tsuaa no tochuu de kankou basu o oriru koto ga dekimasu ka.**

**4**

(1) 芦ノ湖を見ることができます。**Ashinoko o miru koto ga dekimasu.** (2) 温泉に【入ることができます。/入れます。】**Onsen ni 【hairu koto ga dekimasu. / hairemasu.】** (3) ゆっくり体を【休めることができます。/ 休められます。】**Yukkuri karada o 【yasumeru koto ga dekimasu. / yasumeraremasu.】** (4) おいしい料理が食べられます。/おいしい料理を食べるこ とができます。**Oishii ryouri ga taberaremasu. / Oishii ryouri o taberu koto ga dekimasu.** (5) 箱根神社に歩いて【行けます。/行く事ができます。】**Hakone Jinja ni aruite 【ikemasu. / iku koto ga dekimasu.】** (6) モーターボートで芦ノ

湖を一周することができます。**Mootaabooto de Ashinoko o isshuu suru koto ga dekimasu.** (7) 近くでゴルフやテニスもできます。**Chikaku de gorufu ya tenisu mo dekimasu.**

## 52 Needs

**1**

(1) ビザは【いらない／必要ではない】。**Biza wa 【iranai / hitsuyou de wa nai】.** (2) 特急券が【いる／必要だ】。**Tokkyuuken ga 【iru / hitsuyou da】.** (3) 予約は【いらない／必要ではない／しなくてもいい】。**Yoyaku wa 【iranai / hitsuyou de wa nai / shinakute mo ii】.** (4) 資金が【いる／必要だ】。 **Shikin ga 【iru / hitsuyou da.】**

**2**

(1) 敬語を練習【しなくては／しなければ】いけません。or 敬語を練習しなくちゃ（いけない）。**Keigo o renshuu 【shinakute wa / shinakereba】 ikemasen. or Keigo o renshuu shinakucha (ikenai).** (2) スーツを【買わなくては／買わなければ】いけません。or スーツを買わなくちゃ（いけない）。**Suutsu o 【kawanakute wa / kawanakereba】 ikemasen. or Suutsu o kawanakucha (ikenai).** (3) 【会社のことを／会社について】インターネットで調べて【おかなくては／おかなければ】いけません。or …インターネットで調べておかなくちゃ（いけない）。**Kaisha no koto o / Kaisha ni tsuite intaanetto de shirabete 【okanakute wa / okanakereba】 ikemasen. or ... intaanetto de shirabete okanakucha (ikenai).** (4) 申し込みの動機をちゃんとまとめて【おかなくては／おかなければ】いけません。or …まとめておかなくちゃ（いけない）。**Moushikomi no douki o chanto matomete 【okanakute wa / okanakereba】 ikemasen. or ... matomete okanakucha (ikenai).** (5) 面接の練習を【しなくては／しなければ】いけません。or 面接の練習をしなくちゃ（いけない）。**Mensetsu no renshuu o 【shinakute wa / shinakereba】 ikemasen. or Mensetsu no renshuu o shinakucha (ikenai).**

**3**

(1) 変えるには及ばない **kaeru ni wa oyobanai** (2) 乗ることはない **noru koto wa nai** (3) ならなくてもいい **naranakute mo ii** (4) お礼をするまでもない **o-rei o suru made mo nai** (5) 作らなくてもいい **tsukuranakute mo ii**

## 53 Possibility and probability

**1**

③ 晴れ **hare** ④ なく **naku** ⑤ くもり **kumori** ⑥ かもれません **kamo shiremasen** ⑦ 暖かくなる **atatakaku naru** ⑧ 雨が降る **ame ga furu** ⑨ 晴れ **hare** ⑩ 暑い **atsui**

**2**

(1) 住所が間違っていた（の）かもしれません。**Juusho ga machigatte ita (no) kamo shiremasen.** (2) どこかに忘れて来たのかもしれません。／落としたのかもしれません。／盗まれた（の）かもしれません。**Doko ka ni wasurete kita no kamo shiremasen. / Otoshita no kamo shiremasen. / Nusumareta (no) kamo shiremasen.** (3) 道が込んでいるのかもしれません。／仕事が忙しくてオフィスを出られないのかもしれません。／待ち合わせの時間を間違えたのかもしれません。**Michi ga konde iru no kamo shiremasen. / Shigoto ga isogashikute ofisu o derarenai no kamo shiremasen. / Machiawase no jikan o machigaeta no kamo shiremasen.** (4) 事故があったのかもしれません。／電車が故障したのか

もしれません。**Jiko ga atta no kamo shiremasen. / Densha ga koshou shita no kamo shiremasen.** (5) 女性が結婚するのが遅くなっているからかもしれません。/男性が家事や育児を手伝わないからかもしれません。/育児施設が整っていないからかもしれません。**Josei ga kekkon suru no ga osoku natte iru kara kamo shiremasen. / Dansei ga kaji ya ikuji o tetsudawanai kara kamo shiremasen. / Ikuji shisetsu ga totonotte inai kara kamo shiremasen.**

**3** (1) b (2) a (3) f (4) d (5) c (6) e

## 54 Certainty and uncertainty

**1** (1) 絶対に **zettai ni** (2) 間違いなく **machigainaku** (3) きっと **kitto** (4) 決して **kesshite** (5) 決まっています **kimatte imasu**

**2** (1) 信じられません **shinjiraremasen** (2) 分かりません **wakarimasen** (3) 分かりません/あやしいと思います/疑わしいと思います **wakarimasen / ayashii to omoimasu / utagawashii to omoimasu**

## 55 Provisions, conditions, and hypotheses

**1** (1) 天気がよかったら/天気がよければ **Tenki ga yokattara / Tenki ga yokereba** (2) お金がたくさんあったら **O-kane ga takusan attara** (3) その本を読む（ん）なら **Sono hon o yomu (n) nara** (4) 五時になると **goji ni naru to** (5) 急げば/急いだら **Isogeba / isoidara** (6) 部長の前に出ると **buchou no mae ni deru to** (7) 何度も書けば **Nando mo kakeba** (8) 日本に行く（ん）なら **Nihon ni iku (n) nara**

**2** (1) 日本に留学しさえすれば、日本語が上手になりますよ。**Nihon ni ryuugaku shi sae sureba, Nihongo ga jouzu ni narimasu yo.** (2) 日本人と友達になりさえすれば、**Nihonjin to tomodachi ni nari sae sureba,** (3) 毎日日本語を話しさえすれば、**Mainichi nihongo o hanashi sae sureba,** (4) 日本のドラマを見さえすれば、**Nihon no dorama o mi sae sureba,**

**3** (1)（もし）たくさん遺産が入ったとしたら、慈善団体に寄付します。**(Moshi) takusan isan ga haitta to shitara, jizen dantai ni kifu shimasu.** (2) 私の友達は暑くてもクーラーを使わない。**Watashi no tomodachi wa atsukute mo kuuraa o tsukawanai.** (3) 私が間違っている（の）なら、そう言ってください。**Watashi ga machigatte iru (no) nara, sou itte kudasai.** (4) どんなに難しくても、一生懸命やればできます。**Donna ni muzukashikute mo, isshoukenmei yareba dekimasu.** (5) 東京はどこに行っても込んでいます。**Toukyou wa doko ni itte mo konde imasu.** (6) 弟は【暇があるといつも/暇さえあれば】ビデオゲームをしています。**Otouto wa 【hima ga aru to itsumo / hima sae areba】 bideogeemu o shite imasu.** (7) 残り物を【食べなければ/食べなかったら】、お腹が痛くならなかったでしょう。**Nokorimono o 【tabenakereba / tabenakattara】, onaka ga itaku naranakatta deshou.**

## 56  Understanding and knowing

**1**

(1) 知っています **shitte imasu**　(2) わかりません **wakarimasen**　(3) わかります **wakarimasu**　(4) わからなく **wakaranaku**　(5) わかる **wakaru**　(6) 知る **shiru**

**2**

(1) 知らない **shiranai**　(2) わからない **wakaranai**　(3) わかりません **wakarimasen**　(4) わかりません **wakarimasen**　(5) 知っています **shitte imasu**, わからない **wakaranai.**

**3**

(1) エクセルの使い方は知っていますか。**Ekuseru no tsukaikata wa shitte imasu ka.**　(2) 経理の知識はどのぐらいありますか。**Keiri no chishiki wa dono gurai arimasu ka.**　(3) インターンシップの資格要件はわかりますか。**Intaanshippu no shikaku youken wa wakarimasu ka.**

## 57  Remembering and forgetting

**1**

(1) 覚えて **oboete**　(2) 思い出して **omoidashite**　(3) 覚えてる **oboete ru**　(4) 思い出した **omoidashita**　(5) 思い出しました **omoidashimashita**　(6) あります **arimasu**　(7) しています **shite imasu**　(8) おぼえていろ **oboete iro**

**2**

(1) a. 忘れました/忘れてしまいました。**wasuremashita / wasurete shimaimashita.** b. いいえ、【する/やる】のを【忘れた/忘れてしまった】んです。**Iie,【suru / yaru】no o【wasureta / wasurete shimatta】n desu.**　c. 明日は忘れないでください。**Ashita wa wasurenaide kudasai.**

(2) a. ごめん、忘れた/忘れちゃった。**Gomen, wasureta / wasurechatta.** b. 太郎に会うまでは覚えていたんだけど。**Tarou ni au made wa oboete ita n da kedo.**　c. うん、でも洋子さんが来るって言ったかどうか覚えてない。**Un, demo Youko-san ga kuru tte itta ka dou ka oboete nai.**　d. あ、思い出した。**A, omoidashita.**　e. 何のアルバイトをしているか覚えてる？**Nan no arubaito o shite iru ka oboete ru?**　f. ううん、覚えてない。**Uun, oboete nai.**　g. 思い出せない。**Omoidasenai.**

## 59  Gratitude

**1**

(1) してくれて **shite kurete**　(2) いてくれて **ite kurete**　(3) みてくれて **mite kurete**　(4) 連れて行ってくれて **tsurete itte kurete**　(5) Example: いつも学校まで車で送ってくれて **itsumo gakkou made kuruma de okutte kurete**

**2**

(1) 推薦状を書いてくださって、本当にありがとうございました。**Suisenjou o kaite kudasatte, hontou ni arigatou gozaimashita.**　(2) 日本語で 手紙を書くのを手伝ってくれてありがとう。**Nihongo de tegami o kaku no o tetsudatte kurete arigatou.**　(3) 色々お世話になりました。本当にありがとうございました。**Iroiro o-sewa ni narimashita. Hontou ni arigatou gozaimashita.** (4) ありがとうございます。まだまだですけど。**Arigatou gozaimasu. Mada mada desu kedo.**　(5) 弟がいつもお世話になっております。**Otouto ga itsumo osewa ni natte orimasu.**　(6) おつかれさまでした。**O-tsukare-sama deshita.** (7) ごちそうさまでした。**Go-chisou-sama deshita.**　(8) 先日はどうもありがとうございました。**Senjitsu wa doumo arigatou gozaimashita.**

**3**

(1) いいえ、どういたしまして **Iie, dou itashimashite.** (2) そう？よかった。 **Sou? Yokatta.** (3) いえ、こちらこそ（いつもお世話になっております）。 **Ie, kochira koso (itsumo o-sewa ni natte orimasu).** (4) いえ、いえ。お互い さまですから。いつでもどうぞ。 **Ie, ie, o-tagai-sama desu kara. Itsu demo douzo.** (5) いいえ、とんでもありません **Iie, tondemo arimasen.** (6) ありが とうございます。 **Arigatou gozaimasu.** (7) お疲れさまでした！ **Otsukare-sama deshita!** (8) うん。（お洋服、汚さないようにね。） **Un. (O-youfuku yogosanai you ni ne.)**

## 60 Apologies and forgiveness

**1**

(1) h  (2) a  (3) g  (4) d  (5) c

**2**

(1) ① 遅くなってすみません **Osoku natte sumimasen** ② 道が込んでいたので **Michi ga konde ita node** ③ すみません（気をつけます） **sumimasen (Ki o tsukemasu)**

(2) ① すみません **Sumimasen** ② 宿題のこと **Shukudai no koto** ③ 申し訳あ りません **Moushiwake arimasen** ④ 出してもいい **dashitemo ii** ⑤ 具合が悪 くて **guai ga waruku te** ⑥ ん **n** ⑦ ありがとうござい **arigatou gozai**

(3) ① ご迷惑をおかけしてしまっ（て） ② 申し訳ありません **Go-meiwaku o o-kake shite shimat(te) moushiwake arimasen** or ① ご迷惑をおかけし（て） ② すみません **Go-meiwaku o o-kake shi(te) sumimasen** ③ ありがとう **arigatou**

(4) ① 見つからないの **mitsukaranai no** ② ごめんね **Gomen ne.** ③ ごめん **Gomen** ④ 悪い **warui**

(5) ① ごめん **Gomen** ② ごめん **Gomen**

**3**

a. ○  b. ×  c. ○  d. ○

## 61 Empathy

**1**

Sample answers

(1) えー！すごい（じゃない）！よかったねぇ。がんばったもんねぇ。 **Ee! Sugoi (ja nai)! Yokatta nee. Ganbatta mon nee.** (2) ほんと！分かる、その気持ち。 あの人、ぜったいゆるせないよねぇ。 **Honto! Wakaru, sono kimochi. Ano hito, zettai yurusenai yo nee.** (3) あ、ほんとう…。かわいそうだねぇ。家族同然だっ たもんねぇ。 **A, hontou . . . Kawaisou da nee. Kazoku douzen datta mon nee.** (4) へえ、いいなあ。【あたしもやろうかなぁ (F)/へえ、オレも何かやろうかな ぁ (M)】。 **Hee, ii naa. 【Atashi mo yarou kanaa (F) / Hee, ore mo nanka yarou kanaa (M)】.** (5) そうですか。それは大変ですねぇ…。 **Sou desu ka. Sore wa taihen desu nee . . .** (6) あぁ、それは困りますよねぇ。お大事に。 **Aa, sore wa komarimasu yo nee. O-daiji ni.** (7) まだ、わかんないじゃない。 きっと大丈夫だよ。 **Mada wakannai ja nai. Kitto daijoubu da yo.**

## 62 Likes and dislikes

**1**

① ねこ **neko**　② 犬 **inu**　③ 好きな **suki na**　④ 大きらいです **dai kirai desu**
⑤ 好き **suki**　⑥ きらい **kirai**　⑦ 行くの **iku no**　⑧ 好きじゃありません **suki ja arimasen**　⑨ 本を読ん **hon o yon**　⑩ 買い物をし **kaimono o shi**

**3**

Questions and sample answers

(1) Q: どんな食べ物が好きですか。**Donna tabemono ga suki desu ka.**
A: <u>すし</u>が好きです。<u>Sushi</u> **ga suki desu.** (2) Q: どんなスポーツをするのが好きですか。**Donna supootsu o suru no ga suki desu ka.** A: <u>サッカー</u>をするのが好きです。<u>Sakkaa</u> **o suru no ga suki desu.** (3) Q: きらいな食べ物がありますか。**Kirai na tabemono ga arimasu ka.** A: <u>なっとう</u>はあまりすきじゃありません。<u>Nattou</u> **wa amari suki ja arimasen.** (4) A: 暇な時どんなことをするのが好きですか。**Hima na toki donna koto o suru no ga suki desu ka.** A: <u>散歩する</u>のが好きです。<u>Sanpo suru</u> **no ga suki desu.** (5) Q: 魚と肉とどっちの方が好きですか。**Sakana to niku to dotchi no hou ga suki desu ka.** A: <u>魚／肉</u>の方が好きです。<u>Sakana/Niku</u> **no hou ga suki desu.** or どっちも好きです。**Dotchi mo suki desu.** or どっちもあまりすきじゃありません。**Dotchi mo amari suki ja arimasen.** (6) 今使っているコンピューターは気に入っていますか。**Ima tsukatte iru konpyuutaa wa ki ni itte imasu ka.** A: (はい/いいえ) (Hai / Iie, ...)

## 63 Desires and preferences

**1**

(1) 新しい車がほしいです。**Atarashii kuruma ga hoshii desu.** (2) 旅行したいです。**Ryokou shitai desu.** (3) 妹は新しいコンピューターをほしがっています。**Imouto wa atarashii konpyuutaa o hoshi-gatte imasu.** (4) 友達は日本語を勉強したがっています。**Tomodachi wa Nihongo o benkyou shita-gatte imasu.** (5) 友達に遊びに来てほしいです。/友達に遊びに来てもらいたいです。**Tomodachi ni asobi ni kite hoshii desu. / Tomodachi ni asobi ni kite moraitai desu.** (6) 弟は母に動物園に連れて行ってもらいたがっています。**Otouto wa haha ni doubutsuen ni tsurete itte moraita-gatte imasu.**

**2**

(1) ほしい **hoshii** (2) ほしい **hoshii** (3) 行きたい **ikitai** (4) 食べたい **tabetai** (5) 食べたい **tabetai** (6) 行きたい **ikitai**

**3**

(1) 続けたい **tsuzuketai** (2) 手伝ってほしい/手伝ってもらいたい **tetsudatte hoshii / tetsudatte moraitai** (3)【仕事をしたく/働きたく】【**shigoto o shitaku / hatarakitaku**】(4) 続けたい **tsuzuketai** (5) 作ってほしい/作ってもらいたい **tsukutte hoshii / tsukutte moraitai** (6) ほしい **hoshii**

**4**

(1) ネックレスが【ほしいそうだ。/ほしいと言っている。】**Nekkuresu ga**【**hoshii sou da. / hoshii to itte iru.**】(2) 日本食が【食べたいそうだ。/食べたいと言っている。/食べたいらしい。】**Nihonshoku ga**【**tabetai sou da. / tabetai to itte iru. / tabetai rashii.**】(3) 仕事を【続けたいと言っている。/つづけたいらしい。】**Shigoto o**【**tsuzuketai to itte iru. / tsuzuketai rashii.**】(4) 作ってもらいたいそうだ。/作ってほしいと言っている。**tsukutte moraitai sou da. / tsukutte hoshii to itte iru.** (5) ほしいそうだ。/ほしいと言っている。/ほしいらしい。**hoshii sou da. / hoshii to itte iru. / hoshii rashii.**

**5**

(1) うーん、きょうの方がいいんですが。 **Uun, kyou no hou ga ii n desu ga.**
(2) そうですねえ、ステーキの方がいいんですが。 **Sou desu nee, suteeki no hou ga ii n desu ga.** (3) あのう、（できれば）みんなに見せないでもらいたいんですが。 **Anou, (dekireba) minna ni misenaide moraitai n desu ga.** (4) あのう、スーザンを連れて【行って/来て】ほしいんですが。 **Anou, Suuzan o tsurete itte/kite hoshii n desu ga.** (5) そうですねえ、ワインの方がいいですが。 **Sou desu nee, wain no hou ga ii desu ga.**

## 64 Hopes and wishes

**1**

(1) 雨が降らないといいんだけど。 **Ame ga furanai to ii n da kedo.**
(2) いい仕事がみつかるといいんだけど。 **Ii shigoto ga mitsukaru to ii n da kedo.**
(3) 試験にパスするといいんだけど。 **Shiken ni pasu suru to ii n da kedo.**
(4) 風邪がはやく治るといいんだけど。 **Kaze ga hayaku naoru to ii n da kedo.**
(5) 今年卒業できるといいんだけど。 **Kotoshi sotsugyou dekiru to ii n da kedo.**
(6) 【フライト/飛行機】が遅れないといいんだけど。 **Furaito/hikouki ga okurenai to ii n da kedo.**

**2**

(1) 転職しなければよかった。 **Tenshoku shinakereba yokatta.** (2) あんな高い車を買わなければよかった。 **Anna takai kuruma o kawanakereba yokatta.**
(3) 大学でもっと勉強しておけばよかった。 **Daigaku de motto benkyou shite okeba yokatta.** (4) 離婚しなければよかった。 **Rikon shinakereba yokatta.**
(5) 自分の好きなことを【やっておけばよかった/やればよかった】。 **Jibun no suki na koto o 【yatte okeba yokatta./yareba yokatta.】**

## 65 Joy and sorrow

**1**

(1) やったあ！ **Yattaa!** (2) 感激です。/うれしいです。/喜びで胸がいっぱいです。 **Kangeki desu / Ureshii desu / Yorokobi de mune ga ippai desu.**
(3) がっかりだよねえ。 **Gakkari da yo nee.** (4) 悲しい。/辛い。/切ない。 **Kanashii. / Tsurai. / Setsunai.** (5) うれしくてどうしたらいいかわかりません。 **Ureshikute dou shitara ii ka wakarimasen.**

**2**

(1) うれしいようです **ureshii you desu** (2) 残念です **zannen desu** (3) さびしがっています **sabishigatte imasu** (4) 幸せです **shiawase desu** (5) つらそうです **tsurasou desu**

**3**

① c ② c ③ a

## 66 Fear or worry

**1**

① こわいです **kowai desu** ② 不安です **fuan desu** ③ のが **no ga**
④ 悩んでいます **nayande imasu** ⑤ 心配で **shinpai de**

**2**

① おそれています **osorete imasu** ② 不安がっていました **fuan-gatte imashita** ③ こわい **kowai** ④ 悩んでいるそう **nayande iru sou** ⑤ 心配していました **shinpai shite imashita**

**3**

(1) ルームメイトは来週のテニスの試合に勝てるかどうか【不安そうです/心配しているようです】。 Ruumumeito wa raishuu no tenisu no shiai ni kateru ka douka【fuan sou desu / shinpai shite iru you desu】. (2) 両親のレストランがつぶれないかと【心配です/不安です】。 Ryoushin no resutoran ga tsuburenai ka to【shinpai desu / fuan desu】. (3) 自分の決めたことが正しかったかどうか不安です。 Jibun no kimeta koto ga tadashikatta ka dou ka fuan desu. (4) 友達のスーさんは犬が恐いようです。 Tomodachi no Suu-san wa inu ga kowai you desu.

## 67　Distress and regret

**1**

(1) こまったなあ **komatta naa**　(2) どうしよう　**dou shiyou**　(3) 困っている **komatte iru**　(4) 落ち込んでいる **ochikonde iru**

**2**

(1) 大学の時にあまり勉強しなかった【の/こと】を後悔している。 **Daigaku no toki ni amari benkyou shinakatta【no / koto】o koukai shite iru.** (2) 学生時代に留学しなかった【の/こと】はざんねんだなあ。 **Gakusei jidai ni ryuugaku shinakatta【no / koto】wa zannen da naa.**　(3) 勉強ばかりしないで、いろいろな経験をすればよかった。 **Benkyou bakari shinai de, iroiro na keiken o sureba yokatta.**　(4) 車の免許をとらなかった【の/こと】を後悔している。 **Kuruma no menkyo o toranakatta【no / koto】o koukai shite iru.** (5) 何かクラブに入ればよかった。 **Nani ka kurabu ni haireba yokatta.**

**3**

(1) (a) 練習しておけば **renshuu shite okeba**　(b) 残念でした **Zannen deshita** (2) 電話してみれば **denwa shite mireba**　(3) (a) 落ち込んでいる **ochikonde iru** (b) つらいです **tsurai desu**　(4) うそをつかなければ **uso o tsukanakereba**

## 68　Surprise

**1**

(1) え？ **E?**　(2) うそでしょ？ **Uso desho?**　(3) 信じられない！ **Shinjirarenai!** (4) まさか！ **Masaka!**　(5) びっくりしたあ。 **Bikkurishitaa.**

**2**

A: のに **noni**　B: に **ni**　C: で **de**　D: しました **shimashita**　E: 驚きました **odorokimashita**

## 69　Hunger, thirst, and fatigue

**1**

(1) お腹すいた！ **Onaka suita!**　(2) のどかわいた！ **Nodo kawaita!** (3) つかれた！ **Tsukareta!**

**2**

(1) a. おなかすいた？ **Onaka suita?**　b. かわいた？ **kawaita?**　(2) つかれましたか。 **tsukaremashita ka.**　(3) 疲れているんじゃない？ **tsukarete iru n ja nai?**

**3**

(1) 岡本さんはお腹がすいているようです。 **Okamoto-san wa onaka ga suite iru you desu.**　(2) 井上さんはのどがかわいているようです。 **Inoue-san wa nodo ga kawaite iru you desu.**　(3) 久野さんは疲れているようです。 **Kuno-san wa tsukarete iru you desu.**

## 70 Pain or discomfort

**1**

(1) 悪い **warui** (2) 頭が痛く **atama ga itaku** (3) 寒気もする **samuke mo suru** (4) ひどいせきも出る **hidoi seki mo deru** (5) 家に帰って寝 **uchi ni kaette ne**

**2**

(1) 胃が痛むんです。**I ga itamu n desu.** (2) 一週間ぐらい前からです。**Isshuukan gurai mae kara desu.** (3) うーん、しくしくですかね。**U-n, shikushiku desu ka ne.** (4) 食事の後ですね。**Shokuji no ato desu ne.**

**3**

Sample answer:

先生、日本語345の○○ですが、今日は授業を休ませていただけないでしょうか。朝起きたら、体がだるくて、吐き気がしました。熱もあります。多分風邪を引いたのだと思います。本当に申し訳ありません。**Sensei, nihongo 345 no ○○ desu ga, kyou wa jugyou o yasumasete itadakenai deshou ka. Asa okitara, karada ga darukute, hakike ga shimashita. Netsu mo arimasu. Tabun kaze o hiita no da to omoimasu. Hontou ni moushiwake arimasen.**

## 71 Satisfaction and dissatisfaction

**1**

A. ① 便利 **benri** ② 満足しています **manzoku shite imasu** ③ きれいでした **kirei deshita** ④ 親切でした **shinsetsu deshita** B. ① おちた **ochita** ② きれいな **kirei na** ③ きれいでした **kirei deshita** ④ ひどかったです **hidokatta desu** ⑤ 寝られませんでした **neraremasendeshita**

**2**

(a) 5 (b) 6 (c) 8 (d) 1 (e) 2 (f) 7 (g) 4 (h) 3

## 72 Advice and suggestions

**1**

(1) したほうが **shita hou ga** (2) どうしたら **dou shitara** (3) いい方法 **ii houhou** (4) のって **notte**

**2**

(1) したら？/すれば？ **shitara? / sureba?** (2) しないほうが【いいよ。/いいんじゃない？】 **shinai hou ga【ii yo. / ii n ja nai?】** (3) ったほうがいいですよ。/ったほうがいいんじゃないですか。**tta hou ga ii desu yo. / tta hou ga ii n ja nai desu ka.** (4) しないほうがいいよ。**shinai hou ga ii yo.**

**3**

(1) 友達の披露宴に行くんだけど、着るものがないんだよね。お金もないし、【どうすれば/どうしたら】いいと思う？ **Tomodachi no hirouen ni iku n da kedo, kiru mono ga nai n da yo ne. Okane mo nai shi,【dou sureba / dou shitara】ii to omou?** (2) どちらの大学院に行くのがいいか悩んでいるんですが、相談にのっていただけないでしょうか。**Dochira no daigakuin ni iku no ga ii ka nayande iru n desu ga, soudan ni notte itadakenai deshouka.** (3) 同僚をデートに誘いたいんだけど、【彼氏/彼女】がいるかどうかわからなくて、悩んでる【んだ/の】。【どうすれば/どうしたら】いいと思う？ **Douryou o deeto ni sasoitai n dakedo,【kareshi / kanojo】ga iru ka dou ka wakaranakute, nayande ru【n da. / no.】【Dou sureba / dou shitara】ii to omou?**

(4) 子供になにか楽器を習わせたいんですけど、習いたがらなくて困っているんです。何かいい方法はないでしょうか。**Kodomo ni nani ka gakki o narawasetai n desu kedo, naraitagaranakute komatte iru n desu. Nani ka ii houhou wa nai deshou ka.**

## 73 Requests

**1**

(1) すみませんが、写真を【とっていただけないでしょうか。／とっていただけませんか。】**Sumimasen ga, shashin o 【totte itadakenai deshou ka. / totte itadakemasen ka.】** (2) すみませんが、（子供が寝ているものですから）もう少し静かに【していただけませんか。／してもらえないでしょうか。】**Sumimasen ga, (kodomo ga nete iru mono desu kara) mou sukoshi shizuka ni 【shite itadakemasen ka. / shite moraenai deshou ka.】** (3) お忙しいところ申し訳ありませんが、この書類にちょっと目を通していただけないでしょうか。**O-isogashii tokoro moushiwake arimasen ga, kono shorui ni chotto me o tooshite itadakenai deshou ka.** (4) もう一度言って【いただけませんか／いただきたいんですが／いただけないでしょうか】。**Mou ichido itte 【itadakemasen ka. / itadakitai n desu ga. / itadakenai deshou ka.】** (5) 'I love you' は日本語で何と言うか教えていただけませんか。**'I love you' wa Nihongo de nan to iu ka oshiete itadakemasen ka.**

**2**

(1) 宿題手伝って【くれる？／もらえない？】or 宿題手伝ってもらえないかな。**Shukudai tetsudatte 【kureru? / moraenai?] or Shukudai tetsudatte moraenai kana?** (2) お金貸して【くれない？／もらえない？】**O-kane kashite 【kurenai? / moraenai?】** (3) 斉藤さん紹介して【くれない？／もらえない？】**Saitou-san shoukai shite 【kurenai? / moraenai?】** (4) クラスのノート見せて【くれない？／もらえない？】**Kurasu no nooto misete 【kurenai? / moraenai?】** (5) 朝6時に【起こしてくれる？／起こしてね。】**Asa rokuji ni 【okoshite kureru? / okoshite ne.】**

**3**

(A) (1) 奨学金に申し込みたい **Shougakukin ni moushikomitai** (2) 推薦状を書いていただけないでしょうか。**Suisenjou o kaite itadakenai deshou ka.** (3) いたし or (more polite) させていただき **itashi or (more polite) sasete itadaki** (4) 宜しくお願い【します。／いたします。】**Yoroshiku o-negai shimasu/itashimasu.**

(B) (1) 頼みがある **tanomi ga aru** (2) 時間代わってもらえないかな。**jikan kawatte moraenai kana.** (3) ちょっと … **chotto . . .** (4) ほかの約束しちゃったんだ。／ほかの予定が入っちゃってるんだよね。**Hoka no yakusoku shichatta n da / Hoka no yotei ga haitchatte ru n da yo ne.**

(C) (1) お願いします。**O-negai shimasu.** (2) お願いします。**O-negai shimasu.** (3) 届けて【くださいますか。／もらえますか。／もらいたいんですが。】**Todokete 【kudasaimasu ka. / moraemasu ka. / moraitai n desu ga.】** (4) お願いします。**O-negai shimasu.**

**4**

(1) お約束の時間を変えていただくわけにはいかないでしょうか。**O-yakusoku no jikan o kaete itadaku wake ni wa ikanai deshou ka.** (2) 論文を直していただくわけにはいかないでしょうか。**Ronbun o naoshite itadaku wake ni wa ikanai deshou ka.** (3) アンケート調査に協力していただくわけにはいかないでし

ようか。**Ankeeto chousa ni kyouryoku shite itadaku wake ni wa ikanai deshou ka.** (4) あしたまで待っていただくわけにはいかないでしょうか。**Ashita made matte itadaku wake ni wa ikanai deshou ka.** (5) もう一度添付ファイルを送っていただくわけにはいかないでしょうか。**Mou ichido tenpu fairu o okutte itadaku wake ni wa ikanai deshou ka.**

**5** (1) 今日は気分が悪いので、早く帰らせていただけないでしょうか。**Kyou wa kibun ga warui node, hayaku kaerasete itadakenai deshou ka.** (2) 地図を書いていただけないでしょうか。**Chizu o kaite itadakenai deshou ka.** (3) 写真をとらせていただけないでしょうか。**Shashin o torasete itadakenai deshou ka.** (4) 先生、本を貸していただけないでしょうか。**Sensei, hon o kashite itadakenai deshou ka.** (5) 少々お待ちいただけないでしょうか。**Shoushou o-machi itadakenai deshou ka.** (6) 来週休暇を取らせていただけないでしょうか。**Raishuu kyuuka o torasete itadakenai deshou ka.** (7) この部屋で休ませていただけないでしょうか。**Kono heya de yasumasete itadakenai deshou ka.**

## 74  Offers and invitations

**1** (1) 宿題手伝おうか。**Shukudai tetsudaou ka.** (2) 荷物お持ちしましょうか。**Nimotsu o-mochi shimashou ka.** (3) コーヒーお入れしましょうか。**Koohii o-ire shimashou ka.** (4) 空港まで迎えに行きましょうか。**Kuukou made mukae ni ikimashou ka.** (5) ご予約いたしましょうか。**Go-yoyaku itashimashou ka.**

**2** (1) コンサートの【チケット/切符】が二枚あるんだけど、行かない？ **Konsaato no【chiketto/kippu】ga nimai aru n da kedo, ikanai?** (2) 新しい居酒屋がオープンしたんだけど、みんなで飲みに【行かない？/行きませんか。】**Atarashii izakaya ga oopun shita n da kedo, minna de nomi ni【ikanai? / ikimasen ka.】** (3) クラスのみんなでレストランに行くんですが、先生も【一緒にいかがですか/いらっしゃいませんか】**Kurasu no minna de resutoran ni iku n desu ga, sensei mo 【issho ni ikaga desu ka. / irasshaimasen ka.】** (4) 日曜日にゴルフをしませんか。**Nichiyoubi ni gorufu o shimasen ka.** (5) 今度一緒にお茶でもいかがですか。**Kondo issho ni o-cha demo ikaga desu ka.**

**3** (1) Aff: うん、行く。ありがとう。**Un, iku. Arigatou.** Neg: うん、ありがとう。でも、今日はちょっと都合が悪くて … 。**Un, arigatou. Demo, kyou wa chotto tsugou ga warukute ...**

(2) Aff: はい、ありがとうございます。喜んでご一緒させていただきます。**Hai, arigatou gozaimasu. Yorokonde go-issho sasete itadakimasu.** Neg: ありがとうございます。ただ、今日は先約がありまして。すみません。**Arigatou gozaimasu. Tada, kyou wa senyaku ga arimashite. Sumimasen.**

(3) Aff: あ、いいですね。是非。**A, ii desu ne. Zehi.** Neg: あ、ありがとう。でも、今日は子供の誕生パーティーがあるので、ちょっと。**Arigatou. Demo, kyou wa kodomo no tanjou paatii ga aru node, chotto.**

(4) Aff: あ、是非（お願いします）。**A, zehi (o-negai shimasu.)** Neg: あ、ありがとうございます。ただ、日曜日は先約があって。残念です。**A, arigatou gozaimasu. Tada, nichiyoubi wa senyaku ga atte. Zannen desu.**

(5) Aff: あ、喜んで。/是非ご一緒しましょう。**A, yorokonde. / Zehi go-issho shimashou.**　Neg: あ、ありがとうございます。ただ、今日は会議が入っていて、ちょっと …。 **A, arigatou gozaimasu. Tada, kyou wa kaigi ga haitte ite, chotto . . .**

**4**

(1) 課長もいかがですか。**Kachou mo ikaga desu ka.**　(2) 伺います。/お邪魔します。**Ukagaimasu. / O-jama shimasu.**　(3) 持っていきましょうか。**Motte ikimashou ka.**　(4) 楽しみにしています。**Tanoshimi ni shite imasu.**

**5**

(1) いっしょにどう？ **Issho ni dou?**　(2) あしたまでに【仕上げなくちゃ/終わらせなくちゃ】ならない仕事がある【の/んだ】。**Ashita made ni shiagenakucha / owarasenakucha naranai shigoto ga aru【no / n da】.**　(3) 仕方ないね。**Shikata nai ne.**　(4) 誘ってね。**Sasotte ne.**

**6**

> 山下先生、
> 　ご無沙汰しておりますが、お元気でいらっしゃいますか。私は忙しいですが、充実した毎日を過ごしております。
> 　実は、先生もご存知の○○さんがこの度イギリスの大学院で勉強することになったそうです。それで、お別れパーティをしたいと思っておりますが、ご都合がよろしければ、先生もいらっしゃってくださいませんか。お別れパーティーは私の家で、来週の土曜日の午後五時からです。食べ物や飲み物もたくさん用意する予定でおります。
> 　では、ご返事をお待ちしております。○○さんも先生にお会いできれば大変喜ぶと思います。先生のお越しをお待ちしております。
>
> 　　　　　　　　　　　　　　　　　　　　　　　　　　　　（自分の名前）

> Yamashita Sensei,
> 　Gobusata shite orimasu ga, o-genki de irasshaimasu ka. Watashi wa isogashii desu ga, juujitsu shita mainichi o sugoshite orimasu.
> 　Jitsuwa, sensei mo go-zonji no ○○-san ga kono tabi Igirisu no daigakuin de benkyou suru koto ni natta sou desu. Sorede o-wakare paatii o shitai to omotte orimasu ga, go-tsugou ga yoroshikereba, sensei mo irasshatte kudasaimasen ka. Owakare paatii wa watashi no uchi de, raishuu no doyoubi no gogo goji kara desu. Tabemono ya nomimono mo takusan youi suru yotei de orimasu.
> 　Dewa, go-henji o o-machi shite orimasu. ○○-san mo sensei ni o-ai dekireba taihen yorokobu to omoimasu. Sensei no o-koshi o o-machi shite orimasu.
>
> 　　　　　　　　　　　　　　　　　　　　　　　　　　　（your full name）

## 75　Orders (commands)

**1**

(1) しなさい **shinasai**　(2) たべな **tabena**　(3) しゃべるな **shaberuna**
(4) いけ **ike**　(5) くるな **kuruna**　(6) しろ **shiro**　(7) 言わない **iwanai**
(8) 泣かないの **nakanai no**

**2**

(1) 部屋をそうじしなさい/きれいにしなさい。**Heya o souji shinasai / kirei ni shinasai.** (2) 歯をみがきなさい。**Ha o migakinasai.** (3) すぐ服を着なさい。**Sugu fuku o kinasai.** (4) 壁に落書きしちゃ【だめ/いけません】。/壁に落書きしないの！**Kabe ni rakugakishicha【dame / ikemasen】. / Kabe ni rakugaki shinai no!** (5) コンピューターにさわっちゃ【だめ/いけません】。/コンピューターにさわらないの！**Konpyuutaa ni sawatcha【dame / ikemasen.】 / Konpyuutaa ni sawaranai no!** (6) けんか（を）やめなさい。**Kenka (o) yamenasai.**

**3**

(1) 誰にも言うな（よ）。**Darenimo iu na (yo).** (2) 静かにしろ（よ）。**Shizukani shiro (yo).** (3) 俺の部屋に入るな（よ）。**Ore no heya ni hairu na (yo).** (4) 何か飲むもの、もってこい（よ）。**Nanka nomu mono, motte koi (yo).** (5) 俺のゲームをつかうな（よ）。**Ore no geemu o tsukau na (yo).**

## 76 Directions and instructions

**1**

(1) ① まっすぐ行って **massugu itte** ② かど **kado** ③ まがって **magatte** ④ 歩いたら **aruitara** ⑤ 3軒目 **sangen me**

(2) ① あるいて **aruite** ② まがって **magatte** ③ わたります **watarimasu** ④ すぎたら **sugitara** ⑤ 5階 **gokai**

**2**

(1) すみません【お手洗い/トイレ】は【どこ/どちら】ですか。
**Sumimasen,【o-tearai / toire】wa【doko / dochira】desu ka.**
(2) すみません、ちょっとお尋ねしたいんですが。【スイートというケーキ屋さんを探しているんですが/スイートというケーキ屋さん】、どこにあるかご存知ですか。**Sumimasen, chotto o-tazune shitai n desu ga.【Suiito to iu keekiya-san o sagashite iru n desu ga / Suiito to iu keekiya-san】, doko ni aru ka go-zonji desu ka.** (3) その喫茶店（まで）の行き方、教えてくれない？**Sono kissaten (made) no iki kata, oshiete kurenai?** (4) その新興住宅地にはどう行けばいいか教えていただけませんか。**Sono shinkou juutakuchi ni wa dou ikeba ii ka oshiete itadakemasen ka.**

**3**

(1) 新しい携帯電話の使い方 **atarashii keitai denwa no tsukai kata** (2) 縦列駐車のしかた **juuretsu chuusha no shi kata** (3) 着物の着方 **kimono no ki kata** (4) 同僚とのつき合い方 **douryou to no tsukiai kata** (5) 駅への行き方 **eki e no iki kata** (6) 自転車の乗り方 **jitensha no nori kata** (7) 外国人の案内のし方 **gaikokujin no annai no shi kata** (8) 人前での話し方 **hitomae de no hanashi kata**

**4**

Sample answers:

(1) このオムレツの作り方を教えていただけませんか。**Kono omuretsu no tsukuri kata o oshiete itadakemasen ka.** (2) すみません、切符の【買い方が分からないんですけど。/買い方、教えてくれませんか。】**Sumimasen, kippu no【kai kata ga wakaranai n desu kedo. / kai kata, oshiete kuremasen ka.】**
(3) すみません、ご迷惑じゃなかったら、クラブの振り方を教えていただきたいんですけど。**Sumimasen, go-meiwaku ja nakattara, kurabu no furi kata o oshiete itadakitai n desu kedo.**

## 77 Confirmation

**1**

(A) 通行人 :　　　　あのう、あそこに交差点がありますね。
　　あなた :　　　　あそこを右ですね。
　　**Tsuukounin:**　Anoo, asoko ni kousaten ga arimasu <u>ne</u>.
　　**Anata:**　Asoko o migi desu <u>ne</u>.

(B) えり :　　　　ふうん、同じ仕事でも女性の給料の方が男性の給料より低いん
　　　　　　　　　ですね。
　　**Eri:**　Fuun, onaji shigoto demo josei no kyuuryou no hou ga
　　dansei no kyuuryou yori hikui n desu <u>ne</u>.
　　真美 :　　　　仕事が同じなのに、給料が違うのは不公平ですよね。
　　**Mami:**　Shigoto ga onaji na noni, kyuuryou ga chigau no wa
　　fukouhei desu yo <u>ne</u>.
　　えり :　　　　本当にそうですね。
　　**Eri:**　Hontou ni sou desu <u>ne</u>.

**2**

(1) ① よね **yo ne** or ね **ne**　② ね **ne**　③ ね **ne**　(2) でしょ **desho**
(3) よね **yo ne**　(4) でしょ **desho**　(5) ① ね **ne**　② ね **ne**

## 78 Permission

**1**

(1) テレビを見てもいいですか。**Terebi o mite mo ii desu ka.**　(2) 友達を連れて
来てもいいですか。**Tomodachi o tsurete kite mo ii desu ka.**　(3) 【帰るの/帰り】
が遅くなってもいいですか。【**Kaeru no / kaeri**】 **ga osoku natte mo ii desu ka.**
(4) 洗濯をしてもいいですか。**Sentaku o shite mo ii desu ka.**　(5) 冷蔵庫のジュ
ースを飲んでもいいですか。**Reizouko no juusu o nonde mo ii desu ka.**

**2**

(1) コンピューターを使ってもいい？**Konpyuutaa o tsukatte mo ii?**
(2) コンピューターを使ってもいい？**Konpyuutaa o tsukatte mo ii?**
(3) コンピューターを使ってもいいでしょうか。**Konpyuutaa o tsukatte mo ii**
**deshou ka.**　(4) コンピューターを使わせていただけないでしょうか。/コンピュー
ターを使ってもよろしいでしょうか。**Konpyuutaa o tsukawasete itadakenai**
**deshou ka. / Konpyuutaa o tsukatte mo yoroshii deshou ka.**

**3**

(1) 先生、写真をとらせていただけないでしょうか。**Sensei, shashin o torasete**
**itadakenai deshou ka.**　(2) 休暇をとらせていただけないでしょうか。**Kyuuka o**
**torasete itadakenai deshou ka.**　(3) 家に帰らせていただけないでしょうか。
**Uchi ni kaerasete itadakenai deshou ka.**　(4) 使わせてもらえない？**Tsukawasete**
**moraenai?**　(5) コピーさせてくれない？/コピーさせてもらえない？**Kopii sasete**
**kurenai? / Kopii sasete moraenai?**

**4**

(1) うーん、悪いけど、今ちょっと使ってる【んだけど/んで】… 。**Uun, warui**
**kedo, ima chotto tsukatte ru【n da kedo. / n de】...**　(2) あ、すみませんが、
あとから人が来ますので。**A, sumimasen ga, ato kara hito ga kimasu node.**
(3) あのう、申し訳ありませんが、今ちょっと忙しいんですが。**Anou, moushiwake**
**arimasen ga, ima chotto isogashii n desu ga.**　(4) うーん、悪いけど、あした
の午後はちょっと都合が悪いんですが。**Uun, warui kedo, ashita no gogo wa**
**chotto tsugou ga warui n desu ga**

**5**

(1) すみませんが、期末試験を少し早く受けさせていただくわけにはいかないでしょうか。**Sumimasen ga, kimatsu shiken o sukoshi hayaku ukesasete itadaku wake ni wa ikanai deshou ka.** (2) すみませんが、論文を締め切りのあと出させていただくわけにはいかないでしょうか。**Sumimasen ga, ronbun o shimekiri no ato dasasete itadaku wake ni wa ikanai deshou ka.** (3) 悪いけど、車使わせてもらうわけには【いかない？/いかないかな。】**Warui kedo, kuruma tsukawasete morau wake ni wa 【ikanai? / ikanai kana. 】** (4) 恐れ入りますが、今日診ていただくわけにはいかないでしょうか。**Osore irimasu ga, kyou mite itadaku wake ni wa ikanai deshou ka.** (5) すみませんが、少し考えさせていただくわけにはいかないでしょうか。**Sumimasen ga, sukoshi kangaesasete itadaku wake ni wa ikanai deshou ka.**

## 79 Prohibition

**1**

(1) 携帯電話[は／を]使ってはいけません。**Keitai denwa wa/o tsukatte wa ikemasen.** (2) ここに車を止めてはいけません。**Koko ni kuruma o tomete wa ikemasen.** (3) ここに入ってはいけません。**Koko ni haitte wa ikemasen.** (4) ゴミを捨ててはいけません。**Gomi o sutete wa ikemasen.** (5) たばこをすってはいけません。**Tabako o sutte wa ikemasen.**

**2**

(1) 電車の中では携帯電話を使ってはいけないことになっています。**Densha no naka de wa keitai denwa o tsukatte wa ikenai koto ni natte imasu.** (2) 目上の人を「あなた」と呼んではいけないことになっています。**Meue no hito o 'Anata' to yonde wa ikenai koto ni natte imasu.** (3) 他人に自分の家族のことをほめないことになっています。**Tanin ni jibun no kazoku no koto o homenai koto ni natte imasu.** (4) スリッパをはいて畳の部屋に入らないことになっています。**Surippa o haite tatami no heya ni hairanai koto ni natte imasu.**

**3**

(A) (1) 行ってはいけません。**itte wa ikemasen** (2) 食べてはいけません。**tabete wa ikemasen**

(B) (1) でかけちゃだめ **dekakecha dame** (2) 遅くなっちゃだめ **osoku natcha dame**

(C) (1) 【休んでは/サボっては】いけません。**【yasunde wa / sabotte wa】 ikemasen.** (2) 居眠りをしてはいけません **inemuri o shite wa ikemasen** (3) 話をしてはいけません **hanashi o shite wa ikemasen**

## 80 Obligation and duty

**1**

In the following answers, **nakereba** can be replaced by **nakute wa**.

(1) 飲み物をひやしておかなければいけません。**Nomimono o hiyashite okanakereba ikemasen.** (2) 招待状を【書かなければ/出さなければ】いけません。**Shoutaijou o kakanakereba / dasanakereba ikemasen.** (3) 買い物をして、そうじをしなければいけません。**Kaimono o shite, souji o shinakereba ikemasen.** (4) 料理を作っておかなければいけません。**Ryouri o tsukutte okanakereba ikemasen.**

**2**
(1) 作ってもらわなければいけない。 **tsukutte morawanakereba ikenai**
(2) くつをぬがなければならない。 **kutsu o nuganakereba naranai**
(3) 受けなければならない。 **ukenakereba naranai** (4) 勉強しなければいけない。
**benkyou shinakereba ikenai** (5) 払わなければならない。 **harawanakereba
naranai**

**3**
① 持って【行かないと/行かなくちゃ/行かなきゃ】いけない **motte【ikanai
to / ikanakucha / ikanakya】ikenai** ② あげなきゃいけない **agenakya
ikenai** ③ 届けてもらわなきゃいけない **todokete morawanakya ikenai**

**4**
(1) 買わないわけにはいかない **kawanai wake ni wa ikanai** (2) チップをあげな
いわけにはいかない **chippu o agenai wake ni wa ikanai** (3) 行かないわけには
いかない **ikanai wake ni wa ikanai** (4) 漢字を覚えないわけにはいかない **kanji
o oboenai wake ni wa ikanai.** (5) 飲まないわけにはいかない **nomanai wake
ni wa ikanai**

**5**
(1) 仕事をやめざるを得ない **shigoto o yamezaru o enai** (2) 使わざるを得ない
**tsukawazaru o enai** (3) 自分の間違いを認めざるを得ない **jibun no machigai
o mitomezaru o enai** (4) (だれか) ほかの人に頼まざるを得ない **(dare ka) hoka
no hito ni tanomazaru o enai** (5) 徹夜せざるを得ない **tetsuya sezaru o enai**

**6**
(1) 約束は守るべきです。 **Yakusoku wa mamoru beki desu.** (2) 留学するべき
です。/留学すべきです。 **ryuugaku suru beki desu. / ryuugaku su beki
desu.** (3) 育児を助けるべきです。 **ikuji o tasukeru beki desu.** (4) 敬語を使う
べきです。 **Keigo o tsukau beki desu.**

## 81 Complaints

**1**
c. d. e. g. h.

**2**
(1) b (2) a (3) b

**3**
(1) ばっかり **bakkari** (2) くれない **kurenai** (3) される **sareru**
(4) んだから **n da kara** (5) させられたり **saseraretari** (6) つきあわされたり
**tsukiawasaretari** (7) なのに **na noni**

**4**
今のテニス部は多くの問題があります。たとえば、新入部員はお酒を飲まされま
す。それから、1年生が4年生の洗濯や掃除をすべてやらされて、4年生の言うことを
聞かないと暴力をふるわれます。それに、4年生しかコートを使わせてもらえない
し、毎月5千円の部費は4年生の飲み会のために使われています。ほとんどの新入部
員は2週間たらずでやめてしまいます。

**Ima no tenisu bu wa ooku no mondai ga arimasu. Tatoeba, shinnyuubuin
wa o-sake o nomasaremasu. Sore kara, ichinensei ga yonensei no sentaku
ya souji o subete yarasarete, yonensei no iu koto o kikanai to bouryoku
o furuwaremasu. Soreni, yonensei shika kooto o tsukawasete moraenai
shi, maitsuki gosen en no buhi wa yonensei no nomikai no tame ni
tsukawarete imasu. Hotondo no shinnyuubuin wa nishuukan tarazu de
yamete shimaimasu.**

## 82 Compliments

**1**

(1) b   (2) a   (3) b   (4) c   (5) a

**2**

(1) b   (2) a   (3) c   (4) a

## 83 Promises and warnings

**1**

(1) 絶対 **zettai**   (2) する **suru**   (3) ように **you ni**

**2**

(1) 食べなさい **tabenasai**   (2) ほうがいいですよ **hou ga ii desu yo**
(3) 入ってはいけません **haitte wa ikemasen**   (4) ください **kudasai**
(5) と **to**   (6) しない **shinai**

**3**

(1) 絶対誰にも言わないよ。**Zettai darenimo iwanai yo.**   (2) 毎日メールす
る（って約束する）から。**Mainichi meeru suru (tte yakusoku suru) kara.**
(3) もう二度とうそをつかないよ。**Mou nido to uso o tsukanai yo.**   (4) 今年は
絶対タバコをやめるって約束する！**Kotoshi wa zettai tabako o yameru tte
yakusoku suru!**

## 84 Opinions

**1**

a. 4   b. 1   c. 2   d. 3

**2**

(1) と思います。/と考えます。**to omoimasu. / to kangaemasu.**   (2) べきで
す。/べきだと思います。/べきじゃないでしょうか。**beki desu. / beki da to
omoimasu. / beki ja nai deshou ka.**   (3) べきじゃありません。**beki ja
arimasen.**   (4) ほうがいいと思います。**hou ga ii to omoimasu.**   (5) べきで
す。/べきだと思います。/わけにはいきません。**beki desu. / beki da to
omoimasu. / wake ni wa ikimasen.**   (6) 気がします。**ki ga shimasu.**

**3**

(1) じゃないんじゃないでしょうか **ja nai n ja nai deshou ka**   (2) あるんじゃな
いでしょうか **aru n ja nai deshou ka**   (3) じゃないんじゃないでしょうか **ja nai
n ja nai deshou ka**   (4) 解決できないんじゃないでしょうか **kaiketsu dekinai n
ja nai deshou ka**   (5) いいんじゃないでしょうか **ii n ja nai deshou ka**

**4**

Sample answers

(1) 子供が小学校で外国語を習うのはいいことだと思います。外国語を学ぶことによ
り、小さいうちから外国の文化や習慣に触れ、世界の歴史や地理にも興味を持つよ
うになるでしょう。その結果、外国語の学習だけでなく、ほかの教科の学習にも良
い影響を与えます。ですから私は小学校から外国語を教えるべきだと思います。

**Kodomo ga shougakkou de gaikokugo o narau no wa ii koto da to
omoimasu. Gaikokugo o manabu koto ni yori, chiisai uchi kara gaikoku
no bunka ya shuukan ni fure, sekai no rekishi ya chiri ni mo kyoumi o
motsu you ni naru deshou. Sono kekka, gaikokugo no gakushuu dake de
naku, hoka no kyouka no gakushuu ni mo ii eikyou o ataemasu. Desukara
watashi wa shougakkou kara gaikokugo o oshieru beki da to omoimasu.**

(2) お金さえあれば本当に幸せになれるでしょうか。確かにお金のない生活は辛いでしょう。でも、お金だけあっても幸せになれるとはかぎりません。人が幸せを感じるためには、支えてくれる、あるいは支えて上げる人の存在、生きがいなど、お金では買えないものも必要なのではないかと思います。ですから、私はお金さえあれば幸せになれるという考え方には賛成できません。

**O-kane sae areba hontou ni shiawase ni nareru deshou ka. Tashika ni o-kane no nai seikatsu wa tsurai deshou. Demo, o-kane dake atte mo shiawase ni nareru to wa kagirimasen. Hito ga shiawase o kanjiru tame ni wa, sasaete kureru, arui wa sasaete ageru hito no sonzai, ikigai nado, o-kane de wa kaenai mono mo hitsuyou na no dewa nai ka to omoimasu. Desukara, watashi wa o-kane sae areba shiawase ni nareru to iu kangae kata ni wa sansei dekimasen.**

## 85 Agreement, disagreement and indifference

**1** ① そうだね **Sou da ne** ② それは同感 **Sore wa doukan** ③ いいね **ii ne**
④ どっちでもいい **Dotchi de mo ii** ⑤ いい考え **ii kangae**

**2** ① a ② f ③ c ④ d ⑤ e ⑥ b

**3** (1) それはそうかもしれません **Sore wa sou kamo shiremasen.** (2) なるほど **Naruhodo** (3) そうですねえ **Sou desu nee** (4) 私も同感です **Watashi mo doukan desu**

## 86 Choosing and deciding

**1** (1) になさいますか **ni nasaimasu ka** (2) お願いします。**o-negai shimasu.**
(3) どちら **dochira** (4) をお願いします。/にします。**o o-negai shimasu. / ni shimasu.** (5) をお願いします。/にします。**o o-negai shimasu. / ni shimasu.**

**2** (1) 転職しないことにしました。**Tenshoku shinai koto ni shimashita.**
(2) 一年後海外の大学院で勉強することにしました。**Ichinen-go kaigai no daigakuin de benkyou suru koto ni shimashita.** (3) TOEFLでいい成績がとれるように英語をもっと勉強することにしました。**TOEFL de ii seiseki ga toreru you ni Eigo o motto benkyou suru koto ni shimashita.** (4) 両親からお金を借りないことにしました。**Ryoushin kara o-kane o karinai koto ni shimashita.** (5) 結婚はしたいですが、一年待つことにしました。**Kekkon wa shitai desu ga, ichinen matsu koto ni shimashita.**

**3** (A) ② (B) ① (C) ② (D) ①

## 87 Shopping

**1** ① 青いセーター（は）ありますか **Aoi seetaa (wa) arimasu ka** ②（お）いくらですか **(o-)ikura desu ka** ③ Mサイズ（は）ありませんか **Emu saizu (wa) arimasen ka** ④（それは）（お）いくらですか **(Sore wa) (o-)ikura desu ka** ⑤ それ、お願いします **Sore, o-negai shimasu**

**2** ① 穴があいている（みたいな）**ana ga aiteru (mitai na)**　② 取りかえていただきたい **torikaete itadakitai**　③（そちら、）あしたも開いていますか **(Sochira,) ashita mo aite imasu ka**　④ 何時から何時までですか **Nanji kara nanji made desu ka**

## 88　Ordering

**1** ① お願いしたいんです **o-negai shitai n desu**　② 照り焼きチキンを一つ **teriyaki chikin o hitotsu**　③ ちらし寿司を二つ **chirashi zushi o futatsu**　④ 親子どんぶりを一つ **oyako donburi o hitotsu**　⑤ 二つ **futatsu**　⑥ どのぐらい（時間が）かかりますか **dono gurai (jikan ga) kakarimasu ka**　⑦ 急いで【もらえますか/下さいますか】**isoide【moraemasu ka / kudasaimasu ka】.**

**2** (A) a. ×　b. ○　c. ×　d. ○　(B) ① b　② a　③ a　④ a　⑤ a　⑥ b

## 89　Reservation

**1** ① 予約したいんです **yoyaku shitai n desu**　② 8月7日から8月10日までです **hachigatsu nanoka kara hachigatsu tooka made desu**　③ ダブルをお願いします **daburu o o-negai shimasu**　④ お願いしたい **o-negai shitai**

**2** ①【変更したい/変えていただきたい】んですが【**henkou shitai / kaete itadakitai**】**n desu ga**　②【帰ることに/帰って来ないといけなく】なったんです【**kaeru koto ni / kaette konai to ikenaku**】**natta n desu**　③ お願いします **o-negai shimasu**

**3** (A) b

(B) 錦/にしき/**Nishiki**　(C) ① 8、7、2　② 1、2、0　③ c　④ c　⑤ a

# Index

The numbers refer to chapters and exercises. For example, 12.7 refers to Chapter 12, Exercise 7.